NGOs and Globalization

NGOs and Globalization

Developmental and Organizational Facets

Edited by

Asok Kumar Sarkar

RAWAT PUBLICATIONS

Jaipur • New Delhi • Bangalore • Mumbai • Hyderabad • Guwahati

ISBN 81-316-0201-X

Published by
Prem Rawat for **Rawat Publications**
Satyam Apts., Sector 3, Jawahar Nagar, Jaipur - 302 004 (India)
Phone: 0141 265 1748 / 7006 Fax: 0141 265 1748
E-mail : info@rawatbooks.com
Website: rawatbooks.com

New Delhi Office
4858/24, Ansari Road, Daryaganj, New Delhi 110 002
Phone: 011-23263290

Also at Bangalore, Mumbai, Hyderabad and Guwahati

Typeset by Inosoft Systems, Noida
Printed at Chaman Enterprises, New Delhi

Dedicated to Rose who is fighting for the cause of the poor

Contents

Foreword

Dr Asok Kumar Sarkar's edited book, *NGOs and Globalization: Developmental and Organizational Facets* is an ambitious and timely one. With the coming of the 21st century, globalization with both its positive and negative consequences impacts all of our lives. The later part of the 20th century certainly saw the networking of the financial and communication institutions worldwide. Today, for example, Chinese interest rates are examined daily around the world given their potential to impact investment and development globally. Additionally, we have up to the minute televised coverage of events occurring around the world.

In the arena of social development, initial impacts of both the International Monetary Fund and the World Bank, through the use of the ill-fated Structural Adjustment Programs (SAPs) of the 1990s, saw a retreat in the individual nations dedicating their funding and efforts to meet the social needs of their citizens. At the time of move away from government sponsored provisions for education, health care and social services, non-governmental organizations (NGOs) were increasingly stepping into the service delivery gap and were relied upon for funding, planning and service provision. This global movement towards the reliance upon NGOs has only accelerated as we have moved further into the 21st century and therefore makes this book all the more valuable for today's social planners, politicians, social workers, community developers, academicians and concerned participant citizens.

Dr Sarkar details well, in the introductory chapter, the long history of globalization and its impact upon the "haves" and "have-nots". Additionally, this chapter describes the interconnectedness of the globalization process with its influence upon social policy development.

Subsequent chapters focus on developmental facets, including the strategy of structural adjustment practices, sustainability, sex trafficking, biodiversity, urbanization, income maintenance as well as the services provided to the disabled and children. These chapters explore the expanding roles for NGOs in today's world.

Although Dr Sarkar has utilized authors that focus primarily on India, Bangladesh and somewhat wider Asia, the reality of the definition of globalization described by the editor in chapter one indicates the applicability and transferability of this work to all nations.

Furthermore, the description of NGOs in their various social developmental approaches creates a helpful case study-like approach for the readers and provides relevant examples.

The second section of the book explores the organizational facets of NGOs in the 21st century. To accomplish that task, Dr. Sarkar included authors who describe the impacts of funding, ideological concerns, politics, influence peddling, power, the role of the state, foreign aid, NGO worker satisfaction and methods of exploring NGO staff performance.

This description of the organizational aspects impacting currently operating NGOs helps draw attention to the factors that will continue to impinge on the future growth and development of NGOs globally. With the possible exclusion of the influence of armed conflict, the editor has included authors who have highlighted the current and future challenges to NGO development and sustainability worldwide.

In conclusion, Dr Sarkar in this book has edited a major contribution to the growing literature focused on NGOs. It is a recommended reading for all those interested in serving the disenfranchised worldwide. It will also be useful for our globally focused, family centered Master in Social Work (MSW) Program at Dominican University.

October 2007

Mark E. Rodgers. DSW, LCSW, BCD
Dean and Professor of Social Work
Dominican University
Graduate School of Social Work
River Forest, Illinois, USA

Acknowledgements

At the very outset, I am indebted to Prof Swapan Kumar Garain of Tata Institute of Social Sciences, my teacher, who introduced me to the world of NGOs and Dr Rama V. Baru of Jawaharlal Nehru University, my Ph.D. guide, who developed my keen interest in this field and made me understand the importance of NGOs in this age of globalization. Prof N. Sudhakar Rao, Department of Sociology, Assam University, who joined as Professor in the Department of Anthropology, Central University, Hyderabad, collaborated with me in the early stages of this work. I greatly acknowledge his help.

Contributors are the real pillars of this volume. They are drawn from different parts of the country as well as from Bangladesh. For instance, Prof K.K. Mukherjee from Delhi University, Delhi; Dr Rama V. Baru from Jawaharlal Nehru University, New Delhi; Mr Ravindra R. Patil from Jamia Millia Islamia University, New Delhi; Ms Komal Parmar from Ahmedabad; Dr B.T. Lawani from Bharati Vidyapeeth University, Pune; Prof Swapan Kumar Garain from Tata Institute of Social Sciences, Mumbai; Prof D. Rajasekhar from Institute for Social and Economic Change, Bangalore; Prof Sukla Deb Kanango, Dr P.K. Ghosh and Dr Debotosh Sinha from Visva Bharati University, Santinikatan; Dr A.K. Nongkynrih from North Eastern Hill University, Shillong; and Prof Niaz Ahmed Khan from University of Chittagong, Bangladesh. I am obliged to all of them for sending papers on time in spite of their busy schedules and helping me to give final shape to this book.

Prof. Mark E. Rodgers, Dean and Professor of Social Work, Dominican University, Illinois, USA, was very kind to write foreword for this book. He recommended it for the students interested in serving the disenfranchised worldwide. I am really thankful to him. I would also like to place on record my sincere thanks to Prof N.B. Biswas, Prof Gopalji Mishra, Dr B.S.Gunjal, Dr S. Dutta, Mr T.B. Sukai, Ms M. Tineshowri Devi, Mr. M. Gangabhusan, Mr Sanjoy Roy and Mr Ravindra R. Patil, who inspired me during the pursuasion of this work. Last but not the least, my parents, my wife Sulata and my son Teo, in spite of all the taxing time, pressurized me to complete this task. I consider myself fortunate to have had such a loving family support.

Asok Kumar Sarkar

Chapter I

Introduction

Asok Kumar Sarkar

THE term 'globalization' has gained immense popularity over the last decade of 20th century. Though millions of people are unaware about it, globalization is a key issue in the dominant theoretical and political discourses and has become a buzzword among the academics, professionals, social activists, corporate bodies, media institutions and larger civil society organizations. It is an inevitable, irreversible and unavoidable process and harbinger of future prosperity. Though globalization process has reduced poverty in many countries with tangible and intangible positive as well as negative impacts on the people, the ecologists, the environmentalists and the Marxist schools oppose it to prevent ecological degradation, livelihood insecurity and consequently further marginalization of the poor. In common parlance, globalization is a new form of capitalism. This gives impetus to understand the globalization process thoroughly.

There is dispute about the date of beginning of globalization. On the basis of a survey of the world in 1400 AD, anthropologist Eric Wolf argues that there were existence of states and polities in Africa as well as in America and they existed in interconnections. Referring to the argument of Wolf, Prof. T.K. Oommen is of the view that there existed a different mode of globalization prior to 1500 AD. A few authors locate the voyage of discovery during the 15th century as the starting point of globalization (Valaskakis, 1999). Many authors hold the view that globalization emerged in the process of colonialism and industrial revolution during 17th and 18th centuries. Still others aver that globalization is a phenomenon of 1960s with cultural planetarization

(Oommen, 2006). Relevant literature on the issue expresses the view that globalization process has prescribed and described a new economic system with the features of capitalistic mode of production. Hence, the conviction is that globalization has emanated from the 'theory of capitalism'.

Marx has written extensively on the theory of capitalism portraying its long history and various phases. He did not use the term 'globalization' but focused on the advance form of capitalism which would cross boundaries of all the nation-states. Marx delineates, capitalists are more conscious in their own progress, contriving new mechanical arts in order to have large scale production and consequently more profits. The improved production capacity of the capitalists brought the predicament in marketing huge quantity of finished goods among the small population of western countries. With a view to avoid overstock of products, the capitalist countries ensnared markets in the conquered colonies of Asia and Africa. The overseas markets assisted capitalist countries in two ways, i.e., making the raw material available for manufacturing at a cheaper rate and securing markets for finished products. This further reinforced the expansion of international trade, commerce and the tendency to capture world market (Marx and Engels 1969; Giddens 1971; Petras 1999; Sengupta 2001). This advanced form of capitalism and the craze to control world market is one reason for the emergence of globalization process.

Globalization increases hegemony of the 'haves' over the 'have-nots'. Thus, Marxists are of the opinion, in addition to the above reason, 'imperialism' is another factor for the provenance of globalization. Historical evidences reveal that the flow of trade, capital and technology helped the imperialist nations to drain out the resources from the less developed colonial nations (Dutt and Sundaram 2004). This issue was more political in nature than the economic or technological advancement. During the period of imperialism, the world was divided into two political groups based on the ideology; one was led by the USA and the other by the USSR. Consequently, two parallel world markets survived: the imperialist world market and the socialist world market. Since the former group could establish its supremacy in the world, the latter lost. The victory of 'imperialism' and the demise of 'socialism' paved the path for unobstructed growth of the process of globalization (Valaskakis 1999; Petras 1999).

The discussion in the preceding paragraphs shows that different modes of globalization existed before 1500 AD. But, the actual step towards globalization process started after 1500. Of course, the term 'globalization' was not spelt out clearly and the process was latent as well as implicit. During this period, the Europeans intervened in the non-European states to improve the 'standard of civilization' in the international society. The norms and values of the European society and Christianity were the level of standards. When colonialism ended with World War II, the civilizing mission of the West broke down.

With the termination of colonialism, the Cold War started and it persisted till late 1980s. The Cold War was a state of tension or hostility in economic and political terms instead of hot or shooting war between the capitalist countries, i.e., the so-called First World headed by the USA and the socialist countries, i.e., the Second World led by the USSR. The policies adopted were to strengthen the military as well as nuclear weapon superiority and weaken the opposition. Following the break up of political system in the Soviet Union, the West declared that it had won the Cold War.

Oommen (2006) argues, if the motive of colonial era was to civilize the people of less developed colonial nations, move towards 'modernization' was reflected during the Cold War. The capitalist countries thought that their modernity was 'natural' but socialist regimes asserted it as 'enlightened modernity'. The colonial or less developed or third world countries were influenced by these two groups, to follow any one of these modernities during Cold War. The incident of dismantling of the Second World (i.e., collapse of the USSR) has resolved the conflict on modernity. It has made only one world and the world follows one modernity, i.e., capitalist modernity (Oommen 2006). According to it, everybody in the world can be equal, but to become equal, the people of the former Second World and Third World countries should approve and adopt certain values and institutional arrangements, i.e., the Structural Adjustment Programme (SAP) which emphasizes minimum role of the state, a free market and a vibrant civil society. SAP is a prescription of the World Bank (WB) and International Monetary Fund (IMF) which describes the actual policy for Liberalization, Privatization and Globalization (LPG) of economy in the developing countries. Thus, though the origin of globalization is sought in the history of colonialism and industrial revolution, actual roots of it lies in the specific economic and political developments of the world during 1980s and 1990s. It is a fact that the upshots like end of Cold War, dismantling of Soviet Union, collapse of the Berlin Wall, spread of capitalism and liberal democracies around the world and the advancement of information as well as communication technology in creating global connectivity have enormously engendered the emergence of globalization.

What happens in the globalization process or what exactly the globalization is? Actually globalization increases the pace of interconnectedness (http://www.christian_aid.org.uk). On the websites, 'globalization' has been defined in many ways. Some of these definitions are as follows: (a) it is a closer integration of the countries of the world especially the increased level of trade and movements of capital–brought on by lower costs of transportation and communication (http://www.wwnorton.com/stiglitzwalsh/economics/glossary.htm). (b) Globalization may be the increasing integration of national economies into expanding international markets (http://www2.montana.edu/lmyoung/glossary.htm). (c) It is a movement towards (http://www.wcit.org/tradeis/glossary.htm) markets or policies that transcend national borders. (d) It is understood as a process by which nationality becomes increasingly irrelevant in global production and consumption (http://www.agtrade.org/defs.cfm). (e) Globalization is also meant as the worldwide integration of government policies, cultures, social movements and financial markets through trade and the exchange of ideas (http://www.highered.mcgraw_hill.com). It is observed that most of the website definitions prefer to emphasize on economic globalization or economic aspects of globalization.

A few literatures highlight that 'globalization' is both a description and a prescription. As description, it refers to the widening and deepening of the international flow of trade, capital, technology and information within a single integrated global market (UNRISD 1995; Watkins 1995; WCCD 1995). As prescription, globalization involves the liberalization of national and global markets in the belief that free flow of trade, capital and information will produce the best result for growth and human welfare (UNDP 1992). This concept of globalization too has emphasized more on economic aspects.

There are some well-accepted definitions of globalization. Such as, Holm and Sorensen (1995) define globalization as "the intensification of economic, political, social and cultural relations across borders". Robertson has emphasized on political and cultural ideas such as human rights, global environmental responsibility and cosmopolitanism, which, in their various ways, project a sense of one humanity. According to him, 'globalization involves the ways in which we understand, experience and act within the single world and it is an inescapable part of the human condition" (Holton 1998). Malcolm Waters (1995) highlights that "globalization is a social process in which the constraints of geography on social and cultural arrangements recede and in which people become increasingly aware that they are receding."

In brief, globalization does not mean to only economic globalization. It includes three main areas of social life, i.e., the economy, the polity and the culture (Waters 1995). The *economy* refers to social preparation for the production, exchange, distribution and consumption of goods or tangible services at the global level. The *polity* refers to social preparation for the concentration and application of power. The *culture* refers to social preparation for the production, exchange and expression of symbols (i.e., facts, affects, meanings, beliefs, preferences, tastes and values) at the global level. Globalization seeks to enter every sphere of the economy, resulting privatization (and increasing price) even in the areas of basic amenities such as water, health, transport, energy, subsidized food, etc. (http://www.peoplesmarch.com/publications/globalization/chapter15.htm).

The globalization process has brought neo-liberal economy or New Economic Policy (NEP) in the developing countries. Though India embarked on a programme for economic liberalization in the late eighties, practically globalization process started in India in July 1991 when the country became a part of Structural Adjustment Programme (SAP). The present prime minister of India was instrumental to start NEP under the leadership of the then Prime Minister P.V. Narashima Rao. The NEP proposes removal of restriction on import-export and permitting free flow of foreign products, technical know-how as well as foreign capital investments; lifting controls and restrictions on private enterprises and allowing free trade and commerce; privatization of economy of the country by disinvestments in public sector, selling out state holding to the national and international level private corporations, reduction of government subsidies on essential goods and services, retrenchment in the existing government employees, etc. In brief, there is role back of the state and markets get importance.

In India, the first decade of NEP is over and now the country is passing through the second decade. Since July 1991, globalization process has promoted only a few sections of society in India within a mixed environment of political stability and instability. It has strengthened the intellectual capital. Hence, the highly qualified professionals in the fields of information technology (software), management, engineering, medicine, etc., are benefited greatly. Several business enterprises and industries have also been expedient. Of course, income level and general standard of living of the people have been improved, but on the contrary, there is environmental degradation. Practically, globalization process has impoverished the common masses. It has made disastrous impact on different sectors of life such as education, health and various social groups like industrial workers, women, dalits, tribals, etc.

In the field of education, drastic change has been observed in India. The budgetary allocation on education of both Union and State government was 3.6 per cent of GDP in 1992 which should have been minimum of 6 per cent. In the year 2001–02, the same budget was reduced to 2.8 per cent of GDP. The private consumption on education increased from Rs 10,002 crores in 1993–94 to Rs 15,196 crores in 1998–99 (http://www.peoplesmarch.com/publications/globalization/chapter15.htm). It is noticed that, when the government is reducing its expenditure on education, it is handing over the responsibility of elementary or primary education to imperialists or foreign institutions. For instance, among the foreign funded projects, the most popular District Primary Education Programme (DPEP) is funded by the World Bank, *Mahila Samakhya* by the Dutch government, *Shiksha Karmi* and *Lok Jumbish* are funded by SIDA. During the year 2000–01, the total amount (cumulatively) of foreign funded projects was Rs 1,076 crores. In higher education, 214 universities, 16 central universities, 28 deemed universities and thousands of colleges are being forced to mobilize a part of their funds from internal or private sources. The IITs and IIMs are being tied up with NRIs and TNCs (http://www.peoplesmarch.com/publications/globalization/chapter15.htm). The high level research activities in science and social sciences are also being influenced by foreign funding. C.P. Bhambhri (1998) is of the opinion that in the new phase of globalization, the western social science agenda has influenced the upper class academics of the metropolitan universities in India because of external funding in research.

In health sector, the condition is deplorable. During the first plan, the proportion of health budget of the total plan investment was 3.33 per cent which reduced to 1.7 per cent in the Eighth Plan (1992–97) (Padmanabhan 1999). The WHO recommended that health care expenditure should be 5 per cent of GDP. But, during the last few years of 1990s, the same was stagnated to 1.4 per cent of GDP. In fact, this was the result of beginning SAP of World Bank in India. The government reduced its expenditure on health and encouraged privatization of health services. Since, on the one hand, the private sector had excessive emphasis on curative services for profit making as well as was unwilling to invest in unprofitable areas like preventive programmes, and, on the other hand, the total government expenditure on communicable diseases had drastically decreased, the incidence of many communicable diseases (like malaria, *kala-azar*, etc.) rose rapidly and took their toll. Privatization has led to deterioration of health services in the public hospitals too. There is always lack of oxygen, saline and medicine due to shortage of funds which often leads to deaths of patients. For instance, at B.C. Hospital in Kolkata where nine children died on September 1, 2002, 31 died during the week, and 200 died in the month of (http://www.peoplesmarch.com/publications/globalization/chapter15.htm) August 2002. Privatization of health services, on the other hand, has resulted in the entry of international institutions under the domain of pharmaceutical segment, health insurance and corporate hospitals. Imrana Qadeer (2002) comments that corporate involvement in tertiary and secondary level of medical care denies the rights of the poor. While talking about intervention of international institutions in health sector of India, Baru (2006)[1] opines that during the 1970s and 1980s bilateral agencies like DANIDA, ODA, SIDA and NORAD were very active. But during the 1990s there was a decline in bilateral commitments, and an increase in funding by multilateral agencies. The World Bank emerged as the single largest financier of the health sector in India in the 1990s.

Paul Mitchel (http://www.wsws.org/articles/1999/jul1999/who_j23.shtml) feels that effect of globalization has undermined workers' health and safety conditions in many industries, since there is competition to provide the lowest costs to transnational corporations. Regarding women, the condition is extremely poor. In India where the poor families feed their girl children less than their boys on the perception that they would be future breadwinners, there the act of doubling the ration prices of food grains is forcing the women to starve (Desai 1998).[2] The decreasing job opportunities in the local area and the present wave of retrenchments in industries are also pushing women back to their homes which, on the one hand, reduces their possibility of social interaction, strengthen patriarchal values, increase 'dowry deaths' and so on, and on the other hand, prohibits the involvement of women in the organized sector. Apart from economic exploitation, there is further degradation of the social and cultural values of women. The corporate involvement to marketize cosmetic goods has brought the phenomenon of 'beauty contests' even at the *galli* level and 'fashion shows' through media. These have led to commoditification of women (http://www. peoplesmarch.com/publications/globalization/chapter14.htm). So far as dalits and tribals are concerned, globalization process has oppressed them more. On behalf of the World Bank-IMF programme, the government has reduced outlay for SC, ST and OBC welfare from 8 per cent in 1990–91 to 6.7 per cent in 1994–95. Again, as private sector does not follow any job reservation policy, privatization of public sector and massive retrenchment of government jobs put the SCs and STs under the scare of unemployment. Dalits, who are hardly able to afford schooling, under the New Policy Framework for Reforms in Education which seeks to drive privatization, will suffer more. Education will be increasingly inaccessible and unaffordable for them. With a view to reducing social inequality, land reform is suggested for development of dalits. But globalization process ignores the same and proposes corporatization of farming for global agricultural (http://www.peoplesmarch.com/publications/globalization/chapter14. htm) market.

In order to minimize the above-mentioned grim condition of the marginalized people like industrial workers, women, dalits, tribals, etc., many specialized agencies of the United Nations, international voluntary organizations, corporate bodies and central as well as state governments provide grants-in-aid to non-governmental organizations (NGOs). It is believed that NGOs are appropriate means to reach vulnerable sections of society. Under the SAP, along with the minimum role of the state and free market policy, prominent role of NGOs for welfare of the people are also suggested. Entry of voluntary organizations (VOs)/NGOs in the field of welfare is not new, but these organizations, what economists call the 'Third Sector', have proliferated after the process of globalization started. But why? What is the underlying reason for so much of importance to be paid to NGOs? Is there any problem with the concept of 'welfare state'?

The term 'welfare state' evokes images of people receiving handouts from the public dole. Sometimes, it gives impression of wasteful government programmes and undeserving recipients who are content to accept public alms rather than work for their livelihood. In brief, the 'welfare state' commits itself to ensure a minimum level of welfare for its citizens. After the Second World War, the concept of 'welfare state' emerged in order to deal with the social and economic crisis in terms of mass unemployment, fall in production, political unrest and so on. As per the provision, welfare state contributed through investment in infrastructure development, health care, education and other programmes for social integration (Narayana 1991). But this concept did not live more than three decades. The state had to bear the burden of huge expenditure. By the late 1970s, there was a growing recognition of the non-viability of the welfare state. For instance, in Great Britain, the contradiction of national insurance and the widening scope of means tested benefits clearly indicated that the idea of welfare state was under considerable strain (Brown, 1995). The failures of economic management raised questions of ability of the government to secure stable growth in the economy that seemed necessary to fund social welfare programmes adequately. Answer, in order to cure the economic illness, was rolling back of the state.

In the beginning of the 1980s, several developed and developing countries started thinking of privatization, liberalization and withdrawal of the state from the social sector programmes like education, health, nutrition, etc. Because, there was a movement that the state was incapable of tackling the problems of neglected and vulnerable groups of society (Bhambhri 1987). Many Third World countries, which were facing balance of payment problem, reduced their budget from social sector and started taking loan from International Monitory Fund (IMF) as well as the World Bank (WB) for the survival of the country's economy. The policy of the IMF and WB under the SAPs was to give loan to the Third World countries to 'help them adjust'. These money loans were tied to strict conditionalities. Loans were only granted when the countries agreed to the adoption of a compressive programme of macro-economic stabilization and structural economic reform (http://www.phmovement. org/pubs/issuepapers/hong08.html).

Any way, during the implementation of IMF-WB's programme, an understanding was developed that investment in public sector was wasteful and therefore the emphasis on NGOs was better. It was assumed, where government failed to reach out to the marginalized sections and created a gap, NGOs could bridge it. NGOs were preferred because of their special characteristics like small size, more participatory, less bureaucratic, more flexible, cost effectiveness and so on (Vahlhans 1994; Baru 1998; Rajasekhar 2000). Many social activists, who believed in radical change, had seen them as the magic wand that would cut through red-tapism, inefficiency as well as corruption. In the process of development, these NGOs play the role of carrying out various programmes, which are designed by either themselves or the government, related to formal education, non-formal education, adult education, health care, social awareness, income generation training, low cost sanitation, safe drinking water, rural entrepreneurship development, computer training, agro-based training, green house, sustainable agriculture, plantation, mini saving, family counselling, legal aid for women, *mahila mandal*, Khadi training and production, child labour issues, welfare for the handicapped, games and sports, aged welfare and so on (Sarkar 2001). The involvement of NGOs in the above-mentioned programmes helps to create a human society which imbibes the social values of dignity, moral and civic character, social justice, democracy and cultural freedom, etc.

In order to perform the task at the international level, NGOs have also been given importance. They are recognized as highly organized and most influential networking groups. In 1990s, they have helped in the preparatory phase of almost every major U.N. conferences, such as, Conference on Environment and Development in Rio de Janeiro in 1992, the Human Rights Conference in Vienna in 1993, the Population Conference in Cairo in 1994, Conference on Social Development in Copenhagen in 1995, Conference on Women's Development in Beijing in 1995, etc. During globalization, NGOs thus have become one of the few means that manages to maintain a common identity and an agenda from one UN conference to another. It has almost become customary now that every official global conference will be flanked by an NGO forum (Seth 1997).

The discussions in the preceding paragraphs show that NGOs have emerged as important actors in welfare and development and also dependable in undertaking many responsible tasks. These roles of NGOs are the new creation or new prescription of International Monitory Fund and the World Bank. The LPG era has thus brought new NGO enthusiasts.

Very often people question how NGOs emerge. Some of the social scientists feel, NGOs' root lies in the community life. According to P.D. Kulkarni (1984), the process of development involves different sectors in a society, such as, (a) the non-formal sector comprising of family, kith and kin and neighbourhood; (b) the market mechanism consisting of organized economy and the traditional unorganized segments of the economy; (c) the public sector includes civic and political institutions at local, state and national levels, and (d) the community sector which encompasses direct service, co-ordinating agencies and special interest groups. The community sector has the bulk of voluntary action which form or promote or nurture NGOs.

In India, in the context of social, economic and political crisis, NGOs have always been appearing as agents of change since the British regime. When colonial exploitation was on the peak and imperialism was the policy for development, welfare activities for impecunious and stymied people were embarked upon by non-profit organizations that were extraneous to the British Government. During the last hundred years, these non-profit agencies have increased by leaps and bounds and spread out in the form of social organizations, cultural organizations, sports organizations and so on. They are formed either as development agents of the community, or as a result of specialized technical knowledge or induced by the government. In the post independence era, freedom fighters, philanthropists, trained social workers, sociologists, anthropologists, development experts, planners, architects, etc., have contributed to promote NGOs (Kapoor et al. 1997). In fact, unique socio-political forces of any zone or province augment the rise of NGOs (Sarkar 1998). For instance, factors like the existence of Christian missionaries in the wake of natural disaster, etc. have led to the development of NGOs in Krishna and Guntur districts of Andhra Pradesh (Baru 1987). In Assam, various socio-political forces, such as zeal for independence, formation of the Kasturba Gandhi National Memorial Trust, Chinese aggression of Frontier Zone in 1962, cultural attitude of younger generation, women's autonomy movement, welfare tendency of retired officials, Christian missionary activities, professional attitude, natural calamity, Acharya Vinoba Bhave's Gramdan Movement and political instability have contributed to the growth of NGOs (Sarkar 1998). In West Bengal, factors like Christian missionaries, movement against casteism, scouts and guides movement, LIONS movement, Gandhian movement, women's movement, *tebhaga* movement, humanitarian attitude of freedom fighters, Naxalite movement, devastating flood, environmental movement, concern to reduce poverty, youth force, social problems of the handicapped, health care motive, welfare tendency of retired officials and politicians, refugee welfare tendency, minority issue and so on have helped led to form a large number of NGOs (Sarkar 2005).

In India, active involvement and initiatives of NGOs have been occurring since late 1970s. For instance, The Foreign Contribution Regulation Act (1976), the CAARD Report (1985), The Seventh Five Year Plan (1985–1990), etc. motivated the NGO sector for country's all-round development (Garain 1994), i.e., for education, health, income generation, environment upgradation, etc. The National Health Policy (1983) invited the NGO sector in health status development. It recognized the need for greater reliance on the voluntary and private sectors in achieving the goal of "Health for all by 2000 AD" (Duggal 1998). The National Population Policy

(2000) which aims to bring down the fertility rate to replacement levels by 2010 and to achieve a stable population by the year 2045, is also focused on the voluntary and non-profit sectors for population control (Nampudakam 2000). At present, NGOs have become very crucial in the process of decentralization of power and development (Mathew 1999). NGOs encourage the elected representatives to strengthen Panchayats financially by collecting taxes, fees, cesses, etc. from the villages and educate the poor in attending the Gram Sabha meetings to make them vibrant bodies (Rajasekhar, 2000). Thus, it is evident that NGOs in India effectively function as agency of change in the process of development.

The NGOs have also been criticized on various grounds. Truly 'voluntary' or 'independent' NGOs are rare who are involved in development work. Most of the NGOs are dependent on donors for project grants. They change their priorities every year since the funding agencies do the same as a result of various international forces (such as any decision taken at the UN conference, epidemic diseases, international economic scenario, etc.). In fact, this is the effect of globalization. Commenting on the changing nature of NGOs and pulls and pressures faced by them, Edwards and Hulme (1996) said, NGOs are increasingly being seen as contractors in the development business. On account of their popularity, NGOs are under tremendous pressure from the government officials, banks, donor agencies, etc., to extend services to a wider territory. It necessitates engagement of a good number of staff. Having employed so many working hands, authority of the organization gets involved with resource generation to maintain their staff. Power, pay scale, organizational assets, visibility of staff, etc. become the major focus and area of monitoring as compared to the caring the people or beneficiaries. Thus, NGOs deviate from the role of service providers (Ramchandran 1998).

Apart from the aforesaid limitations, inherent contradictions and conflicts like poor salary and long working hours (in most of the NGOs), absence of job security, lack of health care benefits and provident fund, no career advancement scheme for field workers, incidents of corruption, exploitation and sexual harassment of female workers are the common problems in NGOs today.

It is clear that in the age of globalization NGOs have gained popularity to work in the developmental fields such as health, education, income generation, environment, microfinance, social forestry, rural development, etc., and at the same time they encounter difficulties as well as criticisms at organizational level. Therefore, it was felt necessary to bring out this volume with the analysis of the present developmental efforts of NGOs. The chapters are invited papers which examine both relevance and salient features to see what the NGOs can contribute and to what extent the state depends on them in this period of globalization.

There are total fourteen chapters in this volume. The first chapter gives an analytical introduction. Then, the book has been divided into two parts. The first part, comprising ten chapters, deal with developmental facets and the second part including three chapters, focuses on the organizational facets. Rama V. Baru, in the second chapter, briefly tries to trace the changes in the health sector under the structural adjustment period, which has resulted in the restructuring of the public sector, and thereby enlarged spaces for both the private and voluntary sectors. The private sector is restricted essentially to providing curative services, pharmaceutical and medical equipments, while the voluntary or 'non-profit' sector consists of grassroots organizations, service institutions, advocacy and research organizations in the health sector. Since the late seventies both the private and voluntary sectors have gained prominence worldwide as a result of the domination of neo-liberal policies. During the nineties, the World Bank has emerged as the single largest financier of the health sector in India and other developing countries. The loans given by the Bank to the social sectors are tied to policy changes and restructuring of the health sector which is supportive of the non-government sectors, both private and voluntary. Given the heterogeneity in organizational forms, variations in the distribution of organizations, varied ideological and social roots of promoters, it is questionable how effective these NGOs are in their outreach to provide services and as builders of civil society.

Komal Parmar discusses poverty has been an issue of vital concern in India since independence. Poverty alleviation needs to be concerned with a broader understanding of human deprivation of choices and freedoms. Access to credit is such an area of deprivation of the poor. The mainstream sources of financial services have traditionally bypassed the poor or economically very backward people. Since the state is curtailing its role in the social sectors and encouraging initiatives of the civil society, the space for NGOs' interventions in poverty alleviation has widened. It is found, NGOs are fulfilling the credit need of the poor through 'microfinance' programme. Microfinance refers to small-scale financial services for both credits and deposits. Very often, this term is used as "micro-credit for micro-enterprise". While debating the issue in the present paper, the author says, credit offers an opportunity to generate income on a sustainable basis and prevent poor people from falling back into the vicious cycle of poverty. NGOs are better suited to contribute to this area. Though the NGO microfinance sector has made a start in providing 'user-friendly' formal financial services to the poor, its outreach is still miniscule in comparison with the need. Parmer feels, in order to foster poor people's development, along with microfinance programme, NGOs should be able to strengthen capacity of the poor people's own organization.

D. Rajasekhar states, in the context of globalization, where NGOs are preferred by the government and external donors in service provision and poverty alleviation, the delivery of microfinance services through a group-based approach is an important poverty alleviation strategy popularized by the NGOs. Since the late 1980s, a large number of NGOs have been forming microfinance groups consisting of women to enable them to undertake savings and credit activities. Rajasekhar tries to explore, do these microfinance programmes have the capacity to become sustainable in the long run? If not, what constraints do they face in achieving sustainability? Are there tensions and trade-offs between the sustainability of these programmes, and their ability to achieve poverty alleviation and empowerment? What needs to be done to facilitate the NGO microfinance programmes to become sustainable? With evidence collected from microfinance programmes promoted by five NGOs in Kerala, these questions have been examined in his paper. He has also illuminated the impact of microfinance programmes on poverty and gender equality, and the extent to which members' participation contributes to achieving these ends.

Having clarified the context that legitimizes the role of voluntary sector, Sukla Deb Kanango attempts to look into different aspects and issues related to the functions and performance of NGOs in the sphere of socio-economic development. The discussion in her paper is based on empirical data obtained from five well established NGOs, who have been working in the field of social welfare as well as economic development for 25 to 50 years. In her analysis, she argues that in the face of ever-shrinking resources and ever-increasing demand, sustainability of development programmes and welfare services will remain a challenge to voluntary service sector for a long time to come. Autonomy in the real sense and sustainability are intricately related and complex issues for any organization. K.K. Mukherjee and Sutapa Mukherjee describe and explain the programmes/services, organized by governments and voluntary organizations, in connection with welfare, rescue and rehabilitation for the girls/women in prostitution. This has been done based on the secondary and primary data collected for the national study on "Girls/Women in Prostitution in India".

Niaz Ahmed Khan provides a broad overview of the current state of social forestry in Bangladesh. His paper, giving a background, focuses on the government's key development goals and strategies for the forestry sector. Then it examines the performance of selected major SF programmes in the country from the perspective of rural development as well as poverty reduction and the state of NGO involvement in the same area. Khan's paper is primarily based on an extensive review of secondary materials together with an analysis of first-hand governmental records, sundry office and project documents. Besides, the discussion substantially draws on the author's observations and insights gained through personal engagement and involvement in a number of state forestry projects.

Ravindra R. Patil narrates that the globalization process has been running at a high speed and transcending all the boundaries of regions and nations in the globe. The basic tenets of this process, such as liberalization of trade and commerce, free flow of goods and commodity, capitalistic mode of production, etc have created adverse impact on global environment and human survival. The discussion on the massive growth of automobile industry and health hazards caused by vehicular pollution in Delhi is one of the glaring realities posed by the effects of globalization process. There is need to have some check on the harmful effects of this process. The government should enforce and implement stringent rules and regulations to keep check on automobile industry and prevent vehicular pollution in Delhi. Similarly, there is an urgent need that NGOs should take positive steps to reduce vehicular pollution of the city. Patil prescribes prospective roles of NGOs in this regard.

In the next chapter, B.T. Lawani highlights the pressures of globalization and neo-liberalism are felt by all, but these forces hit disabled people especially hard. Disabled people are directly affected when neo-liberal policies push states to cut social supports, and such cuts (for example, to public health programmes) also produce more impairment and more disability. As capital becomes more mobile across all boundaries, mobility becomes one of the few tactics available for labour. Since disabled labour is less mobile, less flexible than non-disabled labour, the demand for flexibility in labour and capital excludes those without flexibility from the market economy. This turns disabled people into unproductive neoliberal subjects. He says, in this context, NGOs have been playing significant worldwide role in the development of rehabilitation services for persons with disabilities. Giving an overview of conceptual clarification of disability, its types, prevalence, national policy and programmes, Lawani delineates the present involvement of NGOs and suggests its prospective roles in India.

Debotosh Sinha points to the fact that India being a vast country with different socio-cultural environment, no single strategy would be good enough to bring success in the field of child health. In the context of globalization, the proportion of plan outlay spent on child health care has been declining from one plan to the other and therefore NGOs are performing an important role in this field. He feels, child health is more of a socio-political problem and unless we integrate socio-political actions and work towards social justice, much cannot be achieved in this direction. Appropriate strategies such as giving recognition to the social workers, improving the status of women in the community, increasing the access to health care and health awareness, enhancing allocation of funds, rationalizing the priorities and so on will result in better child health.

The last chapter in the first part is on the state of Meghalaya where agriculture and horticulture are the major fields of income generation towards sustainable livelihood of the people. While there arise voices which echo across the borders, i.e., globalization, marketization and privatization, NGOs are directly engaged in the promotion of income generating activities. The paper by A.K. Nongkynrih is based on the data collected from twelve NGOs which are registered under the Societies Registration Act, 1976 and Cooperative Societies Act and are mainly engaged in income generation programme. All those NGOs are distributed in four districts such as Jaintia Hills, East Khasi Hills, Ri Bhoi and West Khasi Hills of Meghalaya. Nongkynrih shows that NGOs find it difficult to handle and provide any assistance to the farmers and small growers with pricing of produce. He feels, NGOs' good intention, approach and process of work adopted in meeting the economic difficulties by providing various skill-based training and other linkages to the poor, and those above the poverty line, are ultimately being determined by the global market forces. The power of the global market force is such that it can either increase economic opportunities of the poor, or they become vulnerable by its power and poor people's chance of economic development gets decreased.

Part two begins with Swapan Garain's analysis of the funding issues in Indian NGO sector. He says, in face of globalization, the fund-raising space for NGOs has changed during the last few decades in the wake of the issues like foreign vs. indigenous funds, business funding vs. foundation/trust grant, institutional sources vs. individual contribution, and external vs. internal revenue generation. He argues, though there are thrust areas, the process of funding and the preferred implementation NGO partner may vary across different segment of funding agencies. They all look out for those NGOs which have sustainable objectives, and are capable of creating more social values from limited resources. The area of funding is increasingly getting concentrated on projects that have a long-term vision.

Asok Sarkar, in his paper, tries to explore in his study the nature of job satisfaction of staff members working with NGOs. He observes, most of the staff members (84.44 per cent), are moderately satisfied with their jobs. The paper also indicates, there is a linkage between salary of the staff as well as level of job satisfaction. Staff mobility mainly occurs in NGOs due to low remuneration. Staff disquiets or changeableness or staff related grievances would no longer be problems in NGOs if salary structure is designed properly. NGOs can contribute to social issues well if pay structure is taken care of.

Finally, P.K. Ghosh's paper underlines that of late performance management has become one of the prime activities in industrial and non-industrial organizations of the private and public sectors. The objectives of performance management are to identify the areas of weakness of the employees and plan for improvement over a period of time. He proposes a model for assessing the performance of the employees in CSOs, NGOs, VOs and Trusts of the modern state. The proposed performance appraisal form is illustrative but not exhaustive. The organizations are to make necessary changes and apply according to their requirements and contexts. He feels, the employing organizations can mould and reshape the traits of the personnel through performance feedback at the end of the year.

The chapters, in the present book, call attention to the profound need to reconsider some of the aspects that have been popularized among the academic people, professionals, media, social activists, corporate bodies and civil society organizations during last twenty years. These include the domination of neoliberal policies that emphasizes role back to the state, a free market and a vibrant civil society. NGOs, being a part of civil society organizations, which are patronized by the World Bank and the International Monitory Fund, have gained worldwide prominence in social welfare as a result of their comparative advantage. The volume unfolds that though NGOs have drawn much attention, they are minuscule in number as compared to the needs, their outreach in any corner of the society is subject to socio-economic development of that locality, and autonomy of the organization in real sense and sustainability of NGO programmes are intricately related as well as complex issues. NGOs cannot replace the state, but may perform complementary as well as supplementary role. They can contribute to a great extent by reducing the tension of poverty or improving health status or empowerment etc., if people's participation is ensured. It should be noted that the power of global market force is enormous. Despite active involvement of NGOs in welfare and development, the wave of global market force either improve the condition of the poor or poor becomes vulnerable by its wave.

NOTES

1. Baru, R. (2006), 'Structural Adjustment and Health: Changing Role of Non- Governmental Organizations in India'. This paper has been published in the present book.
2. Desai, R. X. (1998), ' Working Women of India Under IMF Rule'. This paper has been quoted at http://www.peoplesmarch.com/publications/globalization/chapter14.htm and the same has been referred to here.

REFERENCES

Baru, R. (1987), "Factors Influencing Variations in Health Services: A Study of Selected District of Andhra Pradesh", M.Phil Dissertation, CSMCH, SSS, Jawaharlal Nehru University: New Delhi.

Baru, R (1998), "Structural Adjustment and Health: Changing Role of NGOs", Paper Presented at International Seminar on Global Governance and Social Policy, Baltic Sea Centre: Kellokeski.

Bhambhri, C.P. (1987), "The Modern State and Voluntary Societies", *The Indian Journal of Public Administration,* Vol. XXXIII, No. 3, pp. 395–398.

Brown, J. (1995), *The British Welfare State,* Blackwell: Oxford.

Dutt, R. and Sundaram, K.P.M. (2004), *Indian Economy,* S. Chand and Company Ltd: New Delhi.

Duggal, R. (1998), "NGOs, Government and Private Sector in Health", *Economic and Political Weekly,* Vol. 23 (13), pp. 633–636.

Edwards and Hulme (1996), "Too Close for Comfort: The Impact of Official Aid on Non-governmental Organizations", *World Development,* 24 (6).

Garain, S. (1994), "Government–NGO Interface in India: An Overview", *The Indian Journal of Social Work,* Vol. 55 (3), pp. 337–345.

Giddens, A. (1971), *Capitalism and Modern Social Theory: Analysis of the Writings of Marx, Durkheim & Weber,* Cambridge University Press: London.

Holton, J. R. (1998), *Globalization and the Nation-State,* Macmillion Press: New York.

Holm, H.H. & Sorensen, G. (1995), *Whose World Order: Uneven Globalization and the End of the Cold War*, Westview Press: Boulder.
http://www.christian-_aid.org.uk
http://www.wwnorton.com/stiglitzwalsh/economics/glossary.htm
http://www2.montana.edu/lmyoung/glossary.htm
http://www.wcit.org/tradeis/glossary.htm
http://www.highered.mcgraw-_hill.com
http://www.phmovement.org/pubs/issuepapers/hong08.html
http://www.wsws.org/articles/1999/jul1999/who_j23.shtml)
http://www.peoplesmarch.com/publications/globalization/chapter14.htm
http://www.peoplesmarch.com/publications/globalization/chapter15.htm
Kapoor, A.K. and Singh, D. (1997), *Rural Development Through NGOs*, Rawat Publications: Jaipur.
Kulkarni, P.D. (1984), *Voluntary Action: The Myth and Reality,* NIPCCD: New Delhi.
Marx, K. & Engels, F. (1969), *Selected Works,* Vol. I, Progress Publisher: Moscow.
Mathew, G. (1999), "Decentralized Institutions: Governmental and Voluntary Sector", *Economic and Political Weekly*, February 27, 7P–529.
Narayana, K.V. (1991), "Political Economy of State Intervention in Health Care", *Economic and Political Weekly,* Vol. 26 (42), pp. 2427–2433.
Nampudakam, M. (2000), "Views on the Population Policy", *Health For the Millions*, January–February, p. 8.
Oommen, T.K. (2006), "The Trajectory of Globalization: Situating India's North-East", Keynote Address in the National Seminar on Globalization and North-East India: Problems and Possibilities, April 26–28, Department of Sociology, Assam University, Silchar.
Petras, J. (1999), "Globalization: A Socialist Perspective", *Economic and Political Weekly*, February 20.
Padmanabhan, B.S. (1999), "Meeting the Challenges of Health", *Yojana*, January 10, pp. 17–19.
Qadeer, I. (2002), "Debt Payment and Developing Elements of Public Health", *Economic and Political Weekly,* January 5, pp. 12–16.
Rajasekhar, D. (ed) (2000), *Decentralised Government and NGOs: Issues, Strategies and Ways Forward,* Concept: New Delhi.
Rajasekhar, D. (2000), "Non-Governmental Organizations (NGOs) in India: Opportunities and Challenges", *Journal of Rural Development,* Vol. 19 (2), pp. 249–275.
Ramachandran, V. (1998), "NGOs in the Time of Globalization", *Reproductive Health in India's Primary Health Care*, CSMCH, SSS, JNU: New Delhi.
Sarkar, A. (1998), "Characteristics of NGOs: An Exploratory Study in Assam", M. Phil Dissertation, Centre for Social Medicine and Community Health, School of Social Sciences, Jawaharlal Nehru University: New Delhi.
Sarkar, A. (2001), "Development Through NGOs in Barak Valley: A Critical Analysis", *Social Action,* Vol. 51, January to March, pp. 61–73.
Sarkar, A. (2005), *NGOs: The New Lexicon of Health Care,* Concept: New Delhi.
Seth, P. (1997), "An Overview of Non-Governmental Agencies and their Functions", *Non-GovernmentalOrganizations in Development: Theory and Practice,* Kanishka Publishers: New Delhi.

Sengupta, C. (2001), "Conceptualising Globalization: Issues and Implications", *Economic and Political Weekly*, Vol. XXXVI, No. 33.
UNRISD (1995), *States of Disarray: The Social Effects of Globalization,* UNRISD: Geneva.
UNDP (1992), *Human Development Report 1992*: New York.
Valaskakis, K. (1999), "Globalization as Theatre", *International Social Science Journal*, June, No. 160.
Vahlhans, M. (1994), "The New Popularity of NGOs: Will the Enthusiasm Last?", *D + C Development and Co-operation*, May–June, pp. 20–22.
Watkins, K. (1995), *Oxfam Poverty Report*, Oxfam: Oxford.
Waters, M. (1995), *Globalization*, Routledge: New York.
World Commission on Culture and Development [WCCD] (1995), *Our Creative Diversity*, UNESCO: Paris.
World Bank (1993), *World Development Report 1993: Investing in Health*, Oxford University Press: Oxford.

PART I

DEVELOPMENTAL FACETS

Chapter 2

Structural Adjustment and Health: The Changing Role of Non-Governmental Organizations in India

Rama V. Baru

INDIA embarked on a programme for economic liberalization during the late eighties and became a part of the Structural Adjustment Programme (SAP) during the early nineties. During this period the emphasis was on cuts on public expenditure, and a more prominent role was given to markets in the economy and welfare services. The experience of early adjusting countries had clearly indicated that the macroeconomic adjustment policies coupled with blanket privatization of the health sector had a negative impact on indicators like mortality rates in several Latin American and African countries. Privatization of health services had far-reaching consequences in terms of accessibility both physical and social, rising costs and excessive emphasis on curative services and the neglect of preventive programmes. Since the private sector was unwilling to invest in unprofitable areas like preventive and disease control programmes, and given the importance of such programmes in most developing countries, the World Bank saw the necessity to invest in these by the state. As a result, the Bank called for a selective role for the state in health, which was articulated, in the World Development Report 1993 entitled "Investing in Health". Investing in health and education was seen as necessary to cushion the impact of SAP on vulnerable sections of the population where the state would selectively invest in some programmes.

Apart from providing a few inputs for preventive programmes, the private sector would take care of curative services at the primary, secondary and tertiary levels and the NGOs would supplement, and in some cases even supplant the state in providing health care, especially to the vulnerable sections.

The importance given to NGOs was based on the neo-liberal assumption that governments are inefficient, corrupt, inflexible and unresponsive to the needs of people they serve. The NGOs, on the other hand, were characterized as smaller, more participatory, less bureaucratic, more flexible, cost-effective and have an ability to reach vulnerable sections of the population.

Based on this understanding the quantum of aid channels through NGOs during the last two decades has increased dramatically from 2.7 billion dollars in 1970s to 7.2 billion dollars in 1990 (Fowler 1992). Regarding bilateral agencies, 13 per cent of total Overseas Development Aid (ODA) and up to 25 per cent of Scandinavian aid are through NGOs. The trend during the nineties was towards their projects (Marcusen 1996). This aid was then channelled to different levels within the NGO sector, viz., from grassroots organizations to those involved in advocacy to the larger ones in research and training.

In much of the recent literature on the role of NGOs they have been characterized as builders of civil society where the nature of their relationship with the state is crucial. There are broadly three different ways in which NGOs relate to the state by complementing it, by opposing it and by reforming it. The relationship of NGOs to the state is largely defined by the ideology and motivations of individual organizations. It is important to recognize that historically the building of civil society and its institutional form in the Western countries were based more on cooperation than in conflict with the state, and its shaping was determined by social forces internal to it. This is clearly a contrast to the present situation where civil society in developing countries is being shaped by external funding from northern NGOs in the context of pressure to reduce state involvement. This kind of an approach undermines the autonomy of NGOs since they are dependent on foreign funding, and their ability to sustain themselves over a longer period of time is questionable. The role of the state and its relationship to NGOs is extremely crucial in shaping civil society, but in developing countries the effort seems to be to reduce the role for the state. In the context of public health this has serious questions for universal access, equity and availability of service since NGOs are not in a position to replace the state. In addition, they present a great deal of diversity in organizational forms and ideological motivations which will result in variations in access, quality and effectiveness of service. In India, the beneficiaries of NGOs include dispensaries and hospitals promoted by religious organizations, trading communities, political activists, and more recently business houses. There are also community health projects in several states which work largely in urban slums and rural areas. Some of these projects are large and receive substantial aid from both the state and foreign agencies, while others run smaller projects and are therefore less dependent on funding from outside. More recently, there is a growing trend to handover government institutions to be run by NGOs.

The growth of NGOs in health services predates SAP and upto the eighties, their role was seen essential as complementing the state in providing health services. From the sixties the government offered subsidies and grant-in-aid to various NGOs to assist the state in the national health programmes. The most important of these was the family planning programmes where the state actively solicited the assistance from NGOs to conduct sterilization, distribute and promote spacing methods and also impart health education. In addition to family planning, they were also involved with immunization and a few disease control programmes. Right through the seventies, NGOs were not given much importance in the plan documents, and during this period a number of development NGOs addressed issues of health as related to over all development. Several community health projects were inspired by the Chinese experience and experimented with demedicalisation by training and persons from the community to deal with health programmes. Essentially, most of these experiments bypassed the state and it was during this phase that foreign funding came into the health sector. The late seventies were marked by world recession and India like other developing countries faced with a financial crunch. During the early eighties, there was an explicit shift in health policy with the government actively seeking the involvement of the private and voluntary sectors in providing health care. The Health Policy Document of 1982 categorically stated: "with a view to reducing government expenditure and fully utilizing untapped resources, planned programmes may be devised, related to local requirements and potentials, to encourage the establishment of practice by non-governmental agencies establishing curative centres and by offering organized logical, financial and technical support to voluntary agencies active in the health field" (Government of India, 1982). At the policy level, this was an important step in the privatization of health through out the eighties and specially with shifts in the nature of foreign funding during the nineties.

The next section will briefly trace the history and social roots of NGOs in the health sector during the turn of the century. This should provide some insight into the plurality in organizational forms and services.

THE ROLE OF NGOs IN HEALTH CARE DURING THE LATE NINETEENTH AND TWENTIETH CENTURIES

Non-profit institutions in health care were promoted by a number of religious institutions and members of trading communities in different parts of India. Prominent among the religious groups who promoted dispensaries and hospitals were the missionaries, both Christian and Catholic, during mid-nineteenth century. The Christian missionaries first set up their operations in the southern state of Tamil Nadu, and subsequently they started establishing hospitals in Uttar Pradesh, Madhya Pradesh and Punjab. Many of the hospitals in the northern states were set up under the auspices of the Lady Dufferin Fund of Women and Children. They were largely managed by women missionaries who were trained to be doctors. Even during this period mission hospitals which concentrated on service mostly had rural out-reach programmes. Their major sources of funding were from the respective churches of UK and USA, but these were cut back during the 1930s as a result of the great depression. As a result, many of these hospitals faced a financial crunch and had to resort to charging their patients for provideing care. The Catholics also established their earliest hospitals in the southern state of Kerala and then expanded to neighbouring states. They also moved to the poorer states of Bihar and Madhya Pradesh where they mainly opened dispensaries or rural health outposts in some very remote areas. Apart from the missionaries, some Hindu reformists also set up health care institutions in some parts of the country. Prominent among them are the monks of Ramakrishna Mission from West Bengal who set up a network of charitable institutions in a few states. In the western part of India, members of trading communities, especially the Marwaris, invested in setting up Ayurvedic and allopathic dispensaries and hospitals in urban areas of Gujarat and Rajasthan. In Maharashtra the Parsis who were also into business and trade set up charitable dispensaries and hospitals. These were similar to the organization of medical relief by merchant guilds in several English towns during the nineteenth century in Britain (Baru 1996).

Apart from religious groups, Gandhi's philosophy of self-help, cooperatives and involvement of different sections of society in the nationalist movement were a very important components of civil society. A number of groups were organized at local levels to provide service to youth, women and the scheduled castes. These were run as voluntary organizations without charging any payment. All the members offered their labour to run these organizations. In some parts of India, followers of Gandhi went in providing medical relief through dispensaries and rural outreach programmes. These institutions played an important role during the independence movement, since they were intended also for mobilizing the ordinary people. The communists had also created a number of institutions through trade unions, not only for health care but in education, theatre and related areas in different parts of India. Since there is a lack of research in this area, it is difficult to estimate their numbers and distribution across the country. Apart from the missionaries who were dependent on foreign funding from their churches, the other NGOs were largely sustained by contributions from the community and philanphists.

The entry of foreign funding into NGOs in the health sector during the seventies brought about a lot of change in the organizations, scale of operation and introduced the concept of wages in this sector. A number of professionals and political activists were responsible for starting health care and development of NGOs with some foreign funding. At this point, there were debates both within and outside the organizations regarding the impact of foreign funding on this sector and expressed reservations about the dangers of undermining the autonomy of the state. Through out the eighties, the development NGOs expanded and many of them used health care as an entry point along with related inputs like programmes for poverty alleviation, income generation and the like. Apart from foreign funding, many of these organizations also received grant-in-aid for implementing some of the government's poverty alleviation and related programmes. With the increasing trend in availability of funds, many of the smaller NGOs expanded in size and diversified their operations. Very often they became large institutions and developed some of the characteristics that government organizations are accused of. Many of these organizations also started employing professionals paying high salaries; as a result, their culture was much more akin to private organizations than voluntary ones.

These changes occurred largely in the medium and large NGOs who had access to foreign funds; but we do not have the data to assess the number of them who are working for health care. The increase in funding with emphasis on which programmes it is to be spent has distorted programme planning in the NGOs. During the early nineties, several American foundations were initiated through the Voluntary Health Association of India (VHAI), which is an umbrella organization for NGOs working in the health sector. In several meetings of these foundations held at the state level, it was understood that reproductive health was not a priority for the people but could be integrated as one input within a primary health care approach. Despite this view, it is significant that many of the NGOs did take up programmes for reproductive health mainly because they needed funds to sustain themselves.

SHIFTS IN PATTERNS OF FOREIGN FUNDING

During the seventies, the single largest funding for health came directly from the US government constituting 57 per cent of total funding. This was followed by the UNICEF with 15.6 per cent, the World Bank with 10.7 per cent and the WHO with 6.3 per cent. The European bilateral organizations contributed 3.2 per cent and American foundations a mere 1.9 per cent (Jeffery 1986). During this period, these funds were channelled through the government for a variety of disease control programmes and family planning. The major bilateral agencies which were active include USAI based in the US and European organizations like DANIDA, ODA, SIDA and NORAD. During the seventies and eighties, the quantum of funding by the World Bank was indeed small; however during the nineties there was a decline in bilateral commitments, and an increase in funding by multilateral agencies. This is not peculiar to the Indian context but a trend that has been observed in a several developing countries (Michaud and Murray 1994). The rationale for the Bank's entry into the health sector during the nineties has been "influenced by the pressing demand to alleviate the impact of adjustment in this area of social services" (World Bank 1992: 94). With the involvement of India in the Structural Adjustment Programme, there was a cut-back in the health sector specially for curative services and communicable diseases programmes. The cut-back on central outlays had a negative impact on the poorer states which faced serious consequences (Tulsidhar 1993). During this period, there were several epidemics of malaria, gastroenteritis and plague claimed thousands of lives. Some of these epidemics occurred in remote rural areas and poorer states of the country. As a consequence, the Bank started giving loans to make up these cuts and selectively earmarked funds for malaria, tuberculosis, blindness and AIDS. AIDS received priority and a large percentage of the funds were earmarked for it (World Bank 1992: 97). The priorities for funding these diseases seemed more to be the whims of the donors rather than based on any epidemiological assessment of the needs of the Indian population.

With the growing presence of the World Bank during the nineties, the bilaterl role of NGOs has undergone a change. Earlier they interacted directly with concerned governments and worked mostly in poorer states, but now most of them have tied themselves into the Bank's programme and supplement their effort for disease control and family welfare. Michaud and Murray observe: "lending from multilateral banks grew rapidly, from just over 79 million dollars in 1981 to nearly 400 million dollars in 1990. Most of the increase came from the World Bank, whose lending rose from 33 million dollars to 263 million dollars during the same period" (Michaud and Murray 1994: 15). Koivusalo and Ollila (1997) also make similar observations regarding the relationship between bilateral and multilateral agencies. With increase in lending by multilateral institutions, the bilateral agencies tend to play a secondary and supportive role to the former. While the bilateral agencies provided grants to developing countries they did not play any significant role in prescribing policy changes. The World Bank, on the other hand, has provided only loans which need to be paid back, and in addition, developing countries have to accept the conditions under which the loan will be introducing the Revised National Tuberculosis Control Programme which is promoting the use of more expensive second line drugs (Banerji 1996).

Since the World Bank attaches a great deal of importance to NGOs, a substantial amount of the funding is meant for NGOs working in these fields. During the last couple of years, there is a perceptible shift in the priorities of NGOs which were dealing with a number of issues concerning health to focusing on donor-driven priorities. This will essentially result in a fragmented view of health provisioning and clearly undermine the autonomy of NGOs to represent the 'felt needs' of the communities they serve. Another important change that has occurred is that many of the northern NGOs have started funding research studies specially in reproductive health, malaria and AIDS. As a result, priorities in research are also undergoing changes. In many of these programmes, there has been a public-private partnership that have developed with NGOs with varied roles ranging from programme implementation to advocacy, overseeing of programmes and research.

IMPLICATIONS OF CHANGING ROLE OF NGOs FOR PUBLIC HEALTH

The restructuring of the state in the provision of health services has opened avenues for the movement of private capital and enlarged spaces for the NGOs. This trend has serious implications. There is sufficient empirical evidence to suggest that NGOs are heterogonous, and are not evenly spread across the country. District level studies from Andhra Pradesh and Maharasthra suggest that they tend to be located in those areas which are better developed rather than the poorer. This would mean that the presence of NGOs where they are needed the most may in fact be wanting. In the absence of state provisioning, these areas would be denied access to any health services. Apart from the question of distribution of institutions, there is a great deal of variation in the kinds of programmes run by NGOs and the target population they serve. This once again presents a lack of uniformity and the necessary inputs that are necessary for effective public health care, a mix of preventive and curative services with a hierarchy of referral services from the primary to tertiary levels. NGOs are supposed to work with the poorest and help meet their needs, but once again this would vary with the different institutional forms. Many missionary hospitals treat both upper class and poor patients and have to charge fees to sustain their programmes. Similarly, even community health projects are increasingly trying to sustain their programmes by collecting some finance from the community. This kind of an approach has implications for equity and access, since communities in our country are stratified, and there are differential needs depending on the strata people belong to. While it is true that NGOs may be more sensitive to the needs of the poor, majority of them do not address the macro issues regarding the structures that perpetuate poverty inequalities because such questions automatically lead to larger political questions. It is also known that most northern NGOs would prefer to support those organizations which are good at ameliorating poverty rather than those who question the very basis of poverty. From World Bank's approach it is clear what kind of NGOs will get funding. In the given scenario, the role of the state in providing basic services becomes crucial. Despite all its shortcomings, the state has built up an extensive network of health services and the present effort seems to dismantle them and reduce possibilities for universal access to all sections of the population. Given the heterogeneity, variation in distribution and type of services offered by NGOs, there will remain some areas in the country that will be unserved in the coming years. Therefore, it is important to emphasize the need for state intervention in the welfare sector. As Robinson and White observe: "The State is the sole agency capable of providing welfare services on an across-the-board, universalist basis founded on some principle of citizen's rights. Given that the social goods provided by specific civic organizations maybe mutually exclusive or conflicting and may reflect a variety of motives from altruism, the state offers a potential integrating framework to both reinforce, regularize and rationalize civic provision, reflecting some broader notion of public welfare which transcends specific embodiments of social welfare" (Robinson and White 1997).

REFERENCES

Banerji, D. (1996), Serious Implications of the World Bank's Revised National Tuberculosis Programme for India. Mimeo, New Delhi.

Baru, R.(1996), Inter-Regional Variations in Non-Government Health Services in India: An Inter-State Analysis, Report submitted to the UNDP, New Delhi.

Baru, R., Nayar, K.R. and Gopal, M. (1996), Patterns of Foreign Funding to the Health Sector in India from the Mid Eighties to the Nineties, Paper commissioned by the Voluntary Health Association of India for the Independent Health Commission, New Delhi.

Fowler, A. (1992), "The Role of NGOs in Changing State-Society Relations: Perspectives from Eastern and Southern Africa", *Development Policy Review*.

Koivusalo, M. and Ollila, E. (1997), *Making a Healthy World: Agencies, Actors and Policies in International*, Zed, London.

Marcusen, H. (1996), "NGOs, the State and Civil Society", *Review of African Political Economy*, No. 69.

Michaud and Murray (1994), "Aid Flows to the Health sector in Developing Countries: A Detailed Analysis 1972–1990", Background Paper No. 11, *World Development Report 1993: Investing in Health*, The World Bank, Washington, DC.

Robinson, M. and White, G. (1997), *The Role of Civic Organizations in the Provision of Social Services: Towards Synergy*, WIDER, UNU, Helsinki.

Tulsidhar, V.B. (1993), "Expenditure Compression and Health Sector Outlays", *Economic and Political Weekly*, Vol. 28, N. 45.

World Bank (1992), *India: Health Sector Financing: Coping with Adjustment and Opportunities for Reform*, The World Bank, Washington, DC.

Chapter 3

NGOs in Globalization and Sustainable Livelihoods

Komal Parmar

POVERTY has been an issue of vital concern in India since independence. The pace of poverty reduction in the past decades has been slow. While an achievement such as increased life expectancy needs to be acknowledged, but the fight against poverty has not yet been a successful one. The proportion of population living in poverty and the trends in poverty alleviation in India are contested issues. Yet, there is a consensus amongst government and other organizations that poverty continues to be a major problem confronting the country.

Today, the largest number of global poor live in India—40 per cent of 1.3 billion poor worldwide. Although the relative number of the poor in India has steadily declined, the total number of poor people in India has increased from 200 million people in 1950 to 312 million in 1994 (36 per cent of Indian population). Several forms of human deprivation are observed, such as poor survival chances, landlessness, malnutrition, environmental pollution and social exclusion arising out of caste and gender discrimination are not necessarily linked to income in a predictable manner. Also, as land-based resources becoming scarce and more degraded, the balance between what the people need and what they can obtain shifts. At times, the effect on women is particularly severe because women are the primary collectors and users of natural resources in most parts of rural India. Agricultural progress is a social, economic and ecological necessity where farming is the main source of food, work and income. Hence, with the severe water crisis, both for domestic use and irrigation, in many parts of the country, at present and in the foreseeable future, water management is critically important for achieving the goal of food security and sustainable livelihoods.

In the past, India has witnessed the emergence of a large number of people's organizations, self-help groups, cooperatives and trade unions of the 'unorganized sector' in many parts of the country. These often complex and dynamic organizations of the poor had developed strategies for addressing poverty at the local level with the objective of improving people's living and working conditions and enhancing their bargaining power. These experiences have been confined to limited areas and have not been replicated on a large scale. Nevertheless, enabling the poor to form their own organizations has in many cases proved to be most successful and sustainable strategy for fighting conditions of deprivation and poverty.

Non-governmental organizations (NGOs) have often been instrumental for the emergence of these organizations of the poor. In recent years, India has witnessed also a rapid growth in numbers and areas of activities of NGOs or voluntary organizations in many parts of the country. Increasingly, the term 'non-governmental organization' encompasses a large variety of organizations of different origins, sizes, purposes, approaches and structures. Depending on the definition of the term, the estimated number of NGOs in India ranges from 10,000 to 100,000. Among them, few exist only on paper and are predominantly self-serving. However, many genuine organizations have acquired vast experiences in the areas of grassroots development processes, people's participation, empowerment strategies, organization building, etc.

Thus today, poverty alleviation is no longer an exclusive domain of government policies and programmes. Even though NGO intervention can certainly not replace governmental programmes, different actors of civil society are playing an increasingly important role. As the space for NGOs' interventions in poverty alleviation has widened with the state reducing its role in the social sectors and encouraging initiatives of the civil society, expectations vis-à-vis NGOs have also changed. High hopes are being pinned on them. NGOs are often expected to perform better than government agencies in poverty alleviation, to be more responsive to the needs of the poor, more efficient in the implementation of programmes, etc. At the same time, pertinent questions regarding the identity, legitimacy, transparency and accountability of NGOs are being voiced more articulately. With the growing involvement of non-governmental sector in social development and poverty alleviation, the role, relevance and efficacy of non-governmental interventions are also being debated.

GLOBAL AND NATIONAL TRENDS

The international development debates have varied over time. But they nevertheless seem to have come back a full circle in the 1990s, with the resurfacing of emphasis on economic growth-oriented development strategies. In the first development decade (1961–70), development was equated with economic growth, and it was assumed that the benefits of development would automatically trickle down to the poor. Failure of economic growth to trickle down, led to a redefinition of development as growth with equity in the late 1960s, and redistributive strategies with growth were recommended in the second development decade. As redistributive strategies like land reform were difficult to implement, the 1970s saw a further redefinition of development as freedom from poverty. Strategies to directly attack the problem of poverty through targeted poverty alleviation programmes became popular. However, the third development decade—the decade devoted to structural adjustment in most Latin American and African countries – saw the resurfacing of economic growth as the goal and primary strategy of development within purview of institutions like the World Bank. Though the goal of development has been re-cast as human development and poverty alleviation in the 1990s, economic growth persists to be viewed as the primary strategy to further this goal.

However, there is a marked shift in the institutional mechanism, which is seen as best suited to promoting economic growth as well as the nature of growth being advocated. In the 1960s and 1970s emphasis was placed on the role of the state in promoting economic growth, through regulating markets, encouraging import substitution strategies, and investing in public infrastructure. What is now being argued for is the rolling back of the state, greater role for the institution of market, and expansion of exports. That economic growth failed to trickle down to the poor in the past is attributed by the World Bank to undue distortion of market mechanism by the state, especially the labour market through policies such as minimum wages, job security regulations, and social security taxes.

Given the broader changes in the global politico-economic context, it is not surprising that though poverty alleviation has re-emerged as a key concern of mainstream international development agencies over the last 15 years, the origins of this interest, the specific concerns of the poor being emphasized, and strategies being recommended now are vastly different from those advocated in the 1970s. The interest in the 1970s in poverty alleviation emerged out of the realization that benefits of economic growth do not automatically trickle down to the poor, as well as the recognition of the political difficulty of implementing re-distributive measures like land reforms in liberal democratic regimes. Hence, a frontal attack on poverty through the state's poverty alleviation programmes was called for. Even though debates on women in development were just emerging, the diversity amongst the poor on the basis of gender were hardly recognized then. The 1990 poverty agenda, on the other hand, had emerged out of the recognition of the shortcomings of the state's poverty alleviation interventions, as well as the strong international opinion that high fiscal expenditure on the part of the state, state interference in functioning of markets and pursuit of import substitution model of growth have been the major contributory factors for the fiscal and balance of payment deficits in most developing countries. Hence, the principal poverty alleviation strategy being recommended now is labour intensive and export oriented economic growth centring around market, and supported by non-governmental initiatives in local level participatory development projects.

The decade of 1990 has also witnessed several changes, at the national level, towards economic, political and social scenario. Some of these are reflections of the larger global context, while others are unique to the Indian context. Some trends clearly pose threats to the marginalized sections as well as NGOs, while others open up opportunities for these groups. Part of the reason that the process of liberalization, globalization and privatization could not go in full swing after introducing these steps in 1991 is the pluralistic, but unstable, political scenario in India.

The 73rd and 74th constitutional amendments passed in 1993 to institutionalize local self-governance in rural and urban areas respectively have also strengthened the process of democratization and decentralization, though several hurdles still need to be crossed. While Panchayati Raj and Nagarpalika have been functioning in some form or the other in different parts of the country since long, it is only in 1993 that they have received a strong constitutional status. The Acts passed in 1993 provide for one-third reservation for women candidates and proportionate (to their population) representation of dalits and tribals, and thus pave the way for the participation of these marginalized sections in political process at the grassroots for the first time. Another favourable change in the socio-political scenario is the momentum of social movements in different parts of the country. Movements of Dalits, women, tribals, peasants and environmentalists, have grown in strength during the last decade. These movements have quite often challenged the anti-poor policies/legislation of the state and multilateral aid agencies as well as the wielders of power at community level. Though their rate of success has varied, they have played a positive role in upholding the rights of women and Dalits standing up for environmental concerns.

Global environment is affected by three interrelated crises, viz. increasing poverty, collapsing ecological system and pervasive communal violence and each of these to some extent is both, the cause and consequence of the other. Each points to important institutional failures, namely the failure of inter-governmental institutions, nation-states and markets on the one hand, and failure of households and communities, on the other. At a theoretical level, the shift in thinking on the appropriate institution for promoting development (from states to markets) has adverse implications on the poor. This is not to argue that nation states have been effective at addressing poverty, but that markets as institutions have been, and are likely to be, less effective. Markets are not neutral to the poor, but are permeated by power relations of varied kinds: class exploitation, gender subordination, diverse ideologies, ethical and cultural values, and hence it is more difficult to make them accountable to the poor than the state. In fact, for the poor to be able to effectively make use of expanding markets, the state provision of basic services has to expand and not reduce. This is particularly so for poor women, who need access to child care, education, health and financial services if they are to make use of market opportunities for their advancement. Empirical evidence from the developing world and countries in transition also supports this viewpoint.

The mainstream thinking on the role of government and NGOs in poverty alleviation has changed through the decades, at both international and national levels. Though a well-defined policy towards NGOs rarely existed, they were approached by national governments and aid agencies to assist in implementation of the community development and welfare programmes, especially in rural areas. This development model as well as role division was also promoted by the Indian government. Many of the Indian NGOs those were active in the independence movement got involved in the implementation of community development programmes of the government in the post-independence period.

During 1977, hopes were raised amongst the poor and the social action groups by the political parties but soon got dispelled as they did not take a clear-cut stand on the critical economic and political issues. As a result, many social action groups as well as people lost faith in formal political processes as modes of bringing about transformation in society. Further, this period (early 1980s) coincided with the emergence of ideas on the centrality of people's participation, conscientization and empowerment in poverty alleviation as well as the need to take into account the diversity amongst the poor on the basis of class, caste, gender, ethnicity and so on. These trends led to the evolution of two distinct types of NGOs in the 1980s: *development* NGOs, which seek to work around concrete sectoral activities relevant to poverty-stricken groups (agriculture, watershed, environment, non-farm income generation, health, literacy), but adopting participatory and innovative approaches; and *empowerment* NGOs, which seek to form organizations of different poverty groups and strengthen their efforts to address the structural causes of their poverty. A few social action groups however did continue their activism, and saw themselves as non-party political formations. Thus, by the 1980s, there were four different categories of NGOs working at the grassroots level in India: welfare NGOs, development NGOs, empowerment NGOs and Social Action Groups. While the first two categories of NGOs often entered into collaborative relationship with the government, the last two often confronted State policies, legislation and practices. Support and network NGOs also emerged during that time to lend capacity enhancement support to grassroots NGOs and create a platform for them to meet, share experiences, and carry out coordinated action.

The development NGOs, in particular, were called upon by the international aid agencies and the Indian government in mid 1980s to supplement the government's micro-level poverty alleviation and basic needs programmes in spheres where they perceived to have a comparative advantage, namely, reaching the poor, eliciting people's participation, promoting innovative and cost effective approaches to poverty alleviation, identifying and disseminating appropriate technology, making the government delivery system accountable etc. Thus, NGOs were called upon to play a greater role.

By the 1990s, the politico-economic context had changed substantially in India and across the globe. A key change was the liberalization, globalization and privatization of the economy, and the resurfacing of economic growth as a key strategy for poverty alleviation on the part of national governments and the

World Bank. However, the strategy now being promoted for enhancing growth is quite different from that advocated in the 1970s. It is led by the market rather than the state, export oriented rather than import substitution oriented, labour-intensive rather than capital intensive and women inclusive rather than women exclusive. Under this new scenario, the role envisaged for NGOs by the Indian government and the World Bank was quite different from that of the 1980s. They were now being called upon to provide 'delivery services', that is, to implement local development programmes rather than supplement government programmes in the area of operation.

ECONOMIC GROWTH AND MICROFINANCE: AN OVERVIEW

It was expected that the economic growth for 2003–04 would be 7 per cent + as compared to 5 per cent growth in the past. The 'feel good' factor had impacted all sectors of business, be it manufacturing or service. Demand as well as supply both witnessed a rise. It was also expected that the foreign exchange reserve would be reaching to $100 billion by March 2004. Stock markets are on a boom, and India has become an attractive and safe investing location for the world.

Annual demand for credit by poor households in 2004 was estimated to range between Rs 150 billion and Rs 450 billion. During 2003, the total supply of credit to this segment did not exceed Rs 15 billion, which is 3 per cent to 10 per cent share only. Rural penetration of bank accounts is 18 per cent. There is limited access to insurance services. Small deposit mobilization is picking up in a big way and hence proper mechanism with safety and guarantee is required by the poor.

The Reserve Bank, commercial banks, private banks, foreign banks, urban and rural cooperative banks, financial institutions, stock markets, formal lenders, viz., NBFCs/25 section/company for-profit and informal lenders, viz., NGOs/individuals are some of the financial markets of our economy.

It becomes essential to tap the capital markets and the reasons for it is to reduce existing cost of borrowing, establish presence in the capital markets, increase financial flexibility, i.e., diversify funding sources and create partnerships to access broad spectrum market alternatives, match the tenor of financing to operating needs and access funding without limitations of cash collateral and earn a better return.

The microfinance institutions (MFIs) bridge over financial market as bank linkages of SHGs under NABARD refinancing schemes. Licensed MFIs can mobilize deposits/savings and tap the financial market quite independently. As network members of an apex institution, they provide bank guarantee arrangements, on the spot securitization/portfolio buy-out, equity and bond markets (future option) and make foreign funding available towards capital/grant/onlending.

Outreach and sustainability are two main goals of microfinance and both can be achieved if MFIs have large capital base of its own which can be a leverage. However, there are gaps in the supply of formal financial services to the poor and the reason is that the institutional supply is constrained by cost of intermediation, price ceilings, inability of the poor to offer physical collateral, apprehensions about ability and willingness to pay for financial services, bitter experiences of directed credit programmes like IRDP and institutional factors including staff incentives.

The donors/bankers have opened doors to MFIs because priority sector lending is the target for the commercial banks, 5 per cent of net lending portfolio is essential to be invested in Women Entrepreneurs by the commercial banks, microfinance is seen as an impressive repayment proposition with repayment rates of > 95 per cent and < 5 per cent default rate. Thus proving that "poor are bankable" and the big untapped market with the poor is unfolding which may bring in large volumes of business.

There are certain prerequisites for accessing the markets such as clearly articulated credit policy/underwriting criteria, demonstrated ability to manage loan portfolio, experienced and credible management team, efficient tracking of portfolio through adequate information systems, strong capital base, transparency of disclosure and corporate governance. There are also certain limitations in access to financial markets for MFIs, a low level of awareness regarding the availability, source and method of approaching; lack of proper legal structure. With the majority of MFIs are caught in the web of different schools of thought on legal status for providing MF services, low capital adequacy ratio and low or no return on assets for most of the MFIs. Mostly negative returns on assets do not bridge over financial markets and low competence levels of human resources in understanding of financial products available in financial markets.

A boom condition can occur in MFIs provided they can get hold of the opportunity. Large volumes are expected, if the service delivery mechanism is perfect and loan losses are controlled. More business products will come in the next decade and big loan size to the borrowers.

There are certain changes anticipated in the MFIs and these are a must, i.e., a broad client base, look for large volumes of business with fairly high volume of products, new technology adopted like smart card, palmtops, etc., human development, the need for MFIs to be highly efficient and competitive in running the operations and change in legal structures to take care of growth. There are other constraints as well, like pressure on interest rate on lending by MFIs from government and other financial market scenario, service cost could increase due to demand for more skill and competence required to manage growing MFIs. Lower margins do not allow to generate more capital to leverage more funds, commercial banks now see it as an important business portfolio, they either want to enter the market directly or through MFIs, and their money power is higher. ECB is banned and hence only local funds are available and foreign equity is welcome but fortunate organizations are a few.

The banks have evolved a strategy to maximize access in microfinance by building partnerships. The existing partners are too small and are not growing fast enough and the banks' response is catalyzing the growth of partners and creating new partners. Making microfinance mainstream and influencing other players to enter the market where the constraint is that the profitability will have to be demonstrated and the response required is dissemination of methodology and practices, sectoral initiatives like designing innovative loan and savings products and identifying profitable microenterprises.

MICROFINANCE AND POVERTY

Many poverty alleviation programmes seek to improve the income, and consumption of households living below the poverty line, broadly defined as a certain annual income level that separates the poor from the non-poor. This pertains to a level of income that can ensure the subsistence of a household in terms of enabling it to access a "nutritional minimum" or a larger basket of goods and services required to fulfil its "basic needs". The provision of financial services can be seen as a means to achieve high income and consumption standards of such households, and enable them to cross the poverty line.

The answer to the question why people are poor is to be found in structural factors, which include distribution of the ownership of land and assets; economic relations in the process of production and exchange; and super structural factors such as caste, that reinforce the structure of economic and social relationships. These help to explain the inequality in income and wealth that have a bearing on poverty.

Poverty alleviation as a state objective would then be best undertaken through addressing these structural causes of poverty. This would include policies aimed at redistribution of assets, including land. On the one hand, over the years the limitations of the state to act on this front have become clear. Rural credit and now microfinance can be seen as a "surrogate" to redistributive reforms.

The failure of many state interventions based on supply in rural credit involving capital or interest subsidies (like the IRDP) is an established fact. This has been accompanied by the rise of social entrepreneurs, notably in Bangladesh. Using innovative strategies involving groups of women, joint liability, progressive lending, small loans and weekly repayments, they have demonstrated that it is possible to lend to the poor and have high rates of recovery. As a result, a consensus on microfinance has developed, broadly within the neo-liberal framework, which highlights the possibility of profitable banking with the poor. The peer pressure exerted by a "group" and the experience of channelling micro loans, especially to women, through NGOs engaged in microfinance is seen as an important means of alleviating poverty, in urban and rural areas of developing countries.

The lack of ability, or the will of the state to address structural factors causing poverty, and with the example of successful private initiatives, microfinance has emerged as one of the important tools for poverty alleviation.

The potential of microfinance has been posited by many on the ability, especially of women borrowers, organized into groups, to carry out profitable micro-business and microfinance equated with micro-enterprise development. Micro-enterprise development represents the distress-related end of the non-farm sector debates, one that is concerned with unemployment, low productivity and poverty. Micro-enterprises are almost invariably labour-intensive, and own account enterprises generating little income and low returns to family labour, even compared to agricultural wage rates. At the same time, the importance of micro-enterprise in the lives of poor people cannot be denied. It is often a secondary activity that is a part of a survival strategy, seasonally or technologically dovetailed into a more complex set of multiple occupations. With agriculture not being able to absorb the growing rural labour force, the spill-over factor adding to the numbers engaged in micro-enterprise, especially in the services and business segments, is strong. It is also accepted that not all households have the capability to undertake micro-enterprise. Several constraints may be in operation, which may limit the income yielding potential of any investment. This could include the risk-averse behaviour of households. Poorer households are more likely to be disadvantaged in this respect on account of their lack of education, entrepreneurial skills, etc. Finally, demand constraints may be operative for the limited range of feasible micro-enterprise options.

The income-based poverty measure referred to above, which is the basis of demarcating the poverty line in India, is also increasingly being questioned. A uni-dimensional measure based upon an annual figure, which ignores important aspects of the poverty paradigm, is considered to be inadequate. The real manifestations of poverty are better captured by conditions of food insecurity and powerlessness and the vulnerability of livelihoods as it is affected by trend factors, shocks and seasonality. The same phenomenon can also be stated and analysed using concepts of the entitlements approach and social exclusion.

Poverty alleviation thus needs to be concerned with a broader understanding of human deprivation of choices and freedom. Within such a framework, the mere access to credit cannot be seen as addressing their livelihood concerns. Most microfinance products do not address food insecurity, co-variant risks in production and empowerment issues. Nevertheless, it is clear that poor households have substantial financial needs which are either unmet or serviced by financial intermediaries on highly exploitative terms.

IMPORTANCE OF FINANCIAL SERVICES FOR THE POOR

Every household, irrespective of its rural/urban status or its economic status has a set of consumption and investment needs. The only set of needs that the poorer sections may not have would be luxury/leisure related expenditure, but that too is open to question given the (relatively) large sums of money that have been seen to be spent by the poor on the purchase of items like radios, TVs or on festivals and fairs, etc. Nevertheless, the needs for funds that typically arise in a poor family are life cycle needs like marriage, birth, death, education and other family events; emergency needs like medical emergencies, natural calamities, theft, accidents etc.; and investment needs like asset purchase, small business, etc.

All these occasions call for access to funds, which are substantial, unlike what we may expect. It is rare that the poor family has enough funds available to it when many of these occasions arise. There are variety of ways through which the poor try to meet these needs, they save, they borrow and they sell/mortgage assets like land, livestock, valuables, etc. The first two mechanisms represent the two major financial services that are required by the poor, namely saving and credit.

A poor household is characterized by uncertainties in the amount of savings and credit available. The poor save money in small lump sums, as and when they come into it; they take loans of small lump sums because their requirements are small; and they repay loans in small lump sums. The financial services being offered to the poor have to take into account the typically irregular and "small" nature of both income and expenditure, if they are to be useful to the poor. The financial services being offered also have to take into consideration the fact that the poor have no collateral to present as security for the loan taken. Thus, mechanisms have to be evolved where lending could be non-collateral based. Similarly, given the extreme vulnerable nature of the families, timeliness of loan is of paramount importance.

The mainstream sources of financial services have traditionally bypassed the poor. The mainstream financial institutions like the banks, the cooperatives, etc. have neither been designed, nor have they attempted to reach out to the very poor. Thus, it is not surprising to note that only a small proportion of the credit needs of the poor is being met by these mainstream sources. The rest of the funds have typically to come from the informal sources such as moneylenders, friends and relatives, traders, landlords and chit funds, etc.

DEFINITION OF MICROFINANCE

The most important finding during the last two decades in the world of finance did not come from the world of the rich or the relatively well-off. More important than the hedge fund or the liquid-yield option note was the finding that the poor can save, can borrow (can indeed decide on loans to fellow poor) and will certainly repay loans. This is the world of microfinance.

Microfinance refers to small-scale financial services for both credits and deposits that are provided to people who farm or fish or herd, operate small microenterprises where goods are produced, recycled, repaired or traded; provide services, work for wages or commissions, gain income from renting out small amounts of land, vehicles, draft animals, or machinery and tools; and to other individuals and local groups in developing countries, in both rural and urban areas. Often the term microfinance is limited to refer to "micro-credit for micro-enterprise". However, microfinance, in theory and in practice, includes a wider range of services; it represents something more than microcredit; it also refers to savings, products, to insurance, to pawns and remittances, in sum, to a much wider range of financial services. This distinction has at its heart the need to highlight the importance of savings and other financial products for poor people. On the one hand, it addresses the concerns of those development practitioners who are less than enthusiastic about the ability of poor borrowers to absorb credit without first building up the capacity to save. On the other hand, it represents the way forward for the "new wave of financial evangelists" which views the poor as "customers" with a capacity to borrow and save, who are in need of diversified financial products.

For several decades, many economies, including the Indian economy, experimented with subsidized credit for the poor. But the only tangible outcome perhaps was the increase in non-performing assets (NPAs). Then came the realization that the core issue for the poor was access to credit rather than the cost of credit. In fact, one of the contributions of microfinance can possibly be the end of interest rate debate. Microfinance has proved time and again that it is access to credit and not interest rates that are a constraint for the poor. Another discovery followed that the poor *can* and *will* save, and can indeed use a wide range of financial services such as remittances facilities and insurance products. The most well-known and cited international example of a microcredit institution is the Grameen Bank in Bangladesh. But, there are numerous others. Even during the Asian financial crises, Bank Rakyat Indonesia not only survived but thrived; as did Banco Sol in Bolivia.

A vast number of players have jumped on to the microfinance bandwagon – for a variety of reasons. There have been NGOs which gradually metamorphosed into lending institutions, development professionals who have set up microfinance companies and banks that have experimented with working exclusively with groups and therefore have 'microfinance branches'. These range from not-for-profits that see microfinance as having a role in 'development' to commercial banks that view microfinance as 'good, sound banking', an excellent way of raising deposits and lending at low risk. In fact the success of groups in microfinance has attracted the attention of wide-ranging players to use these groups for a range of purposes. Several governmental schemes are being routed through microfinance, including a very large project funded by the World Bank and being implemented in the state of Andhra Pradesh. Similarly, organizations like Hindustan Lever have looked at the potential of these groups as a channel for retailing and have launched a programme called "Project Shakti" to tap the smaller villages through the micro-credit channel. Microfinance leaders are gaining prominence and it is said that some of the leaders, particularly women, have been taking a more active role in other social spheres, including contesting elections for the Panchayat and so on.

SUSTAINABLE LIVELIHOODS AND MICROFINANCE

After decades of limited success in eliminating rural poverty, new ideas about rural development are emerging. A number of prominent agencies are currently revising their rural development strategies in broadly similar directions. So called "livelihoods approaches" work with people, supporting them to build upon their own strengths and realize their potential, while at the same time acknowledging the effects of policies and institutions, external shocks and trends. The aim is to do away with preconceptions about what exactly rural people are seeking and how they are most likely to achieve their goals, and to develop an accurate and dynamic picture of them in environment. This provides the basis for identifying the constraints to livelihood development and poverty reduction. Such constraints can lie at local level or in the broader economic and policy environment. They may relate to the agricultural sector or they may be more to do with social conditions, health, education or rural infrastructure. The new livelihoods approach is non-sectoral and attempt to address these problems by de-linking the concepts 'rural' and 'agricultural' and widening the scope of rural development activity. They see sustainable poverty reduction as achievable only if external support works with people in a way that is congruent with their existing livelihood strategies and ability to adapt. The term "sustainable livelihoods" relates to a wide set of issues which encompass much of the broader debate about the relationship between poverty and environment. A livelihood comprises the capabilities, assets (including both material and social resources) and activities required for a means of living. A livelihood is sustainable when it can cope with and recover from stresses and shocks, maintain or enhance its capabilities and assets, while not undermining the natural resource base.

Sustainable livelihoods approach to development incorporates the concept that it is important to meet the needs of people today without compromising the ability of future generations to meet their need. This approach is not uniform or static but it evolves with the expansion of the understanding of what sustainable livelihood should constitute. It is important for the government and non-governmental organizations to think about sustainable livelihoods in a much larger context.

Credit offers an opportunity for people to generate income on a sustainable basis. Therefore, the task of stakeholders in the development sector is to identify activities which can be taken up by local communities and which can generate sufficient income to prevent them from falling back into the vicious cycle of poverty.

MICROFINANCE AND THE POOR: FINANCIAL SERVICES FOR LOW-INCOME FAMILIES AND THE ROLE OF NGO SECTOR

Informal services have always been an integral part of the traditional economy of India and even semi-formal and formal financial services through agricultural cooperatives and banks are within physical reach (less than 5 kms) of perhaps 99 per cent of the population of the country. A vast network of commercial banks, cooperative banks and regional rural banks (RRBs) as well as other financial institutions provide such services. The other financial institutions include non-banking financial companies (NBFCs), insurance companies, provident funds and mutual funds. The RRBs were established in order to meet the credit requirements of the poor – small and marginal farmers, landless workers, artisans and small entrepreneurs and should therefore have emerged as major source of microfinance. Integraged Rural Development Programme (IRDP) was considered as Government of India's main poverty alleviation programme and the world's largest microfinance programme. But, the problem with IRDP was that its design incorporated a substantial element of subsidy and this resulted in extensive malpractices and misutilization of funds. Thus, the IRDP experience affected the credibility of micro-borrowers in the view of bankers and ultimately hindered access of the less literate poor to banking services.

Microfinance has emerged as a major intervention aimed at poverty reduction. A majority view, reflecting a broad consensus among various stakeholders, is enthusiastically promoting channeling of resources to poor households in urban and rural areas through these NGOs and MFIs engaged in microfinance. A wide range of enabling devices is simultaneously being developed towards ensuring the viability and sustainability of such institutions. These include the documentation of best practices and networks for information sharing, development of financial performance indicators, management standards, training programmes, etc. Besides, attempts are being made to link these institutions to sources of funding, both government and private. Advocacy efforts that are designed to influence the direction of reform of the financial sector in developing countries are also underway.

A feature of modern microfinance is that it is being increasingly considered a part of the discipline of finance, a niche within the financial services sector, rather than a development intervention. Many people now also see microfinance as the preserve of the non-government sector. This is true even for India where the public sector banks and the formal financial sector predominates in lending to the poor. However, linkages with the formal banking system ought to be created, such as self-help group (SHG) is the bank linkage programme of the National Bank for Agriculture and Rural Development (NABARD).

Many features of the present-day microfinance suggest that it is not a part of the modernization project and its objectives of economic growth improved technology and increased labour productivity. Though loans are still ostensibly given for "productive" purposes, it is accepted that they do not necessarily enable investment, but also support consumption needs or debt redemption. The largely homogenous loan products and recovery periods combined with progressive lending confirm the absence of a project approach to loaning. These products can best serve the purpose of financing working capital requirements of trading and service sector activities. Long-term loans are the exception rather than the rule. Capital formation through asset creation is not considered the major objective of credit. Loan utilization and problems related to fungibility of cash loans are no longer issues. Borrowers are not expected to repay loans out of income from productive investments but out of "normal" income.

Microfinance is thus essentially geared to the financial sustainability of the microfinance institution. The lessons from traditional systems, from participatory and bottom-up approaches from flexibility and diversity paradoxically serve to promote a regime of private, professionally managed but expensive institutions primarily for credit delivery. These institutions are increasingly expected to rely on market borrowing or deposits for their resources and offer a range of financial services, though not necessarily within a developmental or even a sound legal framework.

The new ideology of microfinance is clearly centred on the role of NGOs microfinance models and prescriptions are aimed at the present breed of NGOs engaged in development work with the poor. Many of these NGOs are involved in implementing savings and credit schemes as well. These schemes may have had their grounding in group organization and activity or in response to a strong need within the community. In any event the hybrid NGO undertaking microfinance as well as other development activity is a fact of life. Such NGOs are under pressure to respond to the demands of the new consensus on microfinance. This has involved addressing the question of financial sustainability, an issue that is increasingly being raised by international donors.

In a world where grants and soft loans are increasingly being directed to NGOs that can demonstrate that they are operationally self-sufficient, there is soon going to be no room for the traditional NGOs which are engaged in a variety of activities. A process of differentiation is setting in whereby the future lies with the professionally managed exclusively microfinance NGOs, with funding for other NGOs becoming increasingly difficult. This process would particularly affect local NGOs or community-based organizations that are arguably best placed to work with the very poor.

As far as the NGOs themselves are concerned the new agenda serves to create a tension between the imagery of compassion and that of capitalism. This issue, within a more optimistic view of the possibilities of scaling up, is also recognized as the "social development versus profit" dilemma. However, the NGOs that scale up their microfinance activities will inevitably leave themselves less space for social development and institution building in which they have the competitive advantage. The effects of structural adjustments have reinforced the need to create safety nets for those who lose out on market opportunities. NGOs are best placed to contribute in this area but are being forced to reexamine their role at a critical stage. Though the rural poor are rated as credit worthy, their enterprises are mainly engaged in the production of non-tradable outputs, the relative profitability of which is likely to diminish under the macro policy influences of adjustments. In the absence of other public or private investment, especially in backward regions, this could have very harmful consequences for the security of the poor.

Over the past 20–25 years, the resultant vaccum in the financial system has started to be filled, initially with the pioneering efforts of organizations such as SEWA Bank based in Ahmedabad and Working Women's Forum in Chennai, but more vigorously during the 1990s by the entrance of significant numbers of NGOs into microfinance.

Initially, many NGOs' MFIs were funded by donor support in the form of revolving funds and operating grants. In recent years, development finance institutions such as the NARBARD and SIDBI and microfinance promotion organizations such as Rashtriya Mahila Kosh (RMK – the national womens' fund), Friends of Women's World Banking, India based in Ahmedabad have also started providing bulk loans to MFIs. This has resulted in MFIs becoming intermediaries between the large public sector development finance institutions and retail borrowers consisting of groups of poor people or individual borrowers living in rural or urban areas. In another model, NABARD refinances commercial bank loans to self-help groups (SHGs) in order to facilitate relationships between the banks and poor borrowers. Though the NGO microfinance sector has made a start in providing 'user friendly' formal financial services to the poor, its outreach is still miniscule in comparision with the need. Recent compilation of support provided by major financial institutions shows that the microfinance outstandings of domestic financial institutions (including NGO-MFIs) did not exceed Rs 800 crores by March 2002 with an outreach to less than 5.5 million families – at best less than 10 per cent of the 60 million poor families in the country. This includes the NABARD scheme for linking the SHGs directly with banks.

CONCLUSION

In the context of the growing institutionalization of NGOs, it is important that funding agencies, the Indian government and NGOs themselves remember that NGOs are not ends by themselves, but means to addressing wider development goals. The ultimate objective of capacity building of NGOs should be that they in turn are able to strengthen capacity of poor people's organizations at different levels to foster their own development, and withdraw direct operations from their area of work. Studying different ongoing efforts in this direction has received little attention, but may be in particular useful. Advocacy efforts, though few at present, should also ultimately be handed over to mass based people's organizations at state, regional and national level.

NOTES

1. Addressing Poverty: Indian NGOs and their Capacity Enhancement in the 1990s – Ranjini K. Murthy and Nitya Rao.
2. Microfinance and Poverty: Sa-Dhan, New Delhi (*Perspective Paper No. 1*).
3. Sustainable Livelihoods and Microfinance: Sa-Dhan, New Delhi (*Perspective Paper No. 5)*.
4. Round Table on Microfinance Sustainable Livelihoods for Better Tomorrows – by Komal Parmar *(Deccan Herald,* Wednesday, April 24, 2002).

Chapter 4

Globalization, Sustainability and Governance of NGO Programmes: Some Reflections on Microfinance Programmes from Kerala

D. Rajasekhar

SINCE 1991 the Government of India has adopted an economic agenda which sees the markets and private sector as efficient in producing goods and services, and achieving rapid economic growth. The aid agencies prescribed that the Indian government should gradually reduce its role in service provision and development, and leave this task to the local organizations such as decentralized government, non-government organizations (NGOs) and so on. In accordance with the above, NGOs have been assigned an increasing role (Rajasekhar 2000) by the government and external donors in service provision and poverty alleviation. One of the poverty alleviation strategies popularized by NGOs (with the funding support from external donors) has been the delivery of microfinance services through a group-based approach.

Microfinance is aimed at providing the rural and urban poor, especially women, with savings, credit and insurance facilities to set up or expand income-generating activities (IGAs), and to improve household income security. The microfinance programmes are expected to alleviate poverty and empower women in a sustainable manner. This expectation is rooted in the limited success of government policies pursued since independence in alleviating poverty in India, where about 24 per cent of the world's poor live. Since the late 1980s, a large number of NGOs have been forming microfinance groups consisting of women to enable them to undertake savings and credit activities.

The studies on NGO experiments relating to microfinance reveal that NGOs and types of groups were uneven across the regions (Rajasekhar 2002). Yet, their experience positively influenced the government, NABARD, Rashtriya Mahila Kosh, banks and external donors to initiate similar programmes on a wider scale. International donors are enthusiastic about these programmes as they believe that they enable poor women to gain access to credit, and, therefore, progressively result in poverty alleviation and empowerment. The programmes are also expected to become self-reliant and self-sustainable. Do microfinance have the capacity to become sustainable in the long run? If not, what constraints do they face in achieving sustainability? Are there tensions and trade-offs between the sustainability of these programmes, and their ability to achieve poverty alleviation and empowerment? What needs to be done to facilitate the NGO microfinance programmes to become sustainable?

With evidence collected from microfinance programmes promoted by five NGOs in Kerala, these questions have been examined in the following sequels of the present paper. An attempt to study the impact of microfinance programmes on poverty and gender equality, and the extent to which members' participation contributes to achieving these results has also been made. After examining the group formation, savings systems, conditions of credit delivery, poverty reach and loan repayments in these NGO programmes, it is concluded that tensions between sustainability, poverty alleviation and empowerment could be minimized, if the programmes fully encouraged the member's participation in the running of the programme.

MICROFINANCE PROGRAMMES IN INDIA: SOME ISSUES

The studies prepared for the Microcredit Summit in February 1997, sector strategy papers of donor agencies, NGO project proposals and policy statements by the government, all present "an extremely attractive vision of increasing numbers of expanding, financially self-sustainable microfinance programmes reaching large numbers of women borrowers, making a significant contribution to global poverty alleviation and initiating an 'upward virtuous spiral' of women's economic, social and political empowerment" (Mayoux 1998: 4). These programmes were also expected to become increasingly self-reliant and independent of donor funds.

Recent studies, however, questioned this enthusiasm. While noting that the quality of service delivered by the NGOs tended to be good[1], questions were raised on the cost-effectiveness of service delivery (Riddel and Robinson 1992), the programme's success in targeting the poor, the sustainability of the services provided and the ability of the programmes to reduce poverty. In addition, Kabeer and Murthy (1996) noted that there were only limited data on the impact of NGO programmes on poverty and that NGOs' comparative advantage over other service agencies were needed to be investigated rather than assumed.

It is argued (Rajasekhar 1996: 92–95) that the ability of microfinance programmes to provide credit to the poorest was limited because of both structural and technical reasons. The emphasis on savings linked to credit, collateral requirements and short-term credit, prevented the poorest from accessing credit, and enabled the less poor with assets to access more credit. The poorest were also discriminated by the groups' management committees[2] and did not have the confidence to borrow from the groups since a 'minimalist approach'[3] to credit was practised.[4]

Income generating activities (IGAs) undertaken with the help of credit, provided by microfinance programmes, tended to be palliative (Namerta 1998). Riddel and Robinson (1992) argue further that such a minimal impact would be a barrier to achieving the most fundamental structural changes in the ownership of principal productive assets, which were essential if significant economic and political changes were to occur. Namerta (1998) states that although the programmes had succeeded to some extent in alleviating poverty, they had failed to address the more fundamental issue of the poor's vulnerability.[5]

Namerta's study of IGAs (1998) (initiated for women in eight microfinance programmes across India) concludes that less than half of the sample women borrowers were economically empowered or benefited from improved household decision-making due to microfinance services. And more than half of the sample had lost control of the loans and incomes from the enterprises as they were taken over by male family members. Mayoux (1998) and Goetz and Sen Gupta (1996) also question the degree to which microfinance services empowered women, and others argue that microfinance programmes diverted the attention of women from other more effective empowerment strategies (Ebdon 1995), or the resources of donors from more effective methods of poverty alleviation (Rogaly 1996).

On the whole, there is mixed evidence on social and economic benefits of microfinance programmes. While one group of studies (Hashemi, Schuler and Riley 1996; Puhazhendi and Badatya 2002) argue that microfinance was very beneficial for social and economic impact, others cautioned against such optimism (Montgomery et al. 1996; Goetz and Sen Gupta 1996; Buckley 1997; Rogaly 1996; Mayoux 1998; Rajasekhar 2002; Kropp and Suran 2002). Other studies suggest beneficial impact of microfinance programmes, but argue that microfinance did not assist the poorest (Hulme and Mosley 1996) thus questioning the ability of the programmes to target the poor, to sustain the services provided and to reduce poverty.

Thus, it appears that microfinance programmes have not always succeeded in their objectives of sustainable poverty alleviation and empowerment. One of the reasons for this could be the tensions between sustainability and empowerment. Before we examine these, let us examine the concepts of sustainability and empowerment.

Sustainability

Sustainability, in this paper, refers to that of microfinance programmes and not to that of NGOs. Sustainability in the context of microfinance programmes can be defined as the ability of the programme to meet the growing needs (credit and other) of members through resources raised on its own strength or resources available at its command. It has two components: institutional and financial.

Institutional sustainability involves creating, nurturing and sustaining people's institutions at various levels, i.e., village, cluster[6] and project. The important requirements here are capacity building of members for self-management and self-reliance. The other prerequisites are transparency, accountability (Edwards and Hulme 1995), monitoring, self-evaluation and impact assessment.

Financial sustainability implies the ability to meet operating costs, meet the costs of borrowing or raising funds, make provision for inflation, and so on, at the programme level. To achieve financial sustainability, resource mobilization in the form of regular savings from members is essential, and initial resources from banks, the government or other sources are needed. The programme should also ensure a rise in incomes of individual members so that increased contribution towards savings and operating costs of the programme is possible.

Sustainability should be achieved at three levels:

(i) the individual
(ii) the group and
(iii) the programme

Individual sustainability implies that, in addition to a rise in the income of the member's household, a member should gradually acquire skills and knowledge relating to group management, leadership, accounts, marketing, utilization of credit, the ability to deal with socio-economic or political problems within her/his community or society, the participation in political bodies at local level, legal systems, the participation in wider movements by taking part in networks, and so on.

Group sustainability implies the acquisition of skills and knowledge in ensuring that the group is financially and institutionally sustainable. For institutional sustainability, the groups need to be independent in management, accounts, leadership, conflict resolution, monitoring, self-evaluation and impact assessment, skills and confidence to approach local government agencies to mobilize resources for members, the ability to minimize market imperfections preventing the members to undertake IGAs, the ability to challenge the societal structures, and the ability to participate in local political bodies. For financial sustainability, the group should be in a position to meet costs relating to the programme such as meeting the salary of the group accountant and meeting the expenses, and be able to mobilize resources from the members and local government agencies.

Programme sustainability means the ability to meet the operating costs, the costs of raising or borrowing the funds, and make provision for inflation, and so on. Institutionally, the programme should be in a position to assist the needs of and provide support to the members in facing problems in the market, their community and society and in political arenas. It should also have a future vision.

Empowerment

There are different perceptions on the ability of microfinance programmes to contribute to women's empowerment. Mayoux (1998) states that three different approaches to microfinance were followed across countries: (i) the financial self-sustainability approach; (ii) the poverty alleviation approach; and (iii) the feminist empowerment approach. The reasons why women were targeted were consistent with the perception on empowerment adopted in each approach. In the financial sustainability approach "definitions of empowerment are essentially in individualist in terms where the ultimate aim is the expansion of individual choice and capacities for self-reliance. The aim may be to enable people to gain access to existing public allocation of resources or the process of growth itself. In this approach, the main role of microfinance is in contributing to individual economic empowerment. It is assumed that increasing women's access to microfinance, particularly to credit, will enable women to make decisions about its use. It is generally assumed implicitly that microfinance will be used by women to increase their incomes through micro-enterprise and that this will increase their control over income and resources" (Mayoux 1998: 17).

In the feminist empowerment approach, empowerment is defined as "a continuous process where powerless people become conscious of their situation and organize to improve it and access opportunities; an outcome where women take control over their lives; set their own agenda; gain skills; solve problems; develop self-reliance" (Mayoux 1998: 22). Two aspects are distinguished: (i) internal, i.e. issues pertaining to self, such as educational level, health status, gender, natural ability and self-confidence; and (ii) external, i.e., issues outside the self, such as legal frameworks, political, social and cultural environments (Mayoux and Johnson 1997). In this approach, microfinance is seen as contributing to this process through enhancing women's productive role and enabling them to challenge inequities within the household, and as a useful point of entry for wider mobilization. Here, the focus is not on access (to loans) as such, but rather on providing explicit support towards social, economic and political processes that will allow women to contest their subordination.

Participation of Members: Can it Minimize the Tensions between Sustainability and Empowerment?

Sustainability, as defined above, broadly corresponds to the feminist empowerment approach. However, there is a trade-off between the financial and institutional approaches. An emphasis only on financial sustainability can compel the programmes to adopt a business-like approach, by taking stringent lending decisions and enforcing rigid financial discipline. NGOs that have sought to achieve financial sustainability by following such measures have generally alienated the poor in the process. In some programmes, emphasis on financial sustainability has forced NGOs to bring changes in the design and implementation of the programme so that: (a) a top-down decision-making approach gradually came into existence; (b) the needs and aspirations of the members were not taken into consideration; and (c) a minimalist approach to credit was followed. This weakened the focus on participation, empowerment and poverty reduction.

The tensions between financial and institutional sustainability, and also between sustainability and empowerment can be resolved by increasing the participation of members in the microfinance programme. The participation can be by means of: (i) increasing the number of members within a programme; (ii) making decisions over different aspects relating to the programme; (iii) getting organized for other microfinance activities or for wider social and political goals; and (iv) by way of contribution of resources (savings), time and skills to enhance sustainability.

The participation of members in microfinance programmes can decrease costs and increase women's skills. But, members' participation needs to go beyond group formation, namesake membership and contribution of mere time and savings. It also needs to be recognized that participation can have costs as well as benefits to women, and choices would continue to be constrained by sustainability considerations and the resources and capacities of women and programmes (Mayoux 1998). Thus, there are potential linkages and tensions between different dimensions of participation, empowerment and sustainability.

THE CREDIT UNION APPROACH: NGOs FROM KERALA

Background Information on the Selected NGOs

This paper is based on the data[7] collected from five NGOs[8] in Kerala state. These NGOs initiated development interventions in villages, which were difficult to access and had limited infrastructure. Three out of the five NGOs were small and covered 20 to 25 villages in a few panchayats in one or two blocks of a *taluk*, while two NGOs were bigger and covered a larger number of villages and target population (Table 4.1). Three NGOs were formed and supported by the Church Administration, while two were secular.

Formed in the late 1970s[9], three of the NGOs began with a mother and child health care programme, which provided supplementary food and nutrition to mothers with children under three years of age. Although women beneficiaries were organized into groups to collect small savings, and to participate in activities (such as the construction of toilets by some NGOs), the overall approach was charity and welfare.[10] Donor-initiated evaluations of two NGO programmes, in the mid-1980s, concluded that if NGOs did not become "people's organizations" with members' participation in the programmes, their activities would not become sustainable. The evaluations recommended the formation of members' organizations, and the initiation of microfinance and IGAs so that the members could move away from "dependency" to "development" and independence, but declared that funds would only be made available for group formation, microfinance, income generation and skill provision. As a result, these two NGOs formed organizations for men and women at various levels, and from the late 1980s onwards, and started microfinance programmes.

The self-evaluation of one programme, conducted in 1986, revealed that grants provided under the earlier programmes were often not used effectively, that poor households did not benefit from the earlier charitable and welfare activities, and that indebtedness was high. Donor agencies' evaluations also arrived at similar conclusions and recommended the replacement of the mother and child healthcare programme by a microfinance programme.

In another organization, health activities (such as health and vaccination camps, referral services, and health awareness programmes) were set up, but as these were also not needs-based, the programmes were not actually implemented. The women belonging to target families instead requested that the organization start IGAs for young women who had completed school. Responding to this request, the NGO provided skills in mat weaving, tailoring, handicrafts, and the manufacturing of palm leaf products. Young women, after obtaining skills, started producing handicrafts in the production centre established by the organization, which also marketed the products through government and NGO sponsored marketing outlets. In the early 1990s, target families, left out of this programme, started requesting credit and IGAs. The NGO then initiated microfinance activities.

Thus, the development focus of the majority of NGOs shifted from charity and welfare to development, due to donors' insistence, self-evaluation and members' request. This was reflected in the change of activities from women and child welfare to savings and credit, agriculture and animal husbandry (Table 4.1) and in the formation of people's organizations at various levels. All the programmes started credit unions from the mid- to late 1980s.[11]

Two NGOs formed only women groups, one NGO had both male-only and female-only groups, and two NGOs had only mixed groups. The number of groups, and women members in these groups, increased several times between 1992 and 1995.

Table 4.1: Details of the Selected NGOs

NGO	*Important activities*	*Number of villages covered*	*Number groups established*	*Number of members*	*Number of NGO staff*
NGO 1	Education, agriculture and animal husbandry and women's development.	20	65	4,000	127
NGO 2	Agriculture and animal husbandry, alternative energy development and milk project.	83	83	40,000	150
NGO 3	Handicrafts and employment generation, animal husbandry and agriculture.	*	50	7,500	6
NGO 4	Women's development, IGAs and microfinance.	169	409	29,000	24
NGO 5	Vocational training, goat breeding and land development.	24	24	2,500	23

* Information was not available.

In all the NGO programmes, village level organizations formally consisted of farm clubs (only men), credit unions (with both men and women) and women's associations. Unlike credit unions, which met regularly to undertake activities, farm clubs and women's associations met only when there was a programme especially earmarked for them. As a result, they gradually lost prominence.

Formation of Credit Unions

Credit unions were formed for the members' families of the earlier mother and child welfare programme. Generally, any adult in the credit union area (normally a village) could become a member. Although the NGOs claimed that credit unions existed for the poorest, discussions with group members revealed that there was heterogeneity within the groups as the formation process was not based on socio-economic criteria. According to one staff member, "there is a little heterogeneity but the groups do not consist of extremely rich families". Although a socio-economic survey was conducted to collect baseline information in one NGO project area, it was not utilized in the group formation process. According to the organization, about 20–25 per cent of families in the credit unions were better-off.[12]

This was corroborated by information collected from 1,381 members from 14 credit unions (Table 4.2) which showed that about one-third of the members were nearly landless and 39 per cent were marginal farmers. About eight per cent were better-off. The proportion of the nearly landless was more in NGOs 1 and 3, while the proportion of the better-off was higher in the church-based NGOs. A majority of the members were women with their distribution being inversely related to their size of landholding. This suggested that credit unions were preferred by poorer women. The distribution of members by religion showed that a larger proportion of Hindus and Muslims came from the nearly landless and marginal farmer categories and that Christians predominated in the larger land size categories. The proportion of Christians was also higher in Church-based NGOs.

Typically, credit unions were relatively large with an average[13] membership ranging from 100 to 150 people. The groups were larger in those NGOs which formed credit unions with the mother and childcare programme beneficiaries.

The Credit Union Structure

The credit union structure was more or less the same in all the NGO project areas. The general body of the credit union which consisted of all the members in the union was divided into wards

Table 4.2: Distribution (%) of Members in Credit Unions by Sex and Landholding

Size of landholding (cents) and category		*Number of men*	*Number of women*	*Total*
0–25	Nearly landless	13.7	86.3	520 (37.7)
26–100	Marginal farmer	13.6	86.4	538 (39.0)
101–200	Small farmer	24.8	75.2	210 (15.2)
201 +	Middle-large farmer	31.9	68.1	113 (8.2)
Total		16.8	83.2	1,381 (100.0)

Note: Figures in the parentheses denote column percentages.

consisting of 25 to 50 members. From each ward a member was elected to the Executive Committee (EC). The EC consisted of 9 to 15 members depending on the number of wards. In the Church-based NGOs, nominees also came from the Trust Board of the local Parish. In two other NGOs, two prominent members of farm clubs and woman's associations were also nominated.

The EC elected a President, a Vice-President and a Treasurer. Although elections were held once in three years, the same EC tended to continue for a longer time with only one or two changes. In several credit unions, the President remained unchanged because he/she came to be trusted by the members, and others simply were not interested in the job. In one organization, the Parish priest was the President. In all the cases, the EC consisted mainly of men and the post of President was held by men from the mixed groups. The Secretary was permanent and paid either by the NGO or the credit union from profits. The main responsibilities of the Secretary were to keep accounts, collect savings and repayments, run consumer stores (if any) and attend meetings organized by the NGO.

The general body met once in a year. The EC met once or twice a month in connection with either a financial or a non-financial matter (or both). The financial meetings reviewed the activities of the last month, planned activities for the next month, considered new applications for membership and discussed information received through circulars from the NGO. The non-financial meetings, to which most members attended, were organized to provide general information through classroom lectures such as changes in rules. Given the large size of the credit unions, non-financial meetings were held only sparingly.

The role of the EC was to: (i) arrange meetings and awareness programmes in the village; (ii) review savings and take credit decisions; (iii) implement activities; (iv) involve in the selection and prioritisation of loan applicants and beneficiaries of other programmes, and (v) increase the membership and strengthen the groups.

The credit unions also undertook other development activities such as implementing NGO development programmes relating to drinking water and animal husbandry, providing consumer store services and chit funds, and mobilizing government resources for public health.

Systems of Savings Mobilization

The NGOs emphasised savings mobilization in their programmes, and fixed minimum and maximum amounts of savings ranging from Rs 25 to 60. There were three types of savings: (i) small savings (ii) shares and (iii) fixed deposits. Small savings could be contributed at any time and the amounts were flexible. On the other hand, the number of shares (the most predominant form of savings) per month was fixed and could not be withdrawn unless it was an exceptional case or the amount reached a certain limit. Incentives to savers were given either through interest or dividends (Table 4.3).

Amount and Regularity of Savings

Regular and quick mobilization of savings was an important aspect in these savings and credit programmes. This was because it not only indicated greater of members participation, but suggested that the members' stakes in the programme were increasing. It also implied that members were contributing all their savings to the group due to their increased confidence in the availability of credit.

The total amount of savings was larger in the older programmes with larger membership (Table 4.3). Some of these programmes also undertook savings mobilization drives in the form of giving awards to the best savers, and utilized cultural troupes and proverbs[14] to inculcate savings habits.

More than half of the members had saved less than Rs 500 and only 12 per cent had saved more than Rs 1,000. Further, there was no significant correlation between the period of stay in the group and the amount of savings of each member (Table 4.4).

It was stated that low income levels[15] constrained savings mobilization. However, this could not be the sole constraint because there was no perfect relationship between members' economic status and their savings amount. A significant proportion of the poor members saved larger amounts than those who were better-off, and not all of the large farmers were in the higher

Table 4.3: Savings Programmes in the Selected Programmes

NGOs	*Minimum amount of savings (Rs)*	*Interest on savings (%)*	*Dividends provided*	*Total amount of savings (Rs lakhs)*
NGO 1	40	6	Yes	11.89
NGO 2	50	No	Yes	15.90
NGO 3	50	4	No	2.20
NGO 4	50	5	Yes	192.74
NGO 5	25–60	6	No	8.07

Table 4.4: Distribution (%) of Members by Amount of Savings and Period of Stay

Amount of savings (Rs)	*Period of stay in years*					*Number of members*
	0–1	*1–2*	*2–3*	*3–4*	*4–5*	
0–100	33.3	38.1	21.0	5.7	1.9	105 (7.6)
100–500	12.8	37.5	26.9	15.2	7.6	646 (46.8)
500–1,000	1.3	19.2	38.4	21.3	19.8	464 (33.6)
1,000–2,000	1.1	9.9	50.0	19.7	19.0	142 (10.3)
2,000+	0.0	0.0	54.2	25.0	20.8	24 (1.7)
All classes	9.1	27.9	33.2	17.2	12.7	1,381 (100)

Note: Figures in the parentheses denote column percentages.

savings amount category. The reasons for slow and irregular mobilization are discussed below:

- The amount of members' savings depended on their expectations of whether they would be able to get credit or not. For instance, the amount of savings in one credit union was stagnating because many members were not able to receive any or the amount of credit they wanted. A member of the EC stated that only 10 out of 50 members in her ward had contributed savings because others were not hopeful of obtaining credit. According to other staff members, similar situations occurred elsewhere. A member in another credit union started saving as the NGO staff member had promised that she would be given a loan. As the loan was not given becsause of defaults by other members, she stopped saving. She stated that she would not save until she was given a loan. With the poorly financed Revolving Credit Fund (RCF), and the rapid increase in the number of members in recent years, the NGO was unable to provide loans to everyone, even if they were eligible.
- Women members were unable to make independent savings. Women members from several credit unions stated that they depended upon their men to save as they had to wait until their husbands gave them money.
- It was expected that members came to the credit union office to deposit their savings. In Church-based NGOs, the credit union office was normally located on the Church campus, and the EC expected the members to contribute when they came for Sunday Mass. As a majority of the members (including Hindus and Muslims) did not come for mass, the savings mobilization was considerably affected.

- Interest incentives were either not provided or were low (Table 4.3). Dividends, given by some of the NGOs, did not work as incentives because they were only distributed when there were profits and this was dependent upon management capability of the EC. Using dividends as opposed to interest had also made the EC less vigilant regarding the use and recycling of funds.

Credit Operations

The RCF consisted of members' savings and funds mobilized from external agencies (for example, loans and grants from donors or government agencies such as RMK). In the case of some NGOs, the members' savings were kept with the credit unions, while the external resources were with the NGO. These NGOs adopted limited decentralization in decision-making. The members submitted loan applications to the EC, and the EC took decisions by considering the opinions of other ward members. In one programme, borrowers were selected in ward meetings and the applications were then forwarded to the EC, which made the final decision. The loans were disbursed in the village.

Two of the programmes followed a centralized system where the EC made suggestions regarding the loans and sent the list of potential borrowers to the NGO which had the RCF at its disposal. In this case, the role of the EC was only advisory as the NGO sanctioned the loans depending on the availability of funds. Another variant of this system was when the members directly applied to the NGO for a loan through the Secretary. While the Secretary advised the NGO regarding who was to be given a loan, neither the EC nor the members had much of a role in decision-making. The loans in these programmes were disbursed at the NGO office.

Criteria Used in Selecting Borrowers

One of the most important criteria, adopted by the EC or the NGO, was the 'ability to repay', 'credit worthiness' or 'financial soundness'. According to the members of the EC, the repayment capacity of a member was decided by calculating whether a member already had an IGA, a variety of income sources and the ability to contribute monthly instalments. In the case of second or third loan, previous repayment performance was taken into account.

Another important criteria used in all the programmes was the member's past savings record. The EC would not only look at the level of savings but also the regularity of savings both before and after obtaining loans. This was because the amount of savings was required to be a certain ratio of the requested loan amount. The ratio varied from 1: 09 to 1: 5 (Table 4.5). In one project area, where the ratio of savings to credit was 1: 09, the EC did not look into other criterion. It only ensured that the members had the required amount of savings. In those programmes where the ratio of saving to credit exceeded 1:1, the decision-making bodies not only looked at credit worthiness, past repayment performance and savings record, but also insisted that two loan guarantors were provided.

Collateral guarantee had to be provided by one ward member and two other members. Where the ratio of savings to credit was 1:3, loans had to be guaranteed by two members with identical savings amounts. Guarantors could only take out a loan after a portion of the loan had been repaid by the borrower. In addition to other criterion, the decision-making bodies looked at member's attendance at meetings and their participation record in community activities.

Table 4.5: Lending Operations Adopted by the NGOs

NGO	*Source of RCF*	*Minimum loan amount (Rs)*	*Maximum loan amount(Rs)*	*Ratio of savings to credit*	*Interest rate (%)*
NGO 1	MS+EF	1,000	5,000	1 : 5	12–24
NGO 2	MS+EF	500	10,000	1 : 3	12–15
NGO 3	MS	500	5,000	1 : 4	24
NGO 4	MS+EF	*	*	1 : 0.9	12
NGO 5	MS	50	3,000	1 : 3	12

MS = Members' savings
EF = External funds

Loan Conditions

The NGOs did not have fixed maximum loan amounts. Nevertheless, the minimum and maximum loans tended to vary from Rs 50 to Rs 3,000 in one NGO and Rs 500 to Rs 10,000 in another. As the loan amounts were conditioned by the level of savings, the average loans were less than Rs 1,000 in four NGOs and Rs 2,039 in another.

The interest rates were fixed by the NGOs and varied across the project areas from 12 to 24 per cent. One NGO informed that it fixed interest rates to similar levels as were already prevalent in the project areas in the region. Another NGO fixed them on the basis of 'local money transactions'. A couple of NGOs arrived at interest rates after consulting the credit union secretaries. None of the NGOs involved members or the elected leaders in the decision.

Loans had to be repaid in up to 10 equal monthly instalments in three NGO project areas, irrespective of the type of the borrower or the size of the loan. Two NGO fixed a one year repayment period for short-term loans, and three years for long-term loans, but repayments had to be made weekly. In most project areas, weekly or monthly instalments were preferred as this allowed a more rapid recycling of credit, reduced supervision costs, eventually leading to financial sustainability.

Spread and Reach of Credit

The selected NGOs had not succeeded in providing credit to the majority of their members. Out of 1,381 borrowers in the selected groups, over 62 per cent had not borrowed even once (Table 4.6). The proportion of members borrowing only once was 28 per cent, while the proportion of members taking two or more loans was less than 10 per cent. An inverse relationship between the size of landholding and not borrowing from the group suggests that the credit unions adopted positive discrimination towards the poor. But this was only partially true. The better-off members in one credit union stated that the loans of around Rs 3,000 were not attractive to them. Instead they were using the credit union to access government programmes to obtain items, such as free seedlings, to which they weren't otherwise entitled.

Women were slightly more likely than men to receive a first or second loan, and there was a marginally higher proportion of

Table 4.6: Distribution (%) of Members by Number of Loans Received from NGOs

Size of landholding (cents)	*Number of loans (%) received*					*Total number of members*
	None	*One*	*Two*	*Three*	*More than four*	
< 25	51.0	36.9	10.4	1.5	0.2	520 (37.7)
26–100	65.4	27.1	6.5	0.7	0.2	538 (39.0)
101–200	72.9	16.7	7.6	1.9	1.0	210 (15.2)
201 >	78.8	14.2	3.5	2.7	0.9	113 (8.2)
Total	62.2	28.2	7.9	1.4	0.4	1,381 (100)

Note: Figures in the parentheses denote column percentages.

Table 4.7: Gender Differences (%) in Accessing Credit in NGOs

Number of loans received	*Male members from three NGO project areas*	*Female members from from all the project areas*	*Female members from three NGOs which formed mixed groups*
None	65.52	61.53	73.59
One	23.71	29.07	18.43
Two	6.03	8.27	6.46
Three	4.31	0.78	1.06
Four or more	0.43	0.35	0.47
Total	100.00	100.00	100.00
Number	232	1,149	852

men, than women, who had never taken a loan (Table 4.7). This may suggest that the credit facility was positively discriminated towards women. However, the women in mixed groups were less likely to receive a first or second loan, than their male or female counterparts in women-only groups. Men were also generally more likely to receive a third or fourth loan than any of the female members.

Repayment of Loans

The NGOs incorporated certain mechanisms, such as linking savings to credit, to encourage prompt repayment and so on. As shown below, the NGO which had the lowest proportion of overdue payments followed the practice of a high ratio of savings to credit. Secondly, the EC or NGO staff were made responsible for the repayments. They were supposed to keep regular contact, hold meetings with borrowers and provide awareness of the importance of prompt repayment. One NGO made the EC provide a repayment guarantee and obtained assurance for prompt repayment and correct loan utilization. The EC held non-financial meetings to raise awareness of the need to repay on time so that other people could receive credit, and this was found to be effective. Another NGO stated that repayment was ensured through home visits by the office bearers, community organizers and ward leaders. Another approach was to obtain collateral security from two other members and promissory notes.

Information on project level repayment was not available because NGOs did not keep it. Where this information was available it was faulty due to the lack of distinction made between

Table 4.8: The Proportion of Overdue Accounts in NGOs (December 1995)

NGO	Total number of loans	Loans overdue (%)	Distribution of bad debts (%)		Distribution of repaid (%)		
			Six months or less	More than six months	Repaid on time date	30 days after due date	More than 30 days after due date
NGO 1	196	24.49	60.41	39.59	100.00	0.00	0.00
NGO 3	19	21.05	0.00	100.00	100.00	0.00	0.00
NGO 4	149	2.01	66.67	84.93	84.93	2.74	12.32
NGO 5	38	44.74	100.00	66.67	66.67	9.52	23.81
ALL	402	17.91	66.66	91.21	91.21	1.82	6.96

Note: Figures for NGO 2 were not available.

overdue payments and loans outstanding. The information collected from the sample credit unions was, therefore, used for an analysis of repayments. Table 4.8 shows that the proportion of overdue accounts ranged from as high as 44.74 per cent in one area to as low as 2.01 per cent in another area. So, the proportion of repaid loans ranged from as high as 97.99 per cent to as low as 55.26 per cent. Of the total overdue accounts, bad loans (i.e. loans due for over six months) ranged from 40 per cent in one area to 100 per cent in another.

Of the total repaid loans, over 91 per cent were repaid on time (Table 4.8). But in a couple of areas, the loans were repaid very late. The fact that the repayment was high in the area where the ratio of savings to credit was very low (1: 0.9) suggests that the savings linked to credit principle was a successful instrument in ensuring repayment. It was because of the conservative savings to credit ratio that even irregular repayment of loans was tolerated here. The chief of this NGO stated that "we are not worried about repayment; in extreme cases, we adjust savings amounts to defaults".

IMPACT OF MICROFINANCE PROGRAMMES

Financial Sustainability

As discussed earlier, the financial sustainability of credit unions can be achieved at three levels. Three NGO programmes had not achieved programme level sustainability and depended upon continuing donors' financial support. Two NGOs appeared to have achieved project level financial sustainability, and this was reflected in the greater mobilization of savings, higher repayment rates, and resource mobilization from government, banks and donors. One of the organizations was able to cover operational expenses by running its own IGA and another organization, which mobilized Rs 20 million in savings from members, was able to achieve financial sustainability mainly due to the following three practices. First, only a small proportion of the members' savings was utilized for credit (the proportion of members obtaining credit was as low as 22 per cent in the sample villages). As a result, the costs towards lending, supervision and repayment were less. Secondly, rigid rules and regulations were followed. Members were bound to make savings in order to obtain credit in the ratio of 1:0.9, they had to provide collateral and make repayments in 10 instalments. Although a majority of the borrowers (especially the women) were reluctant to borrow due to these rigid rules and regulations, the NGO did not want to relax them as it was feared this would increase supervision costs. The credit union programme's co-ordinator informed us that the 'relaxation of the savings linked to credit principle would throw the programme out of gear' as it would lead to an increase in overdue payments and an excessive demand for credit and the programme did not have enough staff to cope with.[16] Thirdly, the savings mobilized at 6 per cent interest were deposited in the bank for around 10 per cent interest. The difference went towards programme expenses with any surplus given back as dividends. The decisions regarding the utilization of savings and surplus were made by the central committee.

In three programmes, the credit unions achieved partial financial sustainability in terms of meeting some of the operational expenses relating to stationery and travel, but the salary costs were still borne by the NGO. In two programmes, the credit unions achieved complete financial sustainability and this was reflected in their ability to generate profits, distribute dividends and meet expenses such as the secretary's salary, stationery and meetings. Financial sustainability at the credit union level became possible because of the following. First, credit unions undertook additional activities such as consumer stores and chit funds and profit from these activities was relatively high.[17] According to members in this group, chit funds met the credit needs of the better-off group members, such as middle farmers, while those in credit unions tended to be poor agricultural labourers. The middle farmers took the initiative to start chit funds because the credit union borrowing procedures had become lengthy and cumbersome, and their credit needs could not be met by credit unions alone. The emergence of different sources of credit was not altogether negative, as chit funds provided higher returns, but the secretary paid less attention to the 'not-so attractive' credit unions (by not offering additional support) which were more important to the poor. Secondly, by adopting rigid criteria (insistence on repayment capacity, collateral security and savings linked to credit) in lending decisions, the credit unions could only afford to follow a minimalist approach in the selection, monitoring and repayment of loans. A direct implication of this was that the capacities and skills of the members did not improve. This was particularly true for members who did not have any on-going IGAs and as a result they did not often borrow from the credit union or remain as members.

The financial sustainability of members was still to be achieved. This was evident from the small amounts of savings, higher proportion of non-borrowers to borrowers, smaller proportion of repeat loans and the very small loan amounts.

Institutional Sustainability

The programme was not institutionally sustainable because there were no credit union federations[18] attached to any of the four NGOs. One of the older programmes had formed a central committee in which the leaders of some credit unions were represented. But this was a hierarchical organization with no inputs flowing from below as well as from above. In the absence of a federation, the NGOs assumed all the responsibilities of the credit union programme.

Institutional sustainability at the credit union level was only partially achieved because of the marginalization of the management committees and members. The EC and the members did not actively participate in credit unions. In some group meetings, the members of the EC had to be reminded that they were in fact the members of the EC. When members were asked "who would you approach if you wanted a loan", the majority of them said they would approach the secretary or NGO staff. Indeed, some secretaries acknowledged that they played an important role in the decision-making process.

The secretary, who was responsible for day-to-day administration and appeared to hold quite a powerful position, conducted the meetings that we attended, led the discussion and s/he was the most knowledgeable about the credit union's affairs. The EC itself did not have much of a role to play. It appeared to just take orders from above. In most of the programmes, neither the members nor their elected leaders were involved in programme planning, implementation and monitoring.

It is not difficult to understand why the EC was not taking an active role. The EC was involved only in the selection of IGA of beneficiaries and in undertaking any required feasibility studies. Although EC members were involved in issues such as lack of repayment, their interaction with members was much lower than the secretary, who, in addition to taking part in the decision-making process and feasibility studies, was very active in the day-to-day functioning of the credit union. S/he collected savings and loan repayments from members and deposited the proceeds. S/he was a link person between the members and the NGO, and the benefactor to members with regard to loan provision, agricultural inputs and the mobilization of government resources. As the secretary communicated the members' needs to the NGO, it was natural that the members looked up to them, rather than to their elected leaders. In fact, one of the NGOs acknowledged this and was adopting measures to contain the secretary's role.

In some of the credit unions, the leadership seemed to be in the control of the better-off, with the poor not occupying any position of influence. In any case, effective participation of the members was difficult in large groups and most of the members were not even aware of their exact savings amount or the dividend that they received.

The selected NGOs kept in touch more regularly with their paid staff or the secretaries, rather than with the elected leaders or any of the target group. The NGOs sent their own staff to audit the books of credit unions on the ground that the president (Parish priest) did not have time or that other members did not have the technical knowledge. Whenever new policies were formulated by the NGOs, they were communicated to the credit unions through a circular. Even when there were objections to decisions taken by the credit union, the NGO generally went ahead.

Poverty Alleviation

As the results indicate, the members' savings amounts were very small, this was mainly due to systemic problems rather than adverse economic conditions. The proportion of non-borrowing members was also very high across the project areas, and even higher in the case of women members in mixed groups. This had the following impact on poverty. First, as the amount of savings only consisted of less than 10 per cent of the household income, it did not provide security for the members. Secondly, due to the rigid application of the savings linked to credit principle, the maximum amount that could be received only ranged from Rs 450 to Rs 2,500 for half of the members. These amounts did not provide the opportunity to undertake an activity which would rescue the household from poverty.[19]

The proportion of non-borrowing members was high and even higher for the women involved in mixed groups. These women stated that the rules relating to the link between savings and credit, collateral requirements and rigid repayment schedules constrained them from borrowing from the credit unions. Women felt that borrowing resulted in "sleepless nights" as the burden of repayment fell on them. In other households, with non-borrowing women who borrowed from chit funds and finance corporations, the loan repayment responsibility fell on male household members.

The second reason for not borrowing from the groups was that poor women wanted to borrow for consumption. However, the credit unions preferred to lend for agriculture (11.85 per cent), livestock (18.34 per cent) or small business (60.25 per cent). These activities together accounted for over 90 per cent of the total amount lent. A majority of the loans were given for small business establishments and petty trade because households were already involved in them and weekly repayments were possible. Less than three per cent of loans were given for consumption, health and education.

A vast majority of income generation loans were small. In one programme, 29 women were given credit to buy poultry with an average loan of Rs 308. With this amount, each woman obtained and reared 5–6 chicks. One woman stated that she would like to expand to 50 chicks, but in order to do so she would need a larger loan. The credit union turned down her request because of her low savings amount. Six women in another project area, each obtained approximately Rs 945 for goat breeding. One woman had bought two small goats and reared them for six months. According to her, the main benefit was the ability to keep one goat after repaying the loan and also having the proceeds of the sale of the other goat. However, in these cases, the incomes or profits from these activities only formed a small proportion of the total household income. Furthermore, these activities were undertaken as supplementary or additional livelihood strategies. The discussion also suggests that credit union loans were only used for one of several livelihood strategies, and that they could not alleviate poverty in sustainable manner.

In another area, about 60 women obtained loans for bamboo work. The loan amounts (an average of Rs 1,425) were meant primarily for the purchase of raw material from the Government Tribal Co-operative. As the raw material at the disposal of the co-operative was limited, most of the loan was utilized for consumption. Loans were not repaid as the earnings from the activity were small and uncertain due to fluctuations in the raw material supply. For the marketing of the finished products, they depended on middlemen who took a large proportion of their profits for marketing and credit costs.

A significant proportion of women were given larger loan amounts to start petty business and trading, or to by a milch animal. Only in a few cases, repeat loans were given as the credit unions followed the policy of "widening of credit" (larger coverage of members) rather than "deepening of credit" (giving repeat loans to the same borrower). The incomes from these activities were substantial, however, a significant proportion of these women were not ultra-poor.

Empowerment

Women's income opportunities were constrained. As there were few opportunities in many villages other than agriculture, women found it difficult to formulate viable income generation proposals on their own due to a lack of awareness, literacy and confidence.

The EC did not bother about the viability of the loan request if the request was for a small loan for consumption, crop production or an on-going IGA. When the applications involved new IGAs, larger amounts and longer repayment periods, one or two EC members visited the borrower to ascertain the activity's feasibility. Post-approval visits were seldom made to monitor the utilization of a loan. This had adverse implications for capacity building and skill improvement of the members.

Some women did not seem concerned about retaining control over their income and stated that they did not have much influence over loan utilization, management of the activity and income. They were more involved in the production process. As all the women who borrowed for agriculture passed the loans onto their family members and repaid loans from money given by men in the family or from their earnings, this did not appear to lead to an increase in their empowerment.

In some cases women were 'disempowered'. According to one woman, the loan she received for her poultry unit was taken by her husband for cultivation and the rest was used for household expenses. There was a lot of pressure on her from the group on account of diverting the loan. With great difficulty, she repaid the loan out of her earnings from wage labour. After that, she was reluctant to borrow from the group. She also turned down the request of her husband to borrow for cultivation purposes. In another case, a loan was taken for goat fattening. Just one month after purchase, the woman's husband sold the goat to pay for alcohol when she was away. She was yet to repay the loan.

Given that all the members rarely met together, the women did not discuss their social problems. In any case, the large size of the group and the presence of male members did not encourage them to discuss the sensitive issues. Women's associations, separately formed for this purpose, did not function regularly. As ordinary members did not participate in group management, their mobility did not improve.

Nevertheless, some activities gave women confidence to request higher amounts of capital. Savings were valued by many women as a means of accumulating capital for purposes such as buying jewellery, house construction, their children's education and marriage. As one women stated, "I look at the pass books and feel happy. I want it [the amount] to grow". In a significant proportion of cases, men did not even know that their wives were making savings or the amount of the savings. The 'secret savers' purposefully did not tell them because they thought there would be pressure on them to obtain loans for either productive purposes (which may not have been a priority for the women) or for unproductive purposes (such as drinking). In one group, nearly half of the women were 'secret savers'.

CONCLUSIONS

This paper examined the sustainability of microfinance programmes implemented by NGOs. These NGOs, which formed large and heterogeneous credit unions predominantly for women, achieved different results in savings mobilization, access to credit, receiving repayments, sustainability, poverty alleviation and empowerment as the systems and procedures were different to enable the participation of members.

With regards to sustainability, donor pressures (mistakenly understood as financial sustainability) created tensions between financial and institutional sustainability. The pressures relating to cost reduction compelled the programmes to put less emphasis to capacity building, to adopt a minimalist approach to credit, to introduce rigid rules and regulations relating to savings collection, credit delivery, and loan repayment. These had an adverse impact first on members' participation in the microfinance activities including savings mobilization, and then on poverty alleviation and empowerment.

Although financial sustainability at programme and group levels could be achieved, the same could not be achieved at the individual level. Furthermore, institutional sustainability could not be achieved at all levels. This was mainly due to tensions between sustainability and empowerment. In this context, we need to ask the question, how can tensions between sustainability and empowerment be reduced? What lesson does this paper teach us?

First, a programme providing microfinance services to women needs to have a minimum gender component. Such a component is normally influenced by the understanding that why microfinance groups are formed for women, i.e. on the ideology and/or approach of the organizations to gender. The approach followed by the selected NGOs was 'sympathy or charity' to women: This was probably due to the majority of NGOs being attached to Churches which normally adopt a paternalistic attitude towards women. This approach had a strong influence on the way the microfinance programmes were organized from the beginning. It was assumed that the formation of micro finance groups would ensure participation of women, and automatically provide women access to credit, resulting in poverty alleviation and empowerment. Thus, the NGOs did not give sufficient attention to the factors that constrain poverty alleviation and empowerment. Thus, clarity of vision was important, if tensions between sustainability and empowerment had to be reduced.

Secondly, programme and group formulation played an important role in reducing the tensions. Programme formulation in this case was influenced by donor agencies. The donors had recommended microfinance programmes for sustainability, poverty alleviation and empowerment. This had an adverse effect on group formation. The groups were large and heterogeneous which constrained the members in their ability in self-management and participation from the beginning.

Thirdly, the microfinance groups could be imaginatively utilized as: a point of entry for training, a forum for information exchange, a tool for enabling the members to participate in the microfinance programme, a basis for local collective action and collective action beyond the local level, and for the formation of federations to challenge macro-level gender inequities. The selected NGOs, by forming large and heterogeneous groups, could not mobilize the groups for the above objectives. The financial sustainability considerations influenced the policy decisions on group formation from the very beginning (Johnson and Rogaly 1997). The groups, mainly consisting of women, were seen as cost-effective mechanisms to mobilize savings, for disbursement of credit and for repayment. The microfinance groups were formed primarily for reducing costs and for efficiency reasons, rather than utilizing them as vehicles for poverty alleviation and empowerment.

Fourthly, the system of savings mobilization and conditions of credit delivery played an important role in ensuring the members' participation, poverty alleviation and empowerment. These systems needed to be flexible to women's aspirations, needs and existing strategies. As we have analysed, the fixation of savings amounts, systems of collection, interest on savings, loan conditions including loan amounts, repayment schedules and amounts, decision-making and recovery mechanisms were all decided by NGOs and thrust upon members. The net result was that the savings mobilization methods and conditions of credit delivery were not favourable for the poorest women.

Fifthly, the NGOs assumed that mere formation of savings and credit groups would result in poverty alleviation and empowerment. The need for complimentary services (a 'credit-plus approach') was not recognized. In any case, the financial sustainability considerations had put up barriers to these possibilities. This had an adverse impact on poverty alleviation and empowerment.

Finally, the micro-meso-macro linkages would play an important role in enabling the women to participate in wider social and political movements. The strategy that should have been adopted was to build the capacity of members to interact with banks and government agencies on their own, and to mobilize local resources. Local resource mobilization would become a platform around which the women's skills and capacities were to be built to increase their participation. The interface with banks and government would raise their awareness levels regarding their entitlements and what they needed to do to secure them. The women's participation in local decentralized government should be seen from this perspective. Still financial sustainability considerations did not allow the NGOs to build the capacity of the people in this regard and then enable them to access other local resources. The strategies that these NGOs utilized were to deposit members' savings to obtain bank loans, and the NGO itself developing contacts and credibility with the government to obtain resources. The micro-meso-macro linkages through networks, lobbying and advocacy remained as outstanding issues.

Therefore, it can be concluded that a microfinance programme can contribute to sustainability, poverty alleviation and empowerment only if member participation is ensured. If savings and credit were utilized as an instrument of self-help promotion for sustainable poverty alleviation and empowerment, the tensions between sustainability and empowerment could be minimized.

NOTES

1. See, for example, Kothai (1994).
2. A review of the studies by Farrington et al. (1993) also suggests that this is a wide-spread problem.
3. Two approaches are followed. A minimalist approach aims at providing only credit on the assumption that with repeated amounts of credit a member would gradually be able to relieve herself of poverty. A credit-plus approach realises that credit is not a sufficient condition for poverty alleviation, and hence, aims at providing a number of complementary services such as marketing, skills, support services such as a crèche or drinking water facilities, to women producers.
4. Namerta (1998) argues that the NGOs did not perform better than the government in income generation programmes, as the participation of women was minimal in programme planning, implementation and monitoring. They were also not better at providing quality support, to members, apostrophe families undertaking IGAs, in the acquisition of raw materials, skills and marketing.
5. Hulme and Mosley (1996) also make a similar point.
6. A cluster may be of different size depending upon the programme. In some programmes, a cluster incorporates as many as 5 to 8 SHGs within one village, whereas in other programmes, a cluster may incorporate 4 or 5 villages or more.
7. The data collected included detailed interviews with chief functionaries of NGOs, staff members and members in three representative groups. From the project area of each of the NGOs, three groups (very well performing, medium performing and not so good performing) were selected along with the NGO staff with the help of information on the level of members' participation, savings mobilization, loans utilization and loan repayment. The NGOs were also requested to provide basic information on all the members in the three selected groups, covering the details of caste, size of landholdings, date of joining, number of loans

taken and repaid, the purpose of the loan and the last loan received, and repayment details. The field visits to the NGOs and the three selected groups were undertaken during the three-year period beginning with 1996, to cross-check the information provided, and to collect additional information on relevant aspects. In group meetings, Rapid Rural Appraisal (RRA) techniques were used and detailed case studies were made on at least two members in each group.

8. Two NGOs were located in Wayanad district, two in Trivandrum district and one in Kottayam district.
9. Two were formed in 1976, two in 1977 and one in 1979.
10. For instance, one NGO implemented a sponsorship programme under which each family member was given Rs 100 per annum as a gift.
11. The ideas and skills required in the formation, systems and structures of credit unions were obtained in seminars, workshops, exposure visits.
12. 'Better-off' refers to those households possessing assets such as house, land and animals. These households were likely to have regular employment and a better health and education status than the poor, who were unlikely to have a house or any assets. The poor were also likely to suffer from seasonal or chronic unemployment and their health and education levels were poor. The NGO mentioned above stated that its benefits would go only to the poor and the baseline data were used in this regard. Although the better-off individuals remained in the group, they did not take any loans or benefits because they could easily get credit from the banks or access resources from government agencies. The strategy, according to the NGO, was to utilize the resources and goodwill of the better-off for the benefit of the poor or for the over all development of the area. The better-off were said not to be involved in any of the decision-making processes, and the leadership in the groups was said to be mature enough to handle this situation.
13. Credit unions had membership ranging from 20 to 120 people in one project area to 150 to 350 in another project area.
14. Kala Sanghams were cultural troupes developed by an organization to perform plays in the villages, to express the need to save and the ill-effects of overspending. Demonstrations with proverbs written on banners were carried out in the villages to promote saving habits.
15. It was argued that low levels of profit from IGAs, undertaken by members, did not enable them to contribute regular savings. Secondly, as the loans given by the NGOs were small, the members were forced to borrow from informal sources elsewhere. With high interest applied to such loans, the profitability of their ventures was eroded, and thus, their ability to save was reduced further. Thirdly, members with very small landholdings and uncertain employment found it difficult to make regular savings.
16. This NGO had only 24 staff members for 29,000 members in their project area.
17. The credit unions that we visited required Rs 30,000–35,000 to meet their yearly expenses and between 60 to 80 per cent of these amounts were generated from profits of chit funds and consumer stores.

18. A 'federation' is a credit union organization at the project level which provides support services to the members, such as helping in the acquisition of raw materials, skills and credit, as well as policy advocacy through networks and lobbying. These responsibilities were undertaken by the NGO when a credit federation is absent.
19. In contrast, IRDP loan amounts were more than Rs 5,000 in most cases.

REFERENCES

Buckley, G. (1997), "Micro-Finance in Africa: Is it Either the Problem or the Solution?" *World Development*, Vol. 25, No. 7.

Ebdon, R. (1995), "NGO Expansion and the Fight to Reach the Poor: Gender Implications of NGO Scaling up in Bangladesh", *IDS Bulletin*, Vol. 26, No. 3.

Edwards, M. and David Hulme (1995), *Non-Governmental Organisations – Performance and Accountability: Beyond the Magic Bullet*, Earthscan, London.

Farrington, J. et al. (eds.) (1993), *Reluctant Partners? Non-Governmental Organisations, the State and Sustainable Agriculture*, Routledge, London.

Goetz, A. M. and Sen Gupta, R. (1996), "Who Takes the Credit? Gender, Power and Control Over Loan Use in Rural Credit Programmes in Bangladesh", *World Development*, Vol. 24, No. 1.

Hashemi, Syed M., Sidney Ruth Schuler and Ann P. Riley (1996), "Rural Credit Programmes and Women's Empowerment in Bangladesh", *World Development*, Vol. 24, No. 4.

Hulme, David and Paul Mosley (1996), *Finance Against Poverty*, Routledge, London.

Johnson, S. and Ben Rogaly (1997), *Micro-Finance and Poverty Reduction*, Oxfam: Oxford.

Kabeer, Naila and R. K. Murthy (1996), "Compensating for Institutional Reclusion? Lessons from Indian Government and Non-Government Credit Interventions for the Poor", IDS Discussion Paper, No. 356, IDS, Brighton.

Kothai, K. (1994), "Economic Impact of Rural Development Projects on Small Farmers", *Journal of Rural Development*, Vol. 13, No. 2.

Kropp, E.W. and B. S. Suran (2002), *Linking Banks and Self-Help Groups in India: An Assessment*, NABARD, Mumbai.

Mayoux, L. (1998), "Women's Empowerment and Micro-Finance Programmes: Approaches, Evidence and Ways Forward", Discussion Paper, The Open University, Milton Keynes.

Mayoux, L. and S. Johnson (eds.) (1997), "Micro-Finance and Women's Empowerment: Strategies for Increasing Impact", Report of the Workshop held on January 13–15, Addis Ababa, Ethiopia.

Montgomery, R., Bhattacharya, D. and Hulme, D. (1996), *Credit for Poor in Bangladesh*, The BRAC Rural Development Programme and the Government Thana Resource Development and Employment Programme, Bangladesh.

Namerta (1998), *Income and Employment Generation Programmes of NGOs in India*, NOVIB, Bangalore.

Puhazhendi, V. and Badatya, K.C. (2002), *Self-Help Group-Bank Linkage Programme for Rural Poor in India: An Impact Assessment*, NABARD, Mumbai.

Rajasekhar, D. (1996), "Problems and Prospects of Group Lending in NGO Credit Programmes in India", *Savings and Development*, Vol. 20, No. 1.

———. (2000), "Non-Governmental Organisations (NGOs) in India: Opportunities and Challenges", Working Paper No. 66, Institute for Social and Economic Change, Bangalore.

———. (2002), "Impact of Micro-Finance Programmes on Poverty and Gender Equality: Some Evidence from Indian NGOs", in Shahra Razavi (ed.), *Shifting Burdens: Gender and Agrarian Change under Neoliberalism*, Kumarian Press, Bloomfield.

Riddel, R. and Mark, R. (1992), "The Impact of NGO Poverty Alleviation Projects: Results of the Case Study Evaluations", Working Paper No. 68, Overseas Development Institute, London.

Rogaly, B. (1996), "Micro-Finance Evangelism, Destitute Women and the Hard Selling of New Anti-Poverty Formula", *Development in Practice*, Vol. 6, No. 2.

Chapter 5

Sustainability of Development Programmes: Dilemma of Voluntary Social Service Sector

Sukla Deb Kanango

IN contemporary parlance, use of the nomenclature 'voluntary social service sector,' may sound little intriguing and unusual. Popular perception is that there is no voluntary social service organization anymore and all that were two decades ago, have now been clubbed as non-governmental organizations or NGOs, as they are commonly known. Whether social service organizations or business organizations, all organizations in the private sector are non-governmental, therefore, the nomenclature NGO does not correctly signify the nature of voluntary social service organization. Hence, the preference for using the latter expression. Secondly, the title of the paper may also appear somewhat intriguing as development programmes are not the domain of voluntary social service sector, they belong to the development sector. But at this point, some reference to the evolutionary history of voluntary social service sector may be relevant. The role of voluntary social service organizations is no more confined to social welfare services alone, but has transcended it in many ways. In a significant measure they are now engaging themselves in socio-economic development activities with the emphasis on health, education and poverty alleviation.

There is a third factor, which has significantly entered the voluntary social service sector, is the international funding organizations, who themselves are voluntary bodies. Mostly taking cue from the thrust areas, determined by the various organs of the United Nations, the international funding organizations have embarked upon financing social development sector. This sector mainly focuses on three broad aspects: (a) economic regeneration of the poor and deprived through entrepreneurship development among them; (b) facilitating upward mobility of the poor and deprived along with economic upliftment through creating opportunity for education and for maintaining proper health; and lastly, (c) their education in citizenship and integration with the society at large by eliminating their marginalization. And, these funding organizations' major consumers are voluntary social service organizations. Significantly, these funding organizations influence the direction that the recipient organizations should give to their programmes and the grants are tied to this condition.

By way of opening the discourse, I would like to clarify the following points: A few dilemmas relating to development endeavour of voluntary organizations have been analyzed in the present paper keeping in view the broad development scenario in such developing countries as India and others in South and South-East Asia. Hence, some of evolutionary aspects of the phenomenon need to be recalled. Most of the countries, barring a few like China, were under colonial rule till the mid-20th century. By the time these countries achieved independence, they were ravaged countries, both economically and socially. It was not only the colonial rule but the World War II too had its own share.

The post-independence period thus became a period of massive reconstruction efforts on both the fronts. These reconstruction efforts are a real struggle till today. These have been further rendered extremely challenging since when these countries are struggling to get a foothold in their affairs, the world outside has not stood still (more particularly the countries of the developed world). It has moved on, moved very fast—technologically and remarkably as a result of this, socially as well. New innovations provided answer to many old ills but also created new needs and thus the search for finding means to meet these new needs has become a perennial concern for these countries. On the other hand, parameters of development determined by the developed world have become a new concern for the developing countries – "how to reach it", whether they are made to live up to it or choose to do so. In either case, it is a strain on their psyche as well as on their resources which are scarce.

Internally, the developing countries like the ones in South and South-East Asia are beset with following difficult situations: large population; highly inequitable landholdings which is the major sustaining factor of their economies, as most of these are agrarian economies; followers of different political systems (nationally and even within the same nation) which obviously determine both politico-economic as well as social relationships among its masses; etc.These countries are characterized by mass poverty (although it is reducing but very slowly) and uneven development among the regions within the same country coupled with socio-political unrest of various kinds. Diagnosis that has been uniformly made is economic backwardness of the people, and therefore, economic development is thought to be the solution for all their ills.

With the industrialization, which has become another important phenomenon in all developing countries throughout the world, there is a large-scale dislocation or displacement of people from their geographical as well as social roots. The inevitable results of such dislocation are large-scale unemployment, economic deprivation, ill-health, unhygienic living conditions and lack of right type of education. The onus for providing such exigencies thus has fallen on the state. The state of course has assumed the responsibility. But even after nearly four decades of the pursuance of the policy it has been realized that the state also can not provide service for all and for everything unless people themselves contribute. The global economic scenario—marketization and liberalization, have led to the similar kinds of difficulties. These are coupled with another ominous development, though it existed earlier too but was much less intense, that is the violence in both personal and public spheres—crimes of different kinds and magnitude. In the background of these developments, the state's repertoire of tools, techniques and resources did not match the requirements of the period. Voluntary action provided a space within the total state set-up and came to occupy a prime place in the sphere of social service since the inception of the modern democratic state. In the present socio-economic scenario, the role of voluntary action has assumed a special significance. The active role of the voluntary social service sector has become a necessity.

As we know, voluntary organizations "exist for the sake of a mission—they exist to make a difference in society and in the life of the individual" (Drucker 1990). Under the present circumstances, one wonders how far voluntary organizations can bring harmony between their mission and their deed. It is understood that they need not continue with the same programmes and activities. Because of demographic changes, some programmes and activities have become redundant, some programmes need to be discarded as they do not bear the expected results. Their mission therefore, needs refocusing, even needs to be changed. This largely explains why and how the nature and functions of voluntary social service sector have changed and assumed the present character. On the whole, voluntary social service sector has undergone a metamorphosis in a significant measure and manner over the last few decades.

Having made the context clear as to what legitimizes the role of voluntary sector, attempts will now be made to delve into different aspects and issues related to their functions and performance in playing an effective role in the sphere of socio-economic development.

Before proceeding further, some explanations regarding the approach adopted in writing the present paper may be made. The discussion was proposed to be based on empirical data obtained from some well established organizations working in the sphere of social welfare as well as social economic development. Accordingly, data were obtained from five organizations working for 25 and 50 years. While going through their responses it was felt that, while some data satisfied the queries, many left several questions unanswered. Hence, relevant data have been reflected upon, while the questions raised by the other set of data have been transposed to the relevant themes and discussed. Readers are, therefore, requested to bear this point in view.

TRANSCENDENCE OF SOCIAL SERVICE TO DEVELOPMENT SERVICE

In viewing the phenomenon at issue, we may ask the following questions: how have social services transcended to development services, what has been the rationale?

Social services to be meaningfully provided to the general public, need enormous resources. All along it has been the responsibility of the modern state to provide for these services. But a situation had arisen around the last quarter of the twentieth century due to which this responsibility became extremely difficult to be borne by the state alone in the face of ever shrinking resources. What became apparent was that unless production increased and wealth got created, services in social sector could not be provided. It also became obvious that people's dependency on the state for all such services could not continue to be entertained. The solution sought was to reverse the process—reducing people's dependency by making them self-reliant in different aspects of their living, more particularly, in their economic life, as far as possible. This was possible only if people could be persuaded to get involved in the process of creation of wealth, management of that wealth and its distribution. In other words, people's entrepreneurship ability needed to be enhanced. While the state could not totally shirk its responsibility of providing basic social services, it had to provide support to increase people's productivity by engaging them in various economic activities. Thus, the domain of social service sector transcended to economic productivity as well. It came to be recognized that the development endeavour should incorporate both social and economic sectors. While the former was a necessity, it could be in place only if it was backed by necessary economic support.

There was another significant area which became a major concern, the speedy depletion of natural environment and its resources. These were vital to support whatever economic activity or occupation one chose to pursue; more particularly, the poor and the marginalized, whose economy centred mainly around natural resources.

Referring to the phenomenon mentioned above, it can be seen in the Table 5.1 how the voluntary organizations studied are actively involved in the sphere of development activity and not merely social welfare. A few who specialize in the specific area of their activities also have development connotation as they are engaged in a big way in the sphere of development and social welfare. Although factual data have been obtained with the help of mailed questionnaires, the author had, besides it, visited and interacted with these organizations and is also in association with some of them (in non-official capacity). Periodically, the organizations furnish the information about the progress of their work and remain in touch. Even a glance at the activities of the organizations would indicate that most of them transcended the domain of purely social welfare service and went over to development services. For example, the oldest organization (No. 4) established in 1945 by a group of freedom fighters and started working with the disadvantaged sections of society. But before long, the organization moved into the area of education—from pre-primary to higher secondary level in a big way. Not only that, they maintained their focus on the children of disadvantaged groups of society and expanded their services in remote villages also. The organization however, continues with such social wel-

Table 5.1: Voluntary Organizations and their Activities

Sl. No.	*1 (Aliuan RKVYS)*	*2 (Anandaniketan)*	*3 (Indian Institute of Cerebral Palsy)*	*4 (Satya Bharati)*	*5 (Asso. For Social Health)*
Year of establishment	1961	1960	1974	1945	1974
A	Smokeless oven (chulha)	*Ashram* Hostel (for general)	Special School for the Disabled	High and Higher Secondary Schools (3)	Family Counselling Centre
C T I	National Bio-Gas Programme	*Ashram* Hostel for Scheduled Tribes	Family Services for the Disabled	Primary and Junior Basic Schools(3)	Short Stay Home for Girls and Women
V	Crèche	*Anganwadi* Training Centre	Adult Education Services	*Balwadi* Centres (3)	*Anganwadi* Training Centre
I T	Youth Club Development	*Jan Sikshan Sansthan* (People's Education Centre)	Community Based Rehabilitation Services	59 Crèches in 59 Villages	Helpline
I	Value Education	*Kristishala* (Museum)	Residential Services	*Anganwadi* Worker's Training Centre (2)	Working Women's Hostel
E S	Children's Learning Centre	Rural Library		Training Centres for Computer, Tailoring and Wool Knitting	Home for the Elderly Canteen

Cont'd

Cont'd

	Consumer Protection	Bidhan Chandra Seva Sadan		Hindi Language Training Centre
		Awareness Generation about Environment	General Hospital	Sangit Maha – *Vidyalaya* (Music College)
		Improved Chulha		Child Sponsorship Programme
		Swarna Jayanti Gram Swarojgar Yojana		Short Stay Home for Girls in Moral Danger
		Training Hostel		Cottage for Orphan Children
		Water Testing Lab		Working Women's Hostel (2)
		Computer Training		Hostel for Girl Students
		Work with Cerebral Palsied Children		Family Counselling Centre
		Direct Observation and Treatment of T.B. Patients		
		Rabindra Mukta Vidalaya		

fare services as Family Counselling, Home for the Orphans and Destitute, Short Stay Home for Girls in Moral Danger, etc. Similarly, the organization 3, which works specially for the disabled, has kept their focus on drawing the able-bodied, particularly, the parents and siblings of the disabled, within their fold to control and prevent further disability among future generations of their children and in their neighbourhood through creation of awareness and education in relevant areas of prevention of disability, promotion of healthy and creative living atmosphere for already affected children.

The single thread that runs through most of the programmes of all these organizations is education. Education programmes, formal as well as non-formal, have figured in their agenda. Some have initiated vocational training programmes also. It is well-known that economic rehabilitation is facilitated mainly by education, and in this all these organizations have set their priority quite clearly.

Health and health education (and awareness) are an integral part of activities of most of these organizations, either directly, or indirectly. For example, organizations 2 and 3 are directly involved in this, while for the remaining organizations, service in this area is mostly referral in nature and education and awareness agendas are about maintenance of proper health.

Barring organization 5, over the years, the remaining organizations have expanded their area of operation (geographically and population-wise) in a significant measure. Hence, many remote areas and a large number of people have come within the fold of their services. Services have also been diversified.

The above phenomenon is observable in most of the organizations in the voluntary sector as their funding sources are conditioned in the sense that they have to engage in developmental activities since welfare orientation has limited value especially in a developing country like India. Vast sections of population need to be served, and to make them self-reliant it is essential that the aim should be their socio-economic development and not mere welfare. And thus arises the fundamental question: how to sustain these development endeavours and the progressive state of development?

MEANING OF SUSTAINABILITY

Sustainability of the development process, whether in terms of programmes or projects, is the main theme of this paper. It has various other implications which, in the course of discussion, will be dealt with as they come up. Two questions come up here: (1) meaning of sustainability, and (2) application of the concept with reference to development endeavour and development programmes carried out by voluntary organizations. The dictionary gives multiple meanings of the term 'sustainability': to hold up; to bear; to support ; to provide for; to maintain; to sanction; to keep going; to keep up; to prolong. 'Sustain', therefore, in the context of development, would mean to prolong, to keep going, rather than to hold up, bear or provide for. But when the term 'sustainability' is adjectivally referred to, it has other connotations as well. Ability to sustain would imply the process of development being supported to help it keep going. On the other hand, it has another implication, that is, the positive consequences of development are sustained. Sustainability is a long-term maintenance of development efforts as well as positive consequences of a programme or project. Thus, the process of development being sustained as well as its positive consequences are of equal concern when we refer to sustainable development.

In whichever context we use, both development service and social service are required to be sustained, and to do that efforts also need to be sustained. Now, the ability to sustain depends on various factors. The most important factor is the resources: money, material and manpower. If the reference is made to a particular programme or project, as Joseph C. Wheeler (1989) mentioned: "The sustainability of projects is determined by a range of factors—including economic soundness, project design corresponding to the managerial, technical and financial capacity of recipients, compatibility with socio-cultural conditions and, last but not the least, environmental sustainability—all of which must be considered at the appraisal and design stage to ensure project success."

It is important to note Wheeler's reference to project design and environmental sustainability that resources are of crucial importance. But by themselves they are not sufficient to maintain sustainability, unless supported by judicious policy and organization to use them properly. A major part of the resources come from nature, whereas, right now going on is a steady depletion of natural resources all over the world. The crucial factor in this is the human society—how does it conduct itself to sustain the process of development or the positive impact of development? Individual and collective behaviour (including organizations' and institutions') is equally responsible for whatever happens in this sphere. Organizations and institutions are significant as they design the projects and provide the required support for any development endeavour, but they comprise people. Hence, human factor is at the core of sustainability or non-sustainability of development process.

The considerations above bring us to the basic question—is it essential that organizations or institutions are to bear responsibility for sustaining development process?

DEVELOPMENT ENDEAVOUR AND ORGANIZATIONS

Development endeavour is institutionalized. The state shares the major responsibility while a sizeable part of it is also taken care of by voluntary efforts of the people, through organizations and institutions they put up. When the professed goal is all-round development of people, it is imperative that the development process be sustained and the institutions that organizations build, whether by the state or people for the purpose, are ethically responsible to sustain the process. Citing the reasons, Riddell and Robinson (1995) observed: "... there are two reasons for this. One stems from a concern with cost recovery, and the desire among NGOs—to transfer the recurrent costs of project management to the community following the withdrawal of the support agency. This is based on the belief that development interventions can be sustained over the longer term only if the community assumes ownership of the project or programme. A second reason for the interest in sustainability is bound up with the desire to avoid promoting dependence on an external agency. This is based in part on NGOs not wishing to be perceived as benevolent patrons, especially when external dependence simply replaces the influence of locally dominant elites without addressing the structural reasons for such dominance."

While much of what has been said above is true, there are other aspects which require consideration. One question that may be asked here is, can voluntary organizations deliberate on the issue of sustainability independent of the externalities that influence the phenomenon? Organizations may have independent entity, but actions and consequences thereof are externally experienced. There is confluence of the outcome of their activities with that of the wider society including other organizations and the state. Concern about sustainability internally for the organization, and externally for the society as a whole are the two dimensions of the same issue. Therefore, reference to development programmes carried out by voluntary organization calls for careful examination.

GOVERNMENT AND VOLUNTARY EFFORTS CONTINUUM IN DEVELOPMENT ENDEAVOUR

Among the developing countries of Asia, India has one of the most developed voluntary sector. It has a long tradition of voluntary enterprise and all along it has been accorded a special significance. Over the years, voluntary sector's nature and character have undergone a metamorphosis, and one may find wide varieties among them. "Ideologically development oriented voluntary organizations in India are a mixed bag, ranging from service-oriented groups to militant movements, ... The service-oriented groups are incrementalist, non-violent and discourage party affiliations. The militant groups are quite often aligned with left parties, such as some trade unions, or they are 'non-aligned' ... environmental movements for resettlement of persons displaced by large dam projects or tribals fighting to regain control of their land" (Viswanath 1993).

Movements initiated by activitists are generally geared to protect the rights or claim the rights of the poor and deprived. The activists struggle along with the poor—their participation is direct, and activists often play the role of advocates. In the process, if needed, they resort to confrontation with the power that be. This in fact, is regarded as the true foundation for sustaining the development of this section of the society. This is however, a debatable matter. Service-oriented organizations, on the other hand, are gradually moving towards promoting self help among people by enabling them to form their own organizations and manage the same, themselves. However, many among the service-oriented organizations, though aspire and move towards developmental activities, still remain at the helm of affairs of their organizations. They do emphasize on people's participation and involvement, but still, if the term may be used, ownership of the programmes and services rest with them.

With the former type of organizations (movements), government's main responsibility lies in responding to the demands of people in a way that is conducive to the development of the people, provided it subscribes to the basic ideals of the state and respects the law of the land. To the latter group, the government, of late, has entrusted a major responsibility of implementing developmental programmes initiated by the state, for the main reason that the government lacks personnel with sufficient motivation to implement such programmes. Voluntary organizations thus, in a way, become an extension of governmental endeavour, and government provides the major support for resources.

Government-voluntary efforts continuum moves in opposite directions in the two situations mentioned above. Voluntary efforts in mobilizing people and organizing movements culminate in governments' intervention in the sphere, where the state is the sole arbiter and its intervention is fundamental. Hence, both are drawn together albeit at a different stage and level. Partnership between the state (government) and voluntary organizations working in service as well as development oriented programmes is now a familiar phenomenon. The only point to be noted is that traditionally voluntary organizations begin the services and programmes, which the government joins at a later period. However, with over three decades now, the scenario has changed. The voluntary organizations come forward to take the responsibility only when the state assures the resources.

The scenario just described leads us to the vital question of sustainability of development, whether it is to be viewed in terms of the process or its consequences. The section below discusses the various dimensions of this issue.

SUSTAINABLE DEVELOPMENT: VOLUNTARY ORGANIZATIONS' EFFORTS AND THEIR DILEMMA

Sustainability is an outcome which is dependent on a number of factors. Some of these factors, by their very nature, are subjective, and therefore, it is difficult to measure the extent or degree of their contribution to sustainability; for example, people's participation in sustaining the programmes or development level etc., organizations' approach and the like. But, the question still remains whether they can or do ensure sustainability.

It would be advisable here to go into the common feature of selection of programmes and activities by voluntary organizations in India. By and large (till now), the organizations adopt such programmes and activities for which financial resources would be available—either from the government or from non-government funding organizations. The result of this mode of adoption of programmes is that the organizations take up such programmes, which many times, may not be to their liking and they do not have the required expertise to manage them. The sole motivating factor is that the funds are available.

In fact, it is a common observation that during the last three decades, organizations have come into existence because the state (government) initiated many programmes of development, and for which it was seeking voluntary organizations' initiative and collaboration. Such organizations are therefore, dependent on grants-in-aid mainly to continue with their programmes.

This, however, is not to deny the fact that there are a number of organizations which have been in existence since very long, more than thirty, forty, fifty years. A sizeable number of these organizations are the brainchild of individual philanthropists and others. The leadership provided by these individuals has been the driving spirit behind these organizations. Over the period of time, these organizations have also adopted the schemes financed and supported by government.

The services rendered by these organizations can be categorized into broadly three types: (a) poverty alleviation through entrepreneurship development and income generation; (b) alleviation of problems related to health, education, family conflicts; and (c) full time care of the deprived and destitute as children, elderly persons, disabled, etc.

The issue of sustainability comes with reference to all the three categories of services. The desired level of progress achieved in all the cases needs to be sustained—eradication of poverty through maintaining a desired level of income, resolution of problems and prevention of their recurrence means sustaining the positive outcome achieved. In the case of persons needing full-time care, the process of care needs to be sustained. To do this, sustained flow of resources is essential.

One may move on from here to the question of how the organizations strive to address the issue of sustainability. Here two different scenarios exist. One group of organizations vow to make the recipients of their services or aid self-reliant, thereby indicating that they would not like to perpetuate their supportive role forever. There is another group of organizations that have been continuing with same services and programmes for decades, and at times shift their focus from one type of programme to another. In the case of the former, sustainability is deliberated on and they strive to seek some answer to the issue. In the case of latter, a complex situation exists so far as sustainability is concerned. These organizations continue to play a major role in the sustenance of some of their programmes by generating resources through the programmes and services themselves, e.g., running educational institutions and hospitals or other type of health services and charging fees for the same. But these organizations also carry out other programmes and services where very little attention is paid to their sustainability. They are mostly dependent on external assistance, and continue as long as assistance is available, and discontinue once assistance is stopped without paying much attention to the impact and effectiveness of such programmes.

In fact, maintaining the organizations becomes more important than sustainable development accruing from their work. Organizations' survival becomes more crucial. One may argue, when development endeavour is dependent on organizations, should not organizations' survival be crucial? This cannot be denied, but this also cannot be accepted at the cost of the achievement of the developmental goals. After all, organizations are means not ends.

Often, therefore, the common refrain is that organizations can not be held responsible for discontinuation of a programme or project if financial support to the programme is discontinued. These come either from the state or other national or international funding organizations. This argument may have some sense for those who are not beneficiaries of the programmes, but for the beneficiaries these often are a blow. For example, one organization had developed a very meaningful programme of family planning in collaboration with the said department of the government. It designed the programme in such a manner that it had in-built incentive in the form of interest free credit given to beneficiaries to upgrade their existing economic activities or start new ones. This was in addition to the usual incentives given by the health department of the government. The loan amount used to be small (as what the beneficiaries asked for) and most of the beneficiaries came from modest and some even quite poor economic background. The organization, and for that matter even those who were aware of the programme, could not believe when the beneficiaries expressed their dismay at the discontinuation of the programme. They felt that they were deprived of the benefit of the programme. It was really amazing how such a small help could go a long way in mitigating their difficulties, even if not fully. In another instance, in an international conference, a participant made a presentation on a project on preventing violence among adolescent boys and girls. The outcome was very encouraging but had to be dropped as the project was discontinued by the sponsors.

In both the cases, thus, sustainability of such development process was jeopardized owing to the loss of support with resources. A number of questions therefore come up in this context. Do the organizations, while designing their programmes and activities, pay adequate attention as to how they would like to sustain the same or positive outcome of the same? How do the organizations view their existence without themselves being project or programme-oriented? When the organizations make vision statements and decide their mission, do they exercise themselves sufficiently on the question of feasibility of as to how they would achieve what they aspire? Common observation is that the organizations do make vision statements and spell out their mission, but the energy and ability to give concrete shape to the mission is very limited. Often, the way it happens, the organizations are not much concerned about it. One gets the feeling that organizations exist, while some programmes and activities just come and go. These do not seem to perturb the organizations much. Hence, the view of the organization as an entity is hazy, rather fragmented from within, pulled and pushed in different directions. In other words, without any sense of (definite) direction, the organization keeps moving and if debated, there is normally denial of this fact on their part.

It is quite evident that no (voluntary) organization can either come into existence or survive without financial support, whether this is generated from within, which again is very limited in extent, or from outside—either government or non-government or both. Even the most well-intentioned works by social activists, whose mission generally is to bring systemic changes, also need financial support. For example, a well-established organization, consequence of dedicated and determined efforts of social activists in Orissa, at different points of their struggle could sustain their work among the marginalized and exploited people because of the financial support they could mobilize. Of course, money was only one of the contributory factors but a major one no doubt.

This brings us to the issue of organizational maintenance vis-à-vis programme sustainability. These two are complementary, not contradictory to each other. If programmes do not sustain, relevance of the organization is questionable. If organization is maintained at the cost of the programmes, this reduces the credibility of the organizations. Hence, sustenance of both is vital.

Programmes are for whom? Development endeavours are for whom? For the people. With regard to voluntary organizations these are particularly for those sections of society that are poor, vulnerable, exploited and marginalized. Today, sustainability is adjudged with reference to the programmes and project, ability to eliminate poverty, help people lead a life with dignity and self-respect. These are desirable, these are what everyone sincerely and intensely aspire for.

Organizations play a midwife's role. Once they facilitate the development, it is the people who should own it and let it move on. It is here that the biggest stumbling block is encountered. Today, there are leaderships in many organizations who sincerely intend leaving the rein in the hands of the people themselves but not without apprehension. Here it is quoted from the same source noted above. The author says: "This structure has some limitations which I have realized. It is not going to initiate radical social transformation in a time bound way. The system is not going to be totally identified with people. They can't be owned by people. If people don't come up you can't sustain it by leadership from outside. That way I see the danger from outside" (Giri 2005: 61). Here the activist and leader, after more than two decades of struggle and working with people, and even after achieving a remarkable measure of success expresses dissatisfaction. This view has a meaning, when all along he strived to make people get involved, through participation and sharing responsibilities.

It has often been seen that many voluntary organizations undertake projects and programmes which operate geographically over an extensive area covering large size of population and these projects are financed by well-established international organizations. This is seen mostly in developing countries and the projects and programmes are geared for poverty alleviation through different economic activities undertaken by the beneficiaries themselves. In other words, beneficiaries' direct involvement in the process of work is a requisite in these projects. Implementation of these programmes is therefore, subjected to evaluation by the funding organization. Mechanisms of these evaluations are decided by the funding organizations themselves—sometimes they do it or engage some independent evaluator. A number of such evaluations conducted throw valuable light on the question of sustainable development and other related issues.

Brown and Korten (1989) as quoted in Riddell and Robison (1995: 37) mentioned: "Among the most serious problems pinpointed are that the management of projects tends to be weak and in part relatedly that sustainability is very difficult to achieve." With reference to management of the programmes/projects of organizations, an important dimension is leadership in the organizations. Very rarely it is seen that leadership comes out of the people (beneficiaries) themselves. It comes mostly out of the initiator of the projects/programmes or the founder member(s) of the organizations themselves. So much depends on the kind of approach that is adopted by such leaders. The case of an organization and one of the respondents to the queries made by the author, may indicate how they address the challenge of sustaining development initiative and the development process. According to the leaders of this organization, "We are maintaining constant dialogue and interaction with the beneficiaries as also the village level affiliated organizations and our branches. As a result, the projects are being implemented smoothly. We, do not face any problem of sustenance of any project." Mentioning about major challenges to sustain the development process the organization observed that it is important "... to maintain the interest and positive approach on the part of the executive committee members, general members and the paid workers of the organization." For this they encourage involvement of general members and workers to participate in all the programmes of the organization and on important occasions (like when they celebrated the Diamond Jubilee of the organization) they honour all the workers, general members and past workers for their good work by giving them formal recognition. In the organization's view, due recognition and acknowledgement of the workers' contributions are the most important element for "achievement of sustenance of an organization". To be noted here is the "sustenance of an organization" which means programmes, and project's sustainability depends on the organization's sustainability in the first place. This is justified (in a sense) as already explained earlier. But in the case of this organization, the fact that it has completed sixty years of its service and carries out twenty different programmes is a proof enough of its ability to continue its work.

The leadership here plays a very important role. The leadership is highly committed as the founder members were Gandhian constructive workers, and has left behind a legacy of dedicated service by its subsequent generations of leaders. However, one can not generalize the view, nonetheless leadership is a crucial factor in the sustainability of development. A Commonwealth Secretariat, 1987 publication entitled *Strategic Issues in Development Management: Learning from Successful Experiences* (3 volumes) mentioned, "In some cases, however, it is apparent that management per se is sometimes not such a problem, but that, especially in smaller projects, leadership can often be crucial to NGO impact. Indeed a new article of faith is simply that "good leadership is essential to project success."

Here again some reservations are there and are often seen to be true in most of the voluntary organizations, "Though leadership is critical to the success of NGOs, usually little attention is paid to the development of leadership potential or to management training. And, once in post, leadership skills are rarely fostered because most NGOs are poor at delegation" (Clark 1991).

The five voluntary organizations, who have responded to the queries, are all working at the grass-roots level (although a few among them also work at other levels). Looking at the organizations one finds the top level leadership is committed and always striving to sustain the organizations. Among the five it is seen that in only one, the leadership is making conscious efforts to develop the second rung of leaders. As a result, when the rein made over, as it happened in two to three cases in the past, the new incumbents could take charge of their sphere of work very confidently and managed quite efficiently. But these are exceptional cases, as in the other four organizations the leadership is highly centralized. One wonders what would happen to the organizations in the absence of such leaders.

MOTIVATING AND FINANCING SUSTAINABLE DEVELOPMENT

Motivation is a vital factor in sustaining development process and this has been discussed above at some length. Now the issue will be discussed with reference to the organization as an entity, not the persons within the organization, and its motivation to finance its own development programmes and projects. In Table 5.2, the responses received from the five organizations give an indication of their motivation.

It is obvious that to a very great extent, organizations are carrying out programmes and projects which are financially supported by government. Next to government, there are non-governmental funding organizations that support some of the programmes of the organizations. In the organization 3, where sizeable number of programmes are partially financed by government and partially by the beneficiaries, beneficiaries pay service charges. These are mainly for education and health services—since schools, hospitals and health centers are run by the organization. These are such services for which, by and large, beneficiaries are generally willing to pay. Two other organizations also generate their funds to support some of their programmes. Beneficiaries contribute financially mostly in the form of paying charges in those organizations' programmes.

The heavy dependence on governmental support can be gauged from the responses which convey the anguish of the organizations. A few sample answers would be a sufficient indication of these: factors that affect implementation of programmes and

Table 5.2: Financing Projects in Voluntary Organizations

Sl. No.	*Number of programmes/ projects funded by government*	*Partly by government and partly by beneficiaries*	*Number of programmes/ projects funded by non-governmental funding organizations*	*Donation*	*Number of programmes partially financed by the organization itself and partially by the beneficiary*	*Total no. of programmes/ projects*
1.	11	0	3	–	3	17
2.	6	0	3	–	0	09
3.	6	8	4	–	0	18
4.	4	0	0	1	–	5
5.	4	0	0	0	3	7

their sustenance are—'arbitrary cut in the proposed budget', 'inordinate delay in approval and sanctioning of grants', 'self-sustainability of the organization, along with other existing programmes are questionable, should the grant be withdrawn', our experience in implementing the scheme is that the release of grant exclusively depends on the person who is holding a particular post at the time, when the post is held by a non-cooperative type of officer, disorganized way of maintaining the files, files mysteriously disappear. Again in some unknown way the files reappear but in an 'injured state' which ultimately becomes totally 'disabled'. Time and again submitting the proposals also do not bear any result. With government, over the years the collaboration has been one of mistrust.

Non-government funding organizations' share in financing of programmes and projects of voluntary organizations is comparatively much less, both in terms of volume and the amount of aid given. By and large, the recipient organizations' experience with such organizations is quite good. The qualitative aspects of the experiences are: examining the proposals of the recipient organizations closely and minutely; overseeing that the implementation and evaluation of the projects is very good; they also help in the process of implementation; their official procedures are much simpler than governmental procedures, they also lay emphasis on training of project personnel which is very conducive to the improvement in the quality of performance, not only of the employees but also of the projects, their supervision is strong and there is no delay in their functioning; they acknowledge merit and grants projects on the basis of merit.

However, in the experience of one organization its experience with non-government funders has been varied. In their words, "some funders have been flexible and have allowed us to use left over funds in other projects. Other funding agencies have been very authoritarian".

With government, therefore, the relationship of voluntary organizations is one of "love-hate". On one hand, situational compulsions make them go for government funding, on the other hand, there is the feeling, "if we could do without it". Mostly, the human factor is the distinguishing factor, officials involved at the helm of affairs make qualitative difference in the dealing with voluntary organizations. As has been expressed by some organizations, it is found that "even a receptionist, or peon matters in gaining access to the department concern and getting the proposal approved". Truth of this is not debated; it only demonstrates the feeling of helplessness and anguish of voluntary organizations. When so much dependence on government is there, sustainability needs to be considered from another dimension. This is what we propose to do below.

COST PRICING AND THE ROLE OF ECONOMIC INSTRUMENTS

'Economics of care' has always been an issue concerning the social sector. Care at what cost, development at what cost? Are the costs calculable? Mostly, the negative answer to the last question frustrates any attempt at answering the earlier ones. On the basis of the argument that social phenomena and most of the development indicators being subjective, it is futile to attempt costing and pricing as well as benefit, as these are not quantifiable. This has been the thinking the world over. But even with these, notwithstanding some attempts were noticed during the seventies and eighties in some quarters in the west towards working out ways to measure the cost and benefit of care, as the issue of efficiency was intricately linked with the question how economically sound the provision for care was. Sadly, this trend of thinking is lacking in other parts of the world, practically nil in developing countries.

Historically, in India, (may be elsewhere in the world as well) in social service as well as in social development sector the thinking that pervaded was that resources in these sectors were a one way transfer—to the needy and deprived and majority of them being very poor, nothing could be expected in return. Although through various poverty alleviation programmes over the last five decades, some improvement in the situation is discernible, there is however, no fundamental change in the thinking process. It is still 'grant-in-aid' dependence. At no time any attempt has been made either at governmental level or at voluntary service sector level, to assess the cost of services. Neither in return assessed in a manner to pin point the extent to which it has been beneficial. At the most, it is said, "situation/condition improved", which hardly conveys anything concrete.

Of late, many analysts have brought the above issue to the fore—costing and pricing of services, whether at voluntary work level or governmental level. Some of them have endeavored to demonstrate how this factor needs to be taken care of to make development (work and process) sustainable. In fact, they have drawn heavily from the experiences of development work carried out in Third World countries, including India and Bangladesh. It is the contention of the author of the present paper that practically none of the (voluntary) organizations, whether local, regional or national in character, engage themselves in the task of working out the unit cost of the services they provide. Similarly, it is also hardly ever thought of how the pricing (of a service) can be incorporated in the service design, where the recipient can share the cost or even become fully in charge of the programmes which benefit them by providing a steady source of income. Mention here may be made of the work done by Theodore Panayoton (the sub-theme here has been coined after his work) who documented his experience with critical analysis in the book entitled *Instruments of Change, Motivating and Financing Sustainable Development* (1998). His work has been related to the area of conservation of natural resources and how this is to be done. But many of these are quite relevant to the, strictly speaking, social development service sector. It, however, requires change in the mindsets of service providers.

According to Panayoton, "Full-cost pricing of resources, goods and services that all costs, present and future, internal (private) and external to the user that are incurred by society during production and consumption are incorporated and fully covered by the price of the good or service." The thought itself may be repelling to voluntary service sector. But some thinking on this line may be advisable instead of ignoring it. It is a fact, particularly in India, that voluntary organizations' have their backs touching the wall, and how long (more) can they provide services absolutely free of charge? It has become almost impossible. There is another truth which these organizations have to face—many of the recipients of their services continue receiving the services, though they have crossed the eligibility criteria and their conditions have improved. They continue praying for the services and organizations very rarely make a thorough inquiry into the matter. There is an economy. Those who can afford to manage their own affairs must make way for others who need these services urgently. This expands the number of people taken care of by such services and the former group may have a moral responsibility towards the latter. Here comes the relevance of, not only working out the cost at present, but also future costs likely to be incurred, taking into account intermediates and externalities. For instance, will the number of beneficiaries get reduced or increase on a future date and/or different categories of beneficiaries have to be accommodated? What inputs are available now may not be available at the same cost on a future date, and the price of obtaining the same may be higher, but without which complete service may not be possible.

Organizations feel shy of charging for services—whether the service costs are high or low. The common plea is that people are so poor; it is cruel to charge any fee, even nominally. We tend to forget the following facts: (1) all beneficiaries are not 'extremely' poor, only some are; (2) even very poor people, in times of extreme difficulties, borrow and try to tide over the situation, repay the loan at a future date although at high interest rate (heavy cost), nonetheless they venture to do so; (3) survival is a struggle for everybody: the well-off as well as not so well-off; at their own levels each one is struggling, and (4) no attempt is made to inculcate the value that if one is able to manage on his/her own, in spite of being eligible to receive the service, should forgo it for someone else who is less fortunate and is worse-off to need the services urgently.

We talk of self-help but very rarely this value is made use of in designing the services. If this is done, to a certain extent, sustainability of development endeavour can be ensured.

If costing of the services is done, it also enables the organizations to understand its justifiability, and see how long these could be sustained.

Some of the economic instruments that can be of good assistance to organizations may be considered here. Panayoton (1999: 15) mentions seven economic instruments which are of great significance in financing sustainable development. These are:

1. property rights
2. market creation
3. fiscal instruments
4. charge systems
5. financial instruments
6. liability system
7. performance bonds and deposit refund systems

He mentions these in relation to conservation of natural resources and development. Naturally, in his analysis governments' role (state) and non-government users of natural resources and their behavioural dimension have been taken into account. Keeping in view the context of the paper, we propose to consider some of the seven instruments. As for the relevance of instruments in the case of voluntary organizations, Panayoton's suggestions have been revised to some extent.

Economic Instruments

Property rights: include ownership rights to land titles; water rights; user rights—stewardship, licensing, concession/bidding; development rights, and prospecting rights.

Voluntary organizations engaged in economic activities are increasing day by day. On the other hand, with increasing emphasis on local self-government bodies like panchayats to bear the responsibility of development work through economic measures like food for work programme, employment generation programme, etc. are also ever expanding. In both the cases, the often heard criticism, both from articulate public as well as the bureaucrats themselves is that, these programmes have failed to create meaningful assets in villages. Roads once built in rural areas are damaged long before or during the subsequent monsoon, credit facilities for cattle breeding and cattle rearing are given, but no market worth is found. With the spurt in formation of self-help groups (for nearly a decade now), the need for working on the economic instruments has become all the more relevant. The question of property right becomes pertinent to those whose activities are based on land or water, or who need user rights to realize the best results of their efforts. But this also becomes relevant where the beneficiaries/consumers need to be diverted to land or water, depending on their activities, e.g., a beneficiary engaged in compost manure producing needs land rights or land user rights as the case may be. An unemployed youth venturing into pisciculture needs the rights to water sources like ponds or lakes; watershed development programmes often stumble upon an uncertain path, because the people who are both producers and consumers of the programme have no right to the use of the natural resources: the land they need to create and protect the water reservoir or the diversion of the flow of water as required (e.g., through bunding). The above mentioned programmes are mostly carried out by voluntary organizations and are increasingly becoming common features in rural development work.

The issue here is, who will give these rights to the individual(s)? Obviously, it is the state which mostly owns the resources. But then what role can voluntary sector play here? It would be that of facilitating or through advocacy and negotiation with the State that can help getting these rights for the people. However, for this they have to do the salesman's job by way of demonstrating the economics of this strategy. Assignments of property rights have several advantages of internalization of external costs. Of all these, two may be mentioned here which are of special value if we refer to the kind of programmes mentioned above: (a) "It goes to the root of the problem: the absence or malfunctioning of markets due to undefined property rights; (b) unlike taxes and charges, property rights adjust automatically to changing circumstances". However, it must be noted that the property rights approach to internalization of costs is not without limitation, e.g., if the rights are sold or auctioned, the seller is at liberty to enhance his monetary benefit according to his own objective which may put others in a disadvantageous position. If among the farmers, someone having share in the midstream water source decides to sell it, it will obviously put the other farmers of the watershed development project into difficulty. However, if total value of such approach is accounted, the advantages in most circumstances outweigh the disadvantages.

The issue of sustainability is crucial in the case of voluntary organizations who mostly render welfare services free of charge, or render social development services with promotional orientation, like family life education, awareness generation related to many social issues and various other preventive programmes. With reference to the latter, the basic assumptions with which most of the organizations function is that such services are not of immediate benefit, but will have accrued benefit at a future period to the beneficiaries. Therefore, charging money for these is difficult, as beneficiaries would choose not to avail of these services if they are required to pay for them. The reality is that most of the organizations today conduct training programmes, orientation programmes of various kinds, but hardly ever design economically sound programmes where costs, if not fully, to a great extent, can be realized from the beneficiaries. Experiences of some organizations who attempted these, have demonstrated that in course of time such programmes also facilitate introduction of some other vital programmes. For example, organizations who run formal education institutions, in course of time, could introduce counselling services in the institutions, again charging fully or nominally depending on their situation. Often we tend to make the mistake of assuming that beneficiaries would not like to be charged. On the contrary, experiences of some organizations have been highly encouraging. Two instances may be mentioned here. One, a slum development work started by initiating small savings by women of families who contributed only Rs 2 per week. These were families living a hand-to-mouth existence. But before long such women only proposed to the social worker, "why don't you raise the amount from Rs 2 to Rs 5." The social worker could not believe if he was hearing them right. Repeated questioning drew the same answer, and it may be mentioned here that in a matter of five years these women were having a rolling fund of few lakhs of rupees. Borrowing from this fund their men ventured into bigger areas, and proved the adage "money brings money".

Next, a non-formal educational centre for street children is run free of charge, but provides no educational materials except the services of two teachers sponsored by some individuals. It initiated a small savings programme charging only Rs 2 per month per child. The idea was to develop a habit of savings among them and that these savings would come to use in purchasing their required educational materials as well as meeting small treatment charges in times of need. Within a short period they themselves came forward with the proposal of raising the rate of monthly savings. It was beyond the expectation of the social worker.

It is now a reality as well as necessity that voluntary social service sectors change the tradition of providing free service, and in the process leaning heavily on state (and others) sponsorship of the services. To break free of the tradition may not be possible at one go, but a determined effort in this direction is called for. It can be tried with a two-way approach, adopting a combination of programmes: one group of programmes and services that generate resources and income and finance; with the same the other group of services where it is a one-way transfer of resources and money like running an old age home for below the poverty line family member or an orphanage where practically no monetary return is possible nor can be expected.

Cost-benefit analysis, which should become an integral part of planning process of a programme, is hardly undertaken by voluntary organizations. Without these, the earlier suggestion of incorporating economic instruments in service design cannot be expected. And in the absence of these, the organizations will continue to experience the unsustainability of their programmes and services.

With a few exceptions, most of the organizations in the social service sector get into drawing proposals without any kind of systematic need assessments of the people of their operational area. Often it is the enthusiasm that drives them to get into the service provision. The result is that more than one or two organizations could be seen doing the same kind of services, addressing the same issues and problems and if asked for, they rarely are in a position to demarcate, physically as well as socially, the impact of their work on the people. In the fifties and sixties of the last century, it used to be strongly debated that there should be coordination among the organizations and overlapping and duplication of services be avoided. Some conscious efforts used to be made to keep the line of demarcation clear. But of late, with the spurt in privatization and state encouraging more private players in social service sector, such coordination has been thrown to the wind. This has resulted in the waste of the scarce resources. And organizations are rarely sure of the impact of their intervention. Lastly, till now it is the periodic report submitted to the funding organization by the concerned NGO and that is the instrument of programme evaluation. It is a fragmented evaluation, because individual assessment is done for each programme and never of all the service inputs that go to one individual beneficiary and in the process that brings changes to the life of the individual.

Over the period of last two decades, an amusing phenomenon is seen in the public sphere. An incident would be self-explanatory here. An IT (Information Technology) industry of very high repute in the country is cited here. Knowing the said industry's social service orientation and capability of generating huge revolving funds, a voluntary organization approached the industry. In the face of queries made with regard to justifying the organization's claim of rendering good services, the organization failed miserably. The IT authority quipped, "They are after money and not good service," and brushed aside the appeal of the organization (it was verbal). Now this incident brings to the fore a few issues. An organization has to function keeping its self-respect intact. "We beg on behalf of the deprived", this attitude is no more is appreciated. In fact, it is not uncommon to find potential financiers avoiding even normal social contact with social service organizations.

Further, just as demand for services has increased, so also has the number of service-providing organizations in the involuntary sector. And, as it is seen that they are perennially dependent on external financiers, there is bitter pleading with the financier to have a share in the resource. This puts the organizations in very poor light. Their self-respect gets lowered. Finally, because of the above, many organizations are treated with contempt and even suspected of serving their own ends (meaning the persons at the helm of affairs) instead of truly serving the people. Under such circumstances only this can be said—organizations need money to serve and survive but equally important is public's perception of the organization. To function with self-respect in spite of the fact that they have to seek other's assistance is a challenge and has to be met. Credibility that they genuinely serve the people needs to be maintained.

CONCLUSION

In the face of ever-shrinking resources and ever-increasing demand, sustainability of development programmes and welfare services will remain a challenge to voluntary service sectors for a long time. Voluntary social service and development organizations are viewed as a front of the government by the public because of their heavy dependence on state sponsorship for the programmes they carry out. This image is certainly not of any good to them, and image apart, it also constrains the organizations in their functioning in a significant manner and measure. Organizations have to toe the line of the funding body. There are very, very few organizations who claim funds on their own terms and conditions. Autonomy in the real sense and sustainability are intricately related, and is a complex issue for any organization. This needs to be sorted out appropriately. Lastly, voluntary organizations have to review their own culture and tradition. Wherever these are at variance with the reality and requirements of the present day, the values, norms and culture operative till now, would need to have a relook into its operations and make appropriate changes. The clientele and beneficiaries are vital players and working with them for ushering attitudinal change, while remaining compassionate and understanding is the great imperative. In the ultimate analysis, what great achievements can be claimed, if our efforts do not bring positive change both in attitude and in life's condition—organizations' as well as beneficiaries'?

REFERENCES

Brown, L.D. (1990), Bridging Organizations and Sustainable Development, Institute for Development Research, Paper No. A 17, Boston.

Clark, J. (1991), *Democratizing Development: The Role of Voluntary Organizations*, Earthscan Publications: London.

Drucker, Peter F.(1990), *Managing the Non Profit Organization: Principles and Practices*, Butterworth Heinemann Ltd., Oxford, U.K.

Giri, A.K. (2005), *Reflections and Mobilizations: Dialogues with Movements and Voluntary Organizations*, Sage Publications: New Delhi.

Korten, D. (1989), Understanding Voluntary Organizations: Guidelines for Donors, Working Paper WPS 258, World Bank, Washington, D.C.

Viswanath, V. (1993), *NGOs and Womens' Development in Rural South India: A Comparative Analysis*, Vistaar Publications: New Delhi.

Wheler, Joseph C. (1989), *Development Cooperation in the 1990s*, OEDCD, Paris.

Chapter 6

Welfare, Rescue, Rehabilitation and Prevention of Prostitution: Role of Government and Voluntary Organizations

K.K. Mukherjee and Sutapa Mukherjee

THIS paper proposes to describe and explain the programmes/services organized for the girls/women in prostitution by governments, both central and state, and voluntary organizations. This has been done based on secondary and primary data collected in connection with the national study on *Girls/Women in Prostitution in India*. At the outset of this discussion, it is important to explain briefly the phenomenon of prostitution in the country and also the terms, viz., prostitutes, prostitution, protective homes and corrective institution, these have been used all through this paper.

PHENOMENON OF PROSTITUTION

Prostitution has a long history and a universal presence of course with variations. The states/union territories can be classified into three categories according to concentration of the problem. While the high concentration zones comprise 73.44 per cent of the prostitutes, average and low concentration zones comprise of 24.80 and 1.76 per cent of the total prostitutes, respectively. The variation in the level of concentration of prostitutes in states/territories is linked with their existing socio-cultural milieu and factors of economic development, viz., urbanization, trade/business, tourist centres and cantonments/police lines. Information about the number of prostitutes can only be an estimation. This is primarily because of the secrecy that surrounds the practice of the profession, constant process of inclusion and withdrawal of girls/women in and from the profession as well as vastness and diversity of the country. There are about three million girls/women in prostitution; about 2.48 per cent of girls/women in the age group 15–35 years are prostitutes. Ninety per cent of the total prostitutes belong to the age group of 15–35 years. Increase in terms of number of prostitutes per year is five times more than the annual growth of the total population. The number of prostitutes in metro cities has followed the same trend. Comparison with earlier available data reveals that the number of girls/women in prostitution has increased 50 per cent during the period 1997 to 2002–03. Similarly, number of girls/women in prostitution in six metro cities has doubled during the last ten years.

Prominent among the factors for growth of prostitution is globalization/modernization. Many other factors have contributed to the rapid growth of prostitution in the country and these primarily include urbanization/industrialization, change in value system towards sex, increasing apprehension of the youth about their sexual performance, globalization thrusts like meeting business competitions and gaining benefits, increase in hospitality industries, high concentration of armed forces in civil areas, prevailing attitude towards women, promiscuity, myths like sex with virgin increases vitality and keeps one mentally young and also cures various sexually transmitted diseases,etc. Every locality in cities and towns has the potentiality to emerge as a prostitution prone area depending on certain conditions. These includes the growth of the area as a trade, tourist or administrative centre. All these contribute to greater sources of income and give an element of anonymity to the women. Availability of cheap transport and communication facilities further contribute to the emergence of the place as an operational area.

Induction of girl children forms an integral part of the trade. Lower the age, greater the demand and higher the income. About 36 per cent of the girls/women in prostitution have entered the trade before attaining 18 years of age, despite regional variations linked with their socio-economic and cultural conditions. The states where large number of young girls is inducted into the trade include Madhya Pradesh (72.8 per cent), Bihar (72.3 per cent),

Rajasthan (67.4 per cent), Uttar Pradesh (50.6 per cent) and Jharkhand (50 per cent). Manifold reasons for induction of girl children in prostitution are: There is greater demand for girl children in prostitution because of the widely prevalent myth that sex with a virgin/minor can cure sexually transmitted diseases/ increase vitality of a person. Another important reason for induction of girl children into prostitution is the assurance of greater income for longer period as well as their vulnerability and easier handling.

Forms of the practice are many and diversified and have developed over a long period along with the changing situations. The eleven forms of prostitution identified in the study are street/ common prostitute, brothel prostitute—permanent/shifting/mobile, call-girl, commuting prostitute, concubine, cage prostitute, home-based prostitute, highway prostitute, singing and dancing girls and prostitutes working under various garbs. Of these forms the oldest ones are common/street prostitute, singing and dancing girls, concubines and religious prostitutes. Red-light area based brothel prostitution developed along with development of cities and towns and changes in other conditions. The recent emerging forms are call-girl, mobile/shifting brothel prostitute, commuting and highway prostitute and the prostitute working under various garbs. They are mainly the result of decline in livelihood opportunities, increase in road communication and transport facilities, business competitions, hospitality industry, desire for greater income to meet the requirements and changing preferences of the clients.

Mixed form of practice is the emerging trend. Mixed forms of practice are becoming common in recent years in cities/towns because of the desire to derive greater income after entry in to the trade. It often involves working as a call-girl/mobile brothel prostitute along with other forms of practice and it is confined mainly to girls/women who are young, smart, outgoing and with entrepreneurial skills. Both common and region specific forms of practices prevail. Common/street prostitute, call-girl, highway prostitute, semi-shifting and mobile prostitute and concubine can be viewed as common forms of practice prevalent all over the country with some variations. Other forms are region specific. Brothel prostitutes working in established red-light areas are confined to only 10 states. Prostitutes working under various garbs are mainly found in Delhi, Maharashtra and north-eastern states. Similarly, singing and dancing girls are common in Bihar and Uttar Pradesh, while religious prostitution is mainly confined to Andhra Pradesh, Karnataka and Maharashtra.

Prostitutes belong to all major religions. Hindus at 78.88 per cent are less in number in comparison to their strength in total population, while the number of Muslims (12.75 per cent) in prostitution is almost in proportion to their strength in total population. Number of Christian (5.81 per cent) prostitutes is more in comparison to their total strength in population. Hindu prostitutes are comparatively more in Andhra Pradesh, Delhi, Orissa, Tamil Nadu and West Bengal. Bihar, Kerala and Uttar Pradesh have more Muslim prostitutes. Christian prostitutes are predominantly more in Kerala, Nagaland and Meghalaya. This regional variation is linked with religious distribution of population of various groups in the respective regions/states.

Prostitutes are mostly from vulnerable groups – castes and tribes. A little more than half (54 per cent) belong to scheduled castes, tribes and other backward class groups. The continuance of prostitution from among these caste groups, despite some decline during last 20 years, is because of their continued backwardness and vulnerability, low level of education, awareness and resource ownership position. Rise in number of prostitutes from among these caste groups has been contributed to by increase poverty. The globalization process again has aggravated the situation by promoting desire for greater consumption. Diversification in forms of practice has also facilitated entry of general castes into the prostitution.

Prevalence of traditional practice of prostitution by families belonging to certain communities not only continues, but also is increasing. This is mainly due to further decline in existing livelihood opportunities, lure of easy money and growing consumerism. Prostitution has specific age orientation; they are either adolescents or youths. About 90 per cent of the total prostitutes belong to the age group 15 to 35 years because of overwhelming emphasis on physical appearance and endurance capacity to entertain multiple clients.

Prostitutes are either illiterate or functionally literate, with some regional variation. About 62 per cent women in prostitution are illiterate. Of the total literates, the majority has education below primary level. There is regional variation in literacy rate of the prostitutes. For example, while all the prostitutes from Goa, Haryana, Jharkhand, and Punjab are completely illiterate, girls/women in prostitution in Tamil Nadu and Kerala have comparatively better literacy and educational standard. Prostitutes belong mostly to illiterate and poor income families. As high as 90 per cent of the parental families of the prostitutes do not own any land or animals. Nearly 70 per cent of the parents were illiterate.

The literacy rate of their mothers and fathers are respectively 17.3 per cent and 28.8 per cent. The prostitutes have better literacy rate (38 per cent) in comparison to their parents indicating a generational difference in education. Only 10 per cent of the paternal families have income above Rs 3,500 per month.

Prostitutes and people in general, despite some difference in perceptions about causes of entry, recognize that there is no one single reason for prostitution. According to them, it is the result of various socio-economic and cultural factors that often work in an interrelated manner. Existing socio-economic-political processes are influencing entry into prostitution. Increasing consumerism in the context of globalization, declining job opportunities for the uneducated/unskilled youth, growing migration and poverty, insurgency, political instability, erosion of values, desire to earn easy money, etc are also contributing to prostitution.

There are common, region-specific and situational causes that determine entry. The common causes are illiteracy, lack of skills, economic distress, increasing consumerism, ill-treatment by parents/guardian, desertion by spouse, dejection in love and deception. Area-specific factors include family and sociocultural traditions. Situational factors cover natural calamities, communal conflicts and displacement caused by drought, flood, earthquake, militancy, etc.

There are regional variations in persons involved in induction. Mothers are prime inductors in Bihar. Mothers have worked as inductors in 46 per cent, 14 per cent and 13.08 per cent cases respectively in Bihar, Rajasthan and Uttar Pradesh wherein traditional practice of prostitution still continues. Lovers, strangers and pimps were responsible in about 95 per cent of the total cases in Jharkhand. Self-induction has been talked about mainly in Andhra Pradesh, Gujarat, Goa, Meghalaya, Maharashtra and Madhya Pradesh probably because of continuance of religion and community based prostitution.

Induction process is multiple and varied. Parents and relations mainly use the process of socialization and brain-washing for induction. Husbands, lovers, neighbours and strangers lure girls and women in the name of marriage, job, and better opportunities and also pleasure. Orientation and training in management of clients and pattern of sharing of income form an integral part of the process of induction. This is done once the client becomes amenable for practice. It is difficult to indicate the exact incidence of trafficking. Financial gains appear to be main reason of entry for about 70 per cent of the total respondents considering the essential element of trafficking. Profile of traffickers has changed as it includes parents, relatives and others. This makes the task of controlling trafficking furthermore difficult. Approximately, about three-fourths of the total cases can be viewed as victims of trafficking.

THE TERMS

a. *Prostitution:* The term 'prostitution' refers to the act of the prostitutes. This act involves the prostitutes themselves who are involved in the organization of the act and others (brothel keeper, pimps, etc.) who help in furtherance of the act. However, for the purpose of study, prostitution refers to prostitutes only.

b. *Prostitutes:* A 'prostitute', for the purpose of study, refers to a woman who allows the use of her body regularly or intermittently, willingly or under compulsion, for sexual activity either for money or for material considerations. Three things connected with prostitution are:

   (i) Payment, which usually involves receipt of money and gifts for allowing the use of body for the purpose of sex for long/short/one time.
   (ii) Emotional indifference/non-involvement about the act of sex for which payment has been received.
   (iii) Promiscuity with possible exercise of choice.

c. *Health and Welfare:* It refers specifically to those activities which aim at protecting the girls/women in the trade from becoming victims of HIV/AIDS and improving their quality of life including that of their children while in prostitution. A wide range of activities are organized under this heading and these include: awareness generation programmes for HIV/AIDS prevention through popularization of use of condoms for each sex act with clients, condom distribution, health check-up, counselling and education (adult/right oriented education), crèche services for the children, recreation, self-help groups and formation of cooperatives.

d. *Rescue:* It refers to releasing and liberating girls/women, especially those below 18 years, from brothels or brothel-like places and from traffickers wherein they are exposed to exploitation for the purpose of prostitution/flesh trade. They are then placed in places, usually homes maintained by the government/voluntary organizations, which are considered to be free from the risk of such exploitation.

e. *Rehabilitation:* It indicates the efforts of restoration of willing girls/women from prostitution into mainstream society. This covers both economic and social rehabilitation by organizing multiple measures like vocational training, education, marriage, counselling, etc.
f. *Prevention:* It covers programmes/activities organized to check/control the entry of girls/women into prostitution. This is done by dealing with and removing the conditions like poverty (lack of livelihood), illiteracy and ignorance. It also includes changing the mindset of the people as well as socio-cultural factors responsible for the entry into flesh trade. Organizing rescue action for girls/women prior to their becoming victims of the trade so that they are not affected by the stigma attached to the practice of the profession, is also carried out as prevention.
g. *Protective Homes:* Protective homes are statutory homes meant exclusively for girls/women rescued under the Immoral Traffic (Prevention) Act (ITPA), and also those who voluntarily seek protection from being forced into prostitution. There is provision for appropriates technically qualified persons, equipments and other facilities in the protective homes. These provide custodial care and protection, in addition to providing education, vocational training and arranging marriage of the girls. The homes are not meant for keeping undertrial those requiring correction, who are sent to corrective institutions. The prostitutes are placed in the protective homes either after the legal hearings of their cases are over or when they make a special request to the magistrate to be placed in the protective home. They can be placed in the protective home for not less than one year and not more than three years.
h. *Corrective Institution:* It means an institution, established or licensed under Section 21, for persons who are in need of correction and are detained under this Act. It also includes shelter where those undertrial (under this Act) are kept during the course of their legal proceedings. The court has the authority to send the women/girls to the corrective institution in lieu of a sentence of imprisonment, for a period not less than two years, and not more than five years. However, the state/territory government is empowered to discharge the detainee after a period of six months if it is satisfied that the offender will lead a useful life after release.

AGENCIES ORGANIZING PROGRAMMES

Government

Prostitution has existed in India from time immemorial, but it is only after independence that definite legal measures and programmes for welfare/rehabilitation have been initiated to tackle the issue. During the earlier periods, including the British rule, efforts were occasionally made to control prostitution. Two Acts were passed by the British rulers, which indirectly tried to control the sex trade without initiating any specificaction. The first legal provision was Indian Penal Code (1860). It tried to protect girls against forced illicit sexual intercourse. It basically covered offences like kidnapping of girls/women, rape, selling, buying or hiring a girl for the purpose of prostitution, but did not touch the problems of prostitution as such. The other legal provision, which tried to control the use of prostitutes for fulfilling sexual needs was Indian Contagious Diseases Act introduced in 1868, since incidence of STDs among the British officers was increasing rapidly.

After independence, government action in dealing with the problem took shape in the formation of a committee by Central Social Welfare Board, Delhi, in 1954. The committee examined the sociological, commercial and social aspects of the problem and also studied the private institutions providing custodial care and services. Following this, the Act on the Suppression of Immoral Traffic in Girls and Women (SITA) was introduced in 1956 for implementing resolutions of the International Convention for Prohibiting Traffic in Human Beings. A number of homes were later established, and support was provided to the existing institutions organizing services to further strengthen their activities. This Act was modified in 1986 and titled as Immoral Traffic (Prevention) Act. This was done with a view to widen the scope of the law and to make it more stringent and effective. Changes were necessary since the original act (SITA) was not effective in controlling trafficking because of lack of concern on the part of the enforcing institutions to treat this as a social malady. The amendments in the earlier Act have basically provided for:

- Enhancing the penalties for the offences, particularly those involving children and minors.
- Cancellation of licenses of hotels, etc. where children and minors have been found involved in prostitution.

- Compulsory medical examination of all persons rescued from a brothel.
- Appointment of special trafficking police officers and establishment of special courts for inter-state trafficking.
- Extending the Act to cover all persons, female or male, those are exploited for commercial purpose.

Apart from these changes, the amended Act also includes comprehensive schemes for rescue, protection and corrective treatment of prostitutes and a specialized machinery for enforcement. The Immoral Traffic (Prevention) Act (ITPA) prescribes stringent action for the offence of procuring, inducing or using a person for the sake of prostitution. This Act comes down heavily on traffickers, particularly those who involve children in the trade. The punishment for such an offence consists of imprisonment for a period not less than seven years, may be for life, and are also liable to fine.

The ITPA was instrumental in formation of a separate machinery to deal with this issue. It not only provided for appointment of officers, but also institutionalization of services for rescuing and rehabilitation of prostitutes. The anti-trafficking police officers are appointed by the central government, whereas the special police officers are appointed by the respective state governments. These police officers are not below the rank of inspectors and are specially designated for offences under the Act. This Act provides for the establishment of protective homes and corrective institutions for effective rescue and rehabilitation of the prostitutes. All this was done in order to treat prostitutes as a separate category and not as criminal offenders. The running of protective homes and other vocational institutions have basically remained key programmes of the government till 1980s.

Apart from protective homes and corrective institutions, there are other types of homes for destitute women, established under the various acts, wherein prostitutes or girls/women who had been forced to enter into sexual relationships are also kept. During the course of the study, efforts were made to find the total number of such institutions, where prostitutes can be placed after their rescue, based on visits and content analysis of available documents. It has been found that there is an overlap in the functioning of these institutions in the sense that these institutions, at some places keep prostitutes as inmates, whereas at other places do not allow them to stay. This is, particularly true of the various short stay homes, managed by both governmental and non-governmental organizations.

The nature of the institutions set up under the SITA/ITPA varied from state to state. Similarly, the departments looking after these homes are not uniform. In Andhra Pradesh, Karnataka and Maharashtra it is under the Department of Women and Child Development, whereas in states like Delhi, Kerala, Madhya Pradesh, Rajasthan and West Bengal, the Department of Social Welfare is the authority. In Tamil Nadu and Gujarat, all the homes under ITPA are run by the Department of Social Defence. This was also the reason for not having updated information about the homes under the Act.

There are a total of 330 (as per available information) institutions for providing shelter to the women in distress, including the 119 institutions under ITPA. Almost 44 out of these institutions are protective homes (less than 15 per cent). In comparison, the per centage of short stay homes for women is significantly higher. These short stay homes provide shelter to any woman in distress. It usually does not involve any legal proceedings for seeking shelter in these short stay homes, like in the rescue/remand/protective homes. In most of these homes they usually keep the women for a maximum period of two years. Many of the short stay homes restrict the entry of prostitutes.

In Haryana, Himachal Pradesh and the North-Eastern states there are no protective homes at all. This is probably due to relative absence of the problem in these areas. It is the jurisdiction of the state government for establishing and maintaining protective homes in the state. States like Maharashtra, Gujarat, Uttar Pradesh, Karnataka, Tamil Nadu and West Bengal have more than two protective homes each due to a large concentration of prostitutes in these states. In Karnataka, there are protective homes and reception centers, whereas in Tamil Nadu, there are protective homes, rescue, remand, after care and short stay homes under ITPA. In Madhya Pradesh, there are protective homes and Nari Niketans. This explicitly brings out the fact that there is no uniformity across the country with regard to the nature of homes established under the ITPA. There is hardly any corrective institution as per the provisions of the act.

It was also found that in the institutions other than those under ITPA, there were inmates who were former prostitutes. Even among the inmates of the 'homes' there is differentiation between the prostitutes and others, wherein the prostitutes undergo lot of hateful stress not only from the fellow inmates, but also from the staff of the 'home'. Under the Juvenile Justice Act, 1986, the minor girls who are rescued from the trade are usually sent to observation homes or remand homes. Once these girls attain the age of 18 they are sent to protective homes or short stay homes or any other such institutions.

Many homes have been largely found to be underutilized in the sense that the number of occupants in most of the homes is much less than their actual capacity. This observation has been made on the basis of the details about occupant capacity as provided by some of the state departments. In Karnataka, the total capacity of the protective homes was 800 but the number of occupants was just about half. Similarly, in Tamil Nadu, the total number of occupants in all the protective homes was less than their total occupancy capacity. Though the number of occupants varies from time to time, it is never full. In the course of visits to some of the 'homes', it was found that the number of occupants also varied in accordance with the location of the 'homes'. In the metro cities like Mumbai and Kolkata, or places where prostitution is more widespread, the number of inmates in the institutions located at these places is also higher.

Management of the Homes: Management of the 'homes' is mainly the responsibility of the Government departments, but a few of these 'homes' were also run by voluntary organizations. Among the various homes, short stay homes for destitute women were mainly run by non-government organizations. There were very few (less than 10) homes under ITPA being managed by voluntary organizations.

The nature of staff structure varied with the type of institution and place of its location. Protective homes were found to have greater number of staff responsible for its various activities unlike the other institutions. This could be due to the fact that the duration of stay is longer at protective homes than at other institutions.

In some 'homes' it was found that all the positions were not filled up and there were vacancies, since many people were not interested to live in such 'homes' due to the social stigma attached to the inmates of these homes. Except for a few regular staff, even those who were supposed to be full time workers were actually working part-time. This was true particularly for the teachers/ instructors and even case workers (counsellors) at some institutions. Many people were not interested to work in such institutions because these hardly provided any scope for career advancement.

Protective homes had better facilities in comparison to other institutions. Administrative staff of the protective homes were generally of higher grade than other 'homes'. It can therefore be concluded that protective homes are comparatively better managed than other homes.

The staff structure of the various homes on the basis of available information is as follows:

Protective Homes	*Reception Centre*	*Rescue Home*	*Short Stay Home*
Warden/	Superintendent	Superintendent	Office Staff
Superintendent	Asst.	Matron	Matron
Asst.	Superintendent	Instructor	Medical
Superintendent	Teacher	Watchman	Officer
Asst. Teacher/	House Mother/		Chowkidar
Instructors	Matron		Peon
Case Worker	Cook		
Matron	Peon		
Senior Clerk	Ayah		
Store Keeper	Compounder/		
Nurse/	Nurse (Part-time)		
Compounder	Instructor		
Peon	(Part-time)		
Chowkidar			
Cook			
Attendant			
Sweeper			
Doctor			
(Part-time)			
Psychologist			
(Part-time)			

Services Provided: All these institutions were established with the perceived goal of not only providing shelter to its inmates but also helping them in the process of their rehabilitation by providing some vocational skills, training and regular counselling. Counselling is an important function in order to help the inmates to get over their emotional disturbances, mental agony and low self-esteem. This is considered necessary to enable the girl/woman leaving the institution to subsist on her own with a higher self esteem so that she does not have to go back to her previous life. The aim of the 'home' accordingly is to help the girls/women mend their ways and make them accept a better and regulated life.

In reality most of these 'homes' function under jail-like conditions. These homes are generally treated as shelter for those prostitutes who have nowhere to go, and also have no one to bail them out. Hence, most of these institutions function only as shelters providing boarding and lodging and that too of an inferior quality. The inmates are treated with a preconceived notion and are occasionally abused by staff members of the 'homes'.

Counselling services, which are essential in these homes, is the most neglected component. The post of the counsellor often remains vacant in most of the homes, though they have provision for a whole time counsellor. Even the counsellors are not free from bias towards these women. Staff members of the home are not committed to their work and remain indifferent to the feelings of the inmates. Not knowing the language of the inmates further adds to this problem. Only in Mumbai, Chennai and Agartala, the environment of the homes was found to be comparatively better.

As a common practice, basic literacy skills are imparted in most of the homes if the inmates are illiterate. They are mainly taught to read and write and make simple calculations, necessary for day-to-day life. Stitching and tailoring are the most commonly taught vocational skills across the country. Other skills like weaving, knitting, embroidery, basket-making, folder-making, etc. are also taught at some 'homes', depending on the availability of good trained instructors and nature of market for a particular commodity in the area. In some of the 'homes' the goods produced by the inmates are sold by organizing exhibitions and sales from time to time. In other homes, as in Tamil Nadu, laundry services are also provided by the inmates to the various hotels and other institutions. In Kerala, some of the homes have linked up with Khadi Board for weaving handloom saris.

Though the homes try to rehabilitate women by imparting vocational skills, these were not found to be adequate. During visits to some homes, it was found that the age-old stitching and tailoring skills are imparted in a routine manner with no inventiveness or specialization in the vocational training programme. New skills like block printing, screen-printing etc. are not taught. It is very important that the inmate during her stay in the home should be trained adequately in order to look after herself and her children, if any, with confidence after her release by taking on alternate ways of earning income. In these days of stiff competition, only innovative skills and training backed by an element of self-confidence can help one in earning a better livelihood.

Apart from routine vocational training and education, health services particularly for pregnant women are also provided. Most of the homes have to take the women to local hospitals for deliveries. Though there is a provision for full-time nurses/compounders, generally these people work on a part-time basis. Doctors visit the homes, but it is usually once in a week or fortnight, and that too for only 1–2 hours. Some of the homes provide residential facilities to the doctors, but which remain largely unoccupied since the doctors prefer to stay away and practice elsewhere and visit the homes once in a while according to their convenience.

Marriage of the inmates as a means of rehabilitation is undertaken by many homes without making proper verification of the background of the groom. Many a time the same person turns up to marry different girls as reported by some of the home officials. These marriages also lack proper follow-up arrangements and it is not uncommon for the girl to land up in brothel again. Counselling service for facilitating marital adjustment is also completely lacking.

Some of the homes have the provision for paying a monthly stipend of Rs 100–125 to the inmates apart from their food and other facilities, but this is also not paid regularly.

Recreational services are confined within the institution and the inmates are usually not taken out of the 'homes' on outings. In case any inmate has to go out for medical check up or for buying things she is accompanied by a staff member. Watching television, playing carrom, etc. are the main forms of recreation.

Problems Faced: Running and managing the homes is riddled with problems. These are given below:

- The basic problem is the lack of monetary resources and adequate infrastructure facilities. All the homes which were visited, complained that they did not receive their funds on time. In many cases, funds are blocked for more than 3–4 months, before they are released. This directly affects the functioning of the homes. Lack of adequate funds is also a reason for their inability to provide better facilities to the inmates. The maintenance of the institutions is generally very poor. Adequate space is also a problem for many of the homes wherein they have to accommodate a large number of girls within a very small area.
- Despite the government provision for having a proper staff structure, it is usually not implemented. Most of the homes were found to have vacancies, since people are not interested to work in such institutions. Finding full-time instructors for imparting vocational skills is also difficult for most of the homes.

- Most of the homes provide residential quarters to its resident employees, but in reality these quarters remain vacant since the employees do not prefer to live in the same campus due to personal reasons. In many homes, even the superintendents do not live in their official accommodation. Due to this problem, the employees who are supposed to be on full-time duty are not able to function adequately.
- Lack of proper understanding of the term 'protective home' and its provisions was found to be very common among the officials in the various departments of the states. The general idea about a 'protective home' is that of a place "where prostitutes are kept instead of a prison" and the same as a reception centre or Nari Niketan.
- Majority of the inmates are not interested in learning new skills as they are sure of being bailed out in little or no time. This becomes a major problem particularly in the rescue and remand homes, where sometimes the girls stay only for a few hours before they are let off again. In some cases, like the Liluah home, the same place is used as rescue, remand and protective home. This makes it difficult to separate the administrative machinery from the inmates, since all of them are made to stay together.
- Sometimes, the homes are unable to send any intimation to the native place of the girls/women because of language problem, since girls from across the country are in the trade. Even though the inmate wants to send a message to her family members she is unable to do so because the 'home' staff is unable to understand her language.
- Innate and suppressed sexual desires of the inmates also create problems for the home staff, particularly the males. This leads to increase incidences of homosexuality among women also, which were found to be quite common.

With the changing socio-economic situation and increasing attention drawn by the phenomenon of prostitution/trafficking in the context of growing awareness about the importance of human rights and spread of AIDS, the government has started initiating a number of steps to deal with the problem, since 1990, apart from running and managing homes. The factors, which specifically worked in favour of increased initiatives and roles on part of the government to deal with the phenomenon of trafficking/prostitution, especially child trafficking/prostitution, are:

(*a*) *Supreme Court's judgments on child prostitution in 1990 and on the subject of commercial sexual exploitation of children and women in the case of Gaurav Jain vs Union of India, 9th July 1997*: In the case of the former, the court directed that the Central and State governments set up advisory committees to make suggestions for the (i) measures to be taken for eradicating child prostitution; (ii) social welfare programmes to be implemented for the care, protection, treatment, development and rehabilitation of the young fallen victims; (iii) amendment of the existing laws; and (iv) welfare and rehabilitation of *devdasis* and *yogins*. In the second judgment, the Court directed *inter alia*, the constitution of a committee to make an in-depth study of the problem and to evolve suitable schemes for their rescue and rehabilitation.

(*b*) *National and international conventions demanding government intervention in sexual and other exploitation of children*: Central Social Welfare Board organized the first national conference on "Female Prostitution and their Children" in 1989. It was followed by a number of conventions (convention on rights of the child 1991 and Bejing World Conference on Women 1995), meetings and discussions. All these emphasized on governmental intervention to deal with the problem, especially the problem of girl child prostitutes and children of the prostitutes. In August 1996, the First World Congress adopted the Stockholm Declaration and Agenda for action against commercial sexual exploitation of children. It suggested actions at different levels with respect to commercial sexual exploitation of children. There are several other international efforts to combat trafficking including the optional protocol to CRC on the sale of children, child prostitution and child pornography and the protocol to combat trafficking of women and children in the UN convention against transnational organized crime.

(*c*) *Study report on prostitution in six metro cities, viz., Bangalore, Calcutta, Chennai, Delhi, Hyderabad and Mumbai, sponsored by Central Social Welfare Board*: This study brought to light the growing incidence of prostitution in the metro cities, and also the dire need to initiate action to redress the plight of the prostitutes and their children.

(*d*) *India's acceptance of the Convention on the Rights of the Child and subsequently initiating action to protect children from exploitation.*

(*e*) *National Human Rights Commission and National Commission for Women taking up the issue of child trafficking, prostitution through studies/meetings/discussions and publication of posters highlighting "sex with a girl child is a crime".*

(*f*) *Growing involvement of development and action groups in the area and the pressure on government.*

In response to these situations and especially the direction of the Supreme Court, the central government took a number of initiatives and formed a committee. The Committee on Prostitution, Child Prostitution and Children of Prostitutes, under the leadership of the Secretary, Department of Women and Child Development, made an in-depth study of commercial and sexual exploitation and trafficking of women and children based on meetings/discussions with concerned groups (government and non-government) and documentary sources including CSWB's report. It came out with a plan of action to combat trafficking and commercial sexual exploitation of women/children. The Plan of action emphasized on (i) prevention; (ii) trafficking; (iii) awareness generation; (iv) health care; (v) education and child care; (vi) housing, shelter and civic amenities; (vii) economic empowerment; (viii) legal reform and law enforcement; (ix) rescue and rehabilitation; and (x) institutional machinery. The committee also sent its plan of action to different state/territory governments with recommendations to initiate measures to deal with the problem. Many of the state/territory governments have also started taking action in this regard, either by forming state level anti-trafficking committees comprising of representatives of both government and voluntary agencies or by appointing special police officers.

Subsequently, the Department of Women and Child Development, Central Social Welfare Board etc. made provisions for financial assistance to non-governmental organizations to run development and care centres for the children who were victims of prostitution. These centres, which have been basically set up in red-light areas, provide facilities of crèche and day care, educational support programmes, supplementary nutrition, health care and counselling. The ministry of Social Justice and Empowerment also started providing financial assistance to NGOs for rehabilitation of children of prostitutes. In some states, like Andhra Pradesh, Haryana, Himachal Pradesh, Uttaranchal, West Bengal, etc. projects have been sanctioned by the Government of India for starting centres under the ICDS (Integrated Child Development Services Scheme) and "Swadhar Yojana" (a central scheme to provide assistance to organizations for starting residential facilities to protect vulnerable women and to rehabilitate them). Children of the prostitutes are also given preference in admission to schools and vocational training institutions. Some state governments have also taken specific action to deal with the problems, which are very much connected with them. For example, Madhya Pradesh government has initiated *"Jawali Yojna'* to tackle the issue of girl child prostitution among the *'bedia'* community. It is implemented in two stages; the first stage emphasizes on enrolment of six-year-old girls in primary schools and the second stage seeks to admit the girls in the middle school or to provide vocational training. Maharashtra, Tamil Nadu, Karnataka and Andhra Pradesh have started forming Self-Help Groups and thrift and credit groups. Governments are providing funds through Rashtriya Mahila Kosh to voluntary organizations to promote Self-Help Groups (SHGs) of women. Financial assistance and other support has been provided for the welfare of *devdasis, yogins*, etc. in states like Maharastra and Andhra Pradesh. A monthly pension to the tune of Rs 300 is provided since 1997 to the *devdasis*, who are over 40 years of age and do not have income of more than Rs 35,000. Furthermore, seed capital to the tune of Rs 10,000 is sanctioned to *devdasis* to start small businesses. Government also provides financial assistance to the agencies (upto Rs 10,000) that work for eradicating the system of *devdasi* and to *ex-devdasis* to arrange marriages of their daughters.

There is no doubt that these are efforts in the positive direction. However, the actions initiated by state/territory governments, except some states in general, lack uniformity, seriousness of purpose, comprehensiveness, quality and coverage. In absence of definite resources and reorganization of the problem as a priority issue, many of the states governments do not have any specific idea about the types of progeramme they are supposed to organize. Whatever discussions and actions have been initiated are basically confined to limited areas, namely Maharashtra, Karnataka, Delhi, West Bengal, Andhra Pradesh and Tamil Nadu, wherein the problem has reached a stage ahead. These states are identified as high concentration zones in terms of areas of origin/operation of prostitutes. This is evident from the fact that the steps to form anti-trafficking committees have been initiated, as per available information, by about 16 state governments and they are in different stages of formation. It is functional in about 8 to 10 states, though the meetings are not held regularly. Similarly, health and counselling services, which are provided by about 10 states, lack both coverage and quality. Programmes for rehabilitation of the prostitutes are organized only by five state governments. Linkage with voluntary organizations has been established effectively only in these states to deal with the problem. In fact prostitution is not considered as a priority area for action by state/territory governments.

Voluntary Organizations

The issue of prostitution has been spearheaded in terms of research and action in the country mainly by voluntary organizations and activists. There have been changes however in dimensions, intensity and strategies of research and action in this area along with the changing emphasis on the issue. This has been brought about by factors like growing awareness about the importance of women's development and rights, especially for the exploited and marginalized section of society; recognition of the phenomenon of prostitution as a source of exploitation of women for fulfilment of commercial ends, giving rise to an alarming situation, whereby many innocent girls have been found to adopt a way of life against their will; realization that prostitutes are major carriers of diseases like STD/AIDS, and the courts taking up a proactive stand on the issue resulting in the opening up of greater scope of action.

Voluntary action in prostitution before independence and even upto 1980 was primarily limited to research and sporadic action in the area of welfare/rehabilitation. The first organization to initiate action for these groups of women and their children was Association of Social Health in India formed in 1928. It was closely followed by All Bengal Women's Union in 1932. These agencies were mainly concerned with setting up institutional services for the rehabilitation of prostitutes. These efforts were initiated by women, some of whom had returned from England, and perceived prostitution as a social problem. There were not many studies except for a few to understand the background of the prostitutes and causes of their entry and continuance in the profession.

The period following 1980 saw a rapid growth and development of voluntary organizations working among prostitutes because of reasons stated above. During the period of data collection, there were 300 organizations working among prostitutes. About two-thirds of them, i.e., 215 were working among prostitutes primarily with the objective of protecting them from HIV/AIDS, mainly through AIDS awareness and condom distribution programmes. The rest were engaged in a variety of other activities, namely rescue, rehabilitation, welfare and prevention. All these organizations, except for 12 to 15, had come into existence mainly after

1986, i.e., the period when human rights, including child rights, became an emerging concern of the people, and the National AIDS Prevention Programme was started with the formation of National AIDS Control Organisation (NACO).

The organizations established earlier in the country were primarily concerned with either setting up of institutional services as mentioned earlier, or initiating welfare services for the prostitutes. There were also some agencies, like Vimochana Devdasi Punarvasati Sangh, SAVDHAN, which initiated activities in communities where prostitution was traditionally practiced. In recent years, there has been an increase in the number of agencies working in red-light areas serving both the prostitutes and their children.

An overwhelming majority of the agencies (over 70 per cent) are working among the prostitutes to protect them and their clients from AIDS. The motivational factor for the remaining organizations was their earlier experience of welfare activities for women and children of the deprived sections. For a majority of these organizations, concern for the deprived and underprivileged children resulted in undertaking activities for the children of the prostitutes. Subsequently, these activities were extended to cover their mothers also, i.e., the prostitutes themselves.

Some of the organizations like PRAJWALA (Hyderabad, Andhra Pradesh), PRERANA (Mumbai), SAMRIDHI, Gram Niyojan Kendra, (Bharatpur, Rajasthan), Vimochana Devadasi Punarvasati Sangha (Belgaum), IMPULSE (Meghalaya) and STOP (Delhi), SNLAAP (Kolkata), etc. have initiated their activities on the basis of research studies conducted by them or by other agencies against trafficking/prostitution by organizing a wide spectrum of activities in terms of resources, rehabilitation and prevention. Child care and health are the two other major issues which have enabled various organizations to initiate many types of activities for the prostitutes and their children.

The agencies mentioned above have been working with certain general and specific objectives. The general objectives have been given below:

- To provide alternate means of life to children of prostitutes.
- To prevent trafficking of girls/women for prostitution and to rescue the minor girls and also women who want to come out of prostitution.
- To prevent entry of new girls into the trade by generating awareness amongst the prostitutes and the communities

where prostitution as a way of living is traditionally accepted.
- To control and prevent spread of STD-HIV/AIDS among the prostitutes.
- To motivate the present practitioners to leave their trade by providing or linking them with institutions offering shelter and rehabilitation facilities.
- To provide services for the welfare of the prostitutes and their children, viz., organizing crèches, balwadis and counselling centers.
- To make the prostitutes and the community members (where possible) aware of the ill effects of the trade.
- To start a crusade against child abuse and commercial sexual exploitation of children.

These objectives are mainly oriented towards a long-term goal of prevention/control of new entry into the trade through the process of trafficking or other means. Only a few of the objectives, like those related to providing welfare services and awareness generation are short term ones. A look at the common objectives makes it very clear that most of the organizations aim at undertaking activities for the brothel-based prostitutes or communities which have traditionally accepted the trade and not for the prostitutes in general. This means that holistic area development, by initiating action against poverty, social evils and other area-specific problems which in a large way contribute to the entry of girls in the trade, either on their own or by force, are often ignored in the action programmes in the field.

Some of the specific objectives are:

- To arrange boarding facilities for the children of prostitutes so as to take them away from their existing circumstances.
- To marry off young girls, who are rescued from the trade.
- To establish and maintain homes/shelter for rescue and rehabilitation.
- To provide condoms to the prostitutes and their clients.
- To arrange health check-ups and counselling services.
- To forming peer groups from the prostitutes themselves to work as pressure groups and provide solutions to their day-to-day problems.
- To educate and provide some skills to the prostitutes.
- Promoting better health among the prostitutes and their children.

- Advocating the rights and amenities to the prostitutes and their children.
- Linking up the communities/prostitutes with various governmental schemes for their effective rehabilitation and prevention of new entry.
- Undertaking developmental activities in the communities where prostitution is traditionally accepted so as to provide them with alternate means of livelihood.

These specific objectives are micro oriented and are complementary to the general goals. These objectives are basically welfare oriented for both prostitutes and their children. There is some element of similarity in the specific objectives of most organizations since the nature of problem is the same in most areas with a few exceptions.

Three hundred organizations are located in 31 states. Majority of these agencies are in nine states, viz., Andhra Pradesh, Bengal, Delhi, Gujarat, Maharashtra, Kerala, Karnataka, Tamil Nadu and Uttar Pradesh, which have a higher concentration of prostitutes. These states/territories together cover over two-thirds of the total organizations working among prostitutes. There are about 15 states/territories, which do not have any organization working among prostitutes other than those working for AIDS prevention. It is difficult to provide any numeric data about the exact number of beneficiaries covered by the organizations individually/jointly under various activities, because most of them could not provide the exact figure about their beneficiaries.

The coverage of the beneficiaries varies according to the programme of the agencies. Among the various programmes, AIDS prevention and welfare activities have greater number of beneficiaries, since these programmes have a wider reach and easier acceptance among them. Between these two activities, AIDS prevention activity has wider coverage.

The beneficiaries can be divided into four broad categories, i.e., non-brothel-based prostitutes (street/common prostitutes, commuting prostitutes, home-based and highway prostitutes etc.), brothel-based prostitutes (permanent/shifting), traditional/religious prostitutes and the children of the prostitutes. The nature of beneficiaries also varies with the location of the organizations. The metro city based organizations work mainly among the brothel (shifting/permanent) and non-brothel based prostitutes, whereas, the organizations located in small towns and rural areas have also covered traditional, religious prostitutes and other prostitutes.

The nature of activities undertaken by various organizations has been found to be linked with the goals envisaged by them. It also varied with the location of the organizations. The organizations, which are working in the red-light areas, have mainly undertaken activities concerning children, health, counselling, awareness generation, condom distribution and advocacy issues. The activities are different for the organizations working amongst communities that traditionally practiced prostitution. They provide alternate sources of income for both the prostitutes and the communities, undertaking social activities for changing the social orientation of the members of the group through education and awareness generation and also some child welfare activities.

This variation in the nature of activities is not just limited to the location of the organizations but also their years of functioning and philosophy governing the development. The oldest organization in the field was set up to rescue and rehabilitate prostitutes and their children. At that time it was the dominant philosophy of action to start homes/shelters and provide institutional services. In keeping with their tradition, the earlier organizations emphasized more on providing rehabilitative services, and also to some extent undertaking welfare activities for the prostitutes in some of the red-light areas, the first being at G.B. Road, Delhi. The present generation organizations have mainly undertaken programmes for prevention of AIDS, and controlling entry of girls/women into the trade. Health and advocacy issues have also become areas of concern for a large number of organizations in recent years.

These activities have been further classified under the main targets as outlined by the organizations specially AIDS prevention, rescue, rehabilitation then prevention and welfare. These are as follows:

STD/AIDS Prevention

1. STD/AIDS awareness generation and prevention.
2. Health check-up and treatment.
3. Condom distribution.
4. HIV detection and treatment/training in management of disease.
5. Counselling.
6. Forming mutual help groups.

Rescue

1. Identification of minor girls/willing women.
2. Conducting raids with help of the police.

3. Placing rescued girls/women in short stay homes and shelters.
4. Motivating girls/women to leave the trade.
5. Providing shelter/homes for the rescued girls.
6. Counselling services for the girls rescued by the police.
7. Shifting the rescued girls to other agencies for rehabilitation in society with the help of linkage groups.

Rehabilitation

1. Imparting education and skill training to the girls/women.
2. Helping to have an alternate way of living by offering financial help or linking up with government schemes and programmes.
3. Providing institutional services at the homes/shelters.
4. Repatriating the girls belonging to Nepal, Bangladesh, etc.
5. Marrying off the girls/women.
6. Counselling services for enabling them to join the social mainstream.
7. Enabling girls to settle down after training in an anonymous environment, and then, over a period of time, to their own environment.

Prevention

1. Institutionalization of the children of prostitutes.
2. Area development programmes emphasizing on livelihood and education for controlling the entry of girl children into the trade.
3. Awareness among prostitutes, so that they do not bring in new girls, particularly minor girls.
4. Helping the prostitutes to arrange marriage of their daughters or providing some alternate method of living to the children.
5. Networking with the police/NGOs for controlling trafficking.
6. Changing the mindsets of the people in general, and the families traditionally accepting prostitution as a way of life.
7. Organizing surveillance specially on the international and inter-state borders to stop trafficking.

Welfare

1. Providing education and training in various skills to the children.

2. NFE/skill-training to the women/girls.
3. Working on health issues particularly STDs/AIDS.
4. Recreational activities for prostitutes and their children.
5. Formation of peer-groups/forums from amongst the women/ girls.
6. Counselling: Vocational and family.
7. Issuing of birth certificate/ration cards, etc.

The programmes of most of the organizations have been developed based on certain patterns, such as:

1. Identification and understanding of the needs has been mostly found as a first step in initiating any development activity. This is because of the belief that programmes can be effective only if they are tailored to suit the requirements of the target groups.
2. Linking needs with the organization's objectives. Every organization has its own set of goals, which it tries to achieve through various activities. This might, at times cause limiting of the range of activities that can be undertaken by the organization.
3. Planning of programmes according to the needs and objectives. The programmes are designed in a manner that they fulfill the organization's objectives, and at the same time also meet the requirements of the targeted beneficiaries.
4. People's participation is not just limited to their participation as beneficiaries only, but also for effective planning and implementation of the programmes. Most importantly, it is the target groups on whom the programmes are focused. Thus, they should necessary play an important role in the formulation of the programme, keeping their requirements in view.

A study of the achievements shows that the nature of activities under AIDS prevention, rescue, rehabilitation, prevention and welfare has been different for the various organizations.

However, it can be said that the programmes like AIDS awareness activity among the prostitutes and their clients (truck-drivers etc.) have made some impact. These have contributed in popularizing the use of condoms especially in metro cities, despite resistance from the clients. The programmes in general have helped in bringing about some change in the conditions of prostitutes and their children wherever these organizations have initiated their activities. First and foremost, there has been some change in awareness and perception of the prostitutes about themselves and their children. This has been achieved through continuous counselling and awareness generation programmes. Prostitutes have been able to protect themselves from AIDS and rid themselves of the feelings of guilt, and inferiority. This change in self-perception has been so strong that now they are demanding social recognition of their profession by getting their trade licensed. The programmes, like identity cards/ration cards have been able to develop in them some element of identity as an individual.

Secondly, there has been greater realization by the prostitutes themselves of the fact that their children, particularly girls, should not be allowed to enter the trade. This has resulted in at least partial implementation of the programmes for the children, emphasizing on their education, vocational training and organizing counselling services. These programmes are being organized in the form of residential/day services. In addition, many organizations are also trying to get the children admitted to the regular schools inspite of several odds. However, there is some amount of helplessness among the organizations as they are unable to deal with the bias towards the children admitted to the schools. Many of the organizations have thus expressed preference for having their own schools for providing education to these children; but this requires a lot of financial investment and other infrastructure facilities, which are mostly beyond their means.

In many cases, the organizations have functioned as pressure groups in placing the demands of the prostitutes before the government and fulfilling some of their necessities and demands. The supreme court order, which allows a child to be enrolled in any school with mother's name only has helped the matter greatly.

The organizations have also been effective in forming peer-groups, cooperatives and self-help and self-supporting groups amongst the prostitutes for solving their day-to-day problems. In some areas, particularly in Kolkata, peer-groups have a strong hold on the prostitutes and they not only help in providing solutions to the problems, but also are effective in generating awareness among the women in the red-light area.

Effective linkages have been established among the organizations working on the issue both nationally/internationally. This helps in sharing experiences and planning effective strategies of action.

People's perception about the issue has also undergone some change, particularly among the urban educated group, where the feeling of apathy towards these women and their children is being gradually replaced by a feeling of sympathy as well as empathy. The media along with the people involved in the cause have been instrumental in bringing about these changes in people's mindset. But sadly, this change in attitude towards prostitutes is very limited and majority still continue to harbour negative feelings of hatred/condemnation and insensitivity.

Whatever achievements have been made are limited to the areas of operation of the organizations, which in themselves are limited only to some particular areas only. Looking at the magnitude of the problem, the achievements might appear insignificant; nonetheless, they mark the beginning of the concern and appropriate action for the issue.

In the implementation of various programmes, the organizations have to face many problems right from lack of resources to apathetic and indifferent attitude of the people. The organizations also face hardships while initiating their programmes because of the difficulty of being accepted by the prostitutes who always view strangers with suspicion. Under such conditions, it requires a lot of effort in building rapport with the target group before any programme is initiated. Developing a feeling of trust in the organization and its people is important for any activity particularly for those involving the children of the prostitutes. Hence, implementing the programmes is in itself one of the basic difficulty faced by the organizations.

Lack of adequate resources and infrastructure facilities also pose difficulties in proper implementation and expansion of the programme. Inadequacy of resources basically implies shortage or lack of funds for carrying out the activities and manpower in the form of staff and workers particularly at the grassroots level, is also a common problem faced by many of the organizations. This is due to the fact that not many people are inclined to work among the prostitutes or their children because of social stigma. This makes it extremely difficult for the organizations to carry out their activities. There is also a low level of understanding of the issue and skill among the workers; and it takes considerable time to train the workers, and once they are trained, they leave for better job options elsewhere. Casual approach of the workers towards their responsibilities also affects the programmes.

In case of some organizations, there were no specific goals and objectives for their programmes. They started work on the issue either because they had heard about it in various seminars/

workshops or have just undertaken it as any other regular programme, because of availability of resources through friendly contacts, particularly for work related with trafficking. Lack of clear objectives makes it difficult to have centralized and focused activities, and they work at random without having in view any specific programmes.

The organizations also have to face resistance of the vested interest groups who feel that the intervention by the organization is making a dent in their own business. This includes the pimps, brothel keepers, trade managers, people with power and position and in some cases also the police. Rivalry among organizations working in the same area also hinders the activities, particularly those with lesser resources and manpower. Instead of establishing linkages with each other, the organizations develop a complexity towards the activity and the people of other organizations. In most of the cases, the organizations have found to be working in an isolated and ad hoc manner.

Lack of adequate shelter facilities is a problem faced by the organizations working for the rescue and rehabilitation of prostitutes and their children. Most of the time, the facilities provided by the government are not adequate and up to the mark. The organizations face a great deal of problems in placing the prostitutes in some good institution after rescuing them from the brothel.

The nature of issues is such that the activities of the organizations fail to evoke desired response from society at large. There exists a pervasive element of stigma about the prostitutes and even their children do not escape the prejudice.

In addition, there is contradiction in philosophy of action among agencies working with some ideologies. For example, the AIDS prevention agencies do not raise questions about exploitation of women and their control/prevention. They are basically interested in controlling the spread of AIDS, many of them feel that the prostitute should be allowed to practice and given license to carry on the profession. Any effort to control the practice is viewed as a violation of human rights. In contrast, the agencies working for rescue, rehabilitation, welfare, prevention/control are raising the issues about the conditions contributing to women's entry into prostitution and are trying to find out their solutions. Over the period of years, it is believed that the contradiction will increase. AIDS prevention agencies well get the upper hand, which may affect the national approach towards the issue of prostitution. In the long run, even practice of prostitution based on license may also be a possibility.

Chapter 7

Forestry for Rural Development in Bangladesh

Niaz Ahmed Khan

OF late, there has been a growing consensus and recognition among governmental and quarters of civil society to regard forestry as a means of rural development and poverty alleviation in Bangladesh. There have been elaborate policy provisions and frameworks in support of forestry for rural development together with an effort to engage a growing number of NGOs in the forestry programmes and forge a public and NGO partnership.

Programmes and initiatives of forestry as means of rural development and poverty alleviation are popularly referred to social forestry (hereafter, SF) in Bangladesh. Despite the widespread use and popularity of the term, however, SF still defies a universal definition, and entails a number of connotations and ramifications. In Bangladesh, the term is used rather flexibly as an umbrella concept for such public, private and community initiatives as aiming at ensuring "active participation by the rural people in planning, implementation and benefit sharing of tree growing schemes" (Task Force 1987: 1). SF is viewed here within the broader framework of rural development in Bangladesh (Alim 1988; Khan 1998a; 1998b, 2001; Ahmed and Azad 1997). It primarily includes afforestation programmes in marginal and degraded forest lands and community forest lands; village woodlots, farm forestry; strip plantations alongside railways, highways and embankments; 'community plantation' on public or communal lands with joint management and benefit-sharing arrangement between the government and local communities;

homestead forestry (home gardens); and varied other manifestations of agro-forestry.

The principal emphasis of SF is on wider participation of local communities in the protection and regeneration of forest resources. As noted above, SF primarily refers to those public initiatives, which enable local people to participate in the planning, implementation and management of local forests for their own benefits. Some commonly stated objectives of SF programmes include the following: to empower local communities by involving them in the planning, implementation and benefit-distribution of forestry activities in order to cater for local needs (especially the subsistence needs of fuelwood, fodder, timber and poles); to promote self-reliance and social equity among local people; to augment their income, productivity, socio-economic status, and living standard; to check environmental degradation, conserve soil and water resources, and to foster the development of local cooperative institutions (Oakley et al. 1991; Task Force 1987; Arnold et al. 1988, 1990; Alim 1988; Davidson 2000).

The present article proposes to provide a broad overview of the current state of SF in Bangladesh. The article is programmed into the following sections. After the introductory remarks we shall move to the next section focusing on the government's key development goals and strategies for the forestry sector. The study then will examine the performance of selected major SF programmes in the country from the perspective of rural development and poverty reduction. Subsequently, the state of NGO involvement in SF is to be examined in the fourth section. The fifth section will explore the major lessons and observations from Bangladesh's experiences of implementing SF programmes in the field, together with an analysis of the implications of the dynamics of globalization for the development of SF.

The study is primarily based on an extensive review of secondary materials together with an analysis of first hand governmental records, sundry office and project documents. Besides, the discussion substantially draws on the author's observations and insights gained through personal engagement and involvement in a number of SF projects (see, 'Acknowledgements').

CURRENT POLICY SUPPORT FOR THE FORESTRY SECTOR

Poverty alleviation is the stated 'overarching thrust' of Bangladesh government's development philosophy and practice. Developmental programmes in the public sector are committed to contribute to poverty alleviation through the promotion of pro-poor economic growth, social development and good governance. The government's stated vision and strategy of development are astutely summarized in the *National Strategy for Economic Growth, Poverty Reduction and Social Development*, which reads:

> The development vision in the present strategy embraces a comprehensive approach on a rights-based framework that highlights the need of progressive realization of rights in the shortest possible time. For this, poverty reduction and accelerating the pace of social development with particular emphasis on empowering the poor and achieving gender equality have been made the overarching strategic goals. (ERD 2003: 7)

The above development vision conforms to the country's constitution as well as the government's international commitments. The government is obliged by constitutional directives to provide ways and means for the development and sustenance of a society in which the citizens' basic needs are met and every person can prosper in freedom. Among the international development frameworks, the government's commitment to the UN Millennium Development Goals (MDGs) and the social targets laid out in the Partnership Agreement on Poverty Reduction (PAPR with the ADB) are most notable. Some of the key MDGs, which have a direct relevance to government's development vision, include the following: 'Eradicate extreme poverty and hunger'; 'Promote gender equality and empower women'; 'Ensure environmental sustainability'; and 'Develop a global partnership for development'.

Forestry development is viewed within the broader context of the above development vision in general and the rural development in particular. For example, the Forestry Sector Master Plan (FSMP), approved by the government for the period between 1995 and 2015, emphasizes the crucial importance of 'people-oriented programmes' for the development of Bangladesh forestry, and notes:

> The strength of Bangladesh is her people ... Recognizing that tree growing and forestry can contribute to poverty alleviation, The Plan will create conditions where people will benefit directly by participating actively in tree growing and forest management ... Community forestry and socially oriented allotment forestry will be promoted by giving priority to poorer communities and poorer members of the community in the allocation of such contracts for tree plantations. Women and poor people who do not have a land based source of livelihood will be

> employed on priority basis in nurseries, plantations, forest management, harvesting and industrial work. (Government of Bangladesh 1995: 33)

The National Forest Policy (1994), which was formulated in response to the vision and recommendations of the FSMP, identifies five 'preconditions' for the development of forestry sector, which are as follows: meeting basic human needs, continued socio-economic growth, participation in decision making and benefit sharing, sustained political commitment, and sustainable utilization of forest resources.

The policy announces a goal of increasing the forest cover to 20 per cent of the country's land area by the year 2015, and delineates a number of objectives and vision for the forest sector including the following: "To meet the basic needs of the present and future generations ... by taking up various afforestation programmes ... by creating employment opportunities, strengthening the rural and national economy, the scope for poverty alleviation and trees and forest based rural development sectors will be extended and consolidated ... through participation of the local people, illegal occupation of forest lands, illegal tree felling and hunting of wild animals will be prevented" (National Forest Policy 1994 in *Bangladesh Gazette,* 6 July 1995).

The above vision is in conformity with the country's National Rural Development Policy (2001), which underscores the need for exploring all possible means of expanding employment and decent income earning opportunities in rural areas, along with measures to enhance the capacity and power of the rural poor to develop and sustain their livelihoods.

The latest perspective plan document of the country, the Fifth Five-Year Plan, identifies SF as one of the major thrusts of the strategy and programme of the forestry sector. The plan has the following vision for SF development:

> Social Forestry has now become a social movement in Bangladesh. The programme includes expansion and strengthening of 335 *thana* nurseries, establishment of 2000 union level nurseries, expansion and strengthening of 80 forest extension and nursery training centers, distribution of 40 million seedlings and raising 19000 km of strip plantations. The local government bodies will coordinate the afforestation programmes at the grassroots level under this programme. NGOs will be more directly involved in afforestation programmes. (Government of Bangladesh 1997: 259)

The key objectives of the plan include the following: continue and expand people-oriented afforestation programmes; elevate socio-economic well being of the people; achieve meaningful participation of local people, local government bodies, NGOs and government agencies in forestry programmes; and expand and rehabilitate the forest resources to increase productivity (Government of Bangladesh 1997: 258).

A PROBE INTO THE PERFORMANCE OF SELECTED MAJOR SOCIAL FORESTRY PROGRAMMES

This section will now review the major SF activities in Bangladesh. The following review uses a simplistic (yet widely accepted) analytic framework, which is based on such major studies as Poffenberger (1990), Khan (1998a) and Locke (1995) have conducted. The framework includes assessment of project performance in terms of the achievement of 'physical' and 'participatory or social' goals with a focus on the 'regulatory variables' in a particular context. The major sources of information include varied internal documents of the concerned projects (such as the Project Completion Reports, Project Performance Reports, Back to Office Report, Report and Recommendation of President to Board of Directors), relevant commissioned surveys and consultancy reports, and selected independent assessments.

Forestry Sector Project (Asian Development Bank [ADB] Loan No. 1468–BAN[SF]; Duration: 1998–2004, Executing Agency: Forest Department)

The Forest Sector Project (FSP) is currently the largest public sector SF intervention in the country. Its stated aims include: conservation of forests in selected protected areas, increased production of wood, institutionalization of forest resource management through local community participation and institutional capacity building and policy reform. The last (October 2003) ADB Review Mission expressed satisfaction with the recent project progress since the previous review mission in April 2003.

The Project Performance Report and Review Mission (ADB) commented on insufficient progress in meeting plantation (and associated physical) targets. Compared to 10,300 ha of woodlots, agro-forestry, char land and pond plantation, and 3,750 km strip and gully plantation, achievements upto September 2003 are 7,776 ha woodlots, 2,509 ha agro-forestry, and 9,990 km of strip plantations. The component of afforestation of unused tea estate lands in Sylhet has been dropped. The component of Participatory Natural Forest Rehabilitation and Management through local community also lagged behind the targets due to delay in government's approval of the project. The strip and institutional plantations showed good progress. ADB Mission found the overall achievements to be fairly good.

Considerable progress has been achieved in initiating reform of the institutions and policies. The government has amended the Forest Act in the year 2000 and undertaken multi-stakeholder consultations to finalize the draft rules and regulations to institutionalize social forestry. However, some indigenous and ethnic minority associations and environmental advocacy groups have expressed concern about the efficacy of the regulations and the mode and inclusiveness of the consultative meetings (Roy and Halim 2000). A considerable number (460) of NGOs have been involved as partners of FD in implementing the project activities. On the project's poverty reduction and gender development impacts, the ADB Review Mission (October 2003) noted the following: After getting benefits from the first rotation wood felling, participants have gained confidence in FD and have become more eager to participate in the Project through Participatory Benefit Sharing Agreement (PBSA). The SF participants in the Dinajpur and Sylhet Forest Divisions are well aware of the Project activities, and expect to receive benefits from these social forestry activities. The PBSAs have been revised to include spouses as equal partners, and verified the requirement of the spouses to sign the PBSAs as being adhered to. FD has increased the number of female staff in professional staff category from 4 to 19.

Community Forestry Project (ADB Loan No. 555–BAN; Executing Agency (EA): FD; Duration: 1981–1988)

The project represents one of the earliest attempts towards introducing a participatory approach to forest resource generation and management in the country. Its primary objectives included benefiting the rural poor by producing fuelwood for domestic uses, fruits, construction timber and fodder, catalyzing community awareness of the value of tree planting and developing a permanent institutional capacity within the FD to undertake social forestry throughout the country. The project area encompassed seven north-western districts of Rangpur, Dinajpur, Pabna, Rajshahi, Bogra, Kustia and Jessore. The project was considered "generally successful".

The physical targets, such as establishment of strip plantations, fuel wood plantations, agro-forestry, training, institutional support, were mostly achieved. A summary of the project's achievements is given in Table 7.1.

Limited headway was of course made in achieving the social goals. Farmers were generally indifferent to the timber species promoted by FD. Seedlings distribution to homesteads lagged far behind the target. Only 3.4 m seedlings were distributed as against a target of 10.9 m. The extension services of FD were inadequate and while selecting the species farmer's preference was not duly attended to. Farmers were generally suspicious of the intention of the government in the absence of written and formal assurance of specific rights to benefits (land and products) once the trees had matured. Fuelwood grown in the project was not used by farmers for domestic consumption, but fulfilled the need of industrial uses.

The project provided employment to several thousand labourers in nurseries and plantations and contributed to an increase in the biomass production.

Upazila Afforestation and Nursery Development Project (ADB Loan No. 0956–BAN[SF]; EA: FD; Duration: 1989–1996)

This project was basically a sequel to the Community Forestry Project and aimed at increasing the production of biomass fuel and enhancing the institutional capacity of FD to implement a self-sustaining nation-wide social forestry programme. The project covered 61 out of 64 districts, i.e., 85 per cent of the total land area of Bangladesh. The project was judged as "partially successful" by various assessment reports.

The physical targets were fully achieved (see Table 7.2). The level and content of farmers' participation in the project activities varied immensely. The contribution of expected participants was mainly to protect the plantations. Generally, farmers actively participated in protecting trees in their agroforestry plots. In the woodlots, the intensity of participant protection and involvement varied with the degree of fuel scarcity and the value they attached to the provision of tree by-products (e.g., leaves and twigs). In some instances, the project's preference and perception of benefits and use of products were not in conformity with farmers' views and field realities. The project, for example, promoted the production of fuelwood for domestic use and meeting household demands of the local poor. However, it was found that the majority of these poor farmers considered it a luxury to burn wood for their domestic use and desired to sell fuelwood for cash earning. Based on intensive interviews with 50 participants,

Table7.1. A Summary of the Community Forestry Project's Achievements (by Component)

Component	*Unit*	*Number*		*%*
		Appraisal	*Actual*	*Achievement*
1. Homestead Woodlots and Community Forestry Growth Centers (CFGCs)				
–Village supported	(no)	4650	4060	87
–Seedlings planted	(million)	10.9	3.4	31
–Newly constructed CFGCs	(no)	19	19	100
–Rehabilitated CFGCs	(no)	21	21	100
2. Strip Plantation				
–Highways(km)		800 (500 miles)	810 (506 miles)	101
–Railways(km)		400 (250 miles)	408 (255 miles)	102
–Canal embankments	(km)	400 (250 miles)	408 (255 miles)	102
–Union council road	(km)	3200 (2000 miles)	2587 (1617 miles)	81
3. Fuelwood Plantation	(ha)	4850 (12000 acres)	4898 (12083 acres)	101
4. Agroforestry Plantation	(ha)	121 (300 acres)	121 (300 acres)	100
5. Institutional Supports				
–Construction of buildings	(no)	272	236	87
–Rajshahi school	(no)	1	1	100
6. Fuelwood Conservation/Research	n/a		(deleted from the project)	
7. Consultants				
–Institutions	(man-month)	36	36	100
–Monitoring and evaluation	(man-month)	36	34	94
–Training	(man-month)	12	46	383
–Agroforestry	(man-month)	36	30	83
8. Training				
–Local	(persons)	15776	22158	140
–Overseas	(persons)	65	22	34

Based on ADB 2001

Table 7.2. A Summary of the Upazila Afforestation and Nursery Development Project's Achievements

Component	Target Appraised Feb 89	Achievement Revised Jun 95	% of revised Actual	% of revised Target
1. Woodplot Plantation (ha)	16000	20225	19415	96
2. Agroforestry Plantations (ha)	3200	4200	5110	122
3. Strip Plantation (km)	17750	17272	17809	103
4. Block Plantation	800	1282	1342	105
5. Seeding Distribution (million)	70	88	99	113
6. FENTCs	40	40	46	115
7. Upazila Nurseries	346	346	345	100
8. Training FD Staff and rural Communities ('000)	76	76	91	120
9. Consulting services				
a. International (person-month)	72	84	84	100
b. Domestic (person-month)	12	16	16	100

Based on ADB 2001

representing different areas of the project jurisdiction, it was found that none of the respondents preferred fuelwood for domestic use (based on Chowdhury 1993). The worst performance was noted in the case of strip plantations. This failure was mainly because the participants considered the future share of harvesting revenue to be inadequate; they did not dare encounter the local elites' use of the strip plantations for livestock pasturage. The poor and landless participants had traditionally been dependent on the local rich and influential families for financial and employment support, especially during periods of crisis. The rich families owned cattle, which were tended by the poor participant farmers and were grazed on the communal grazing land on the road, rail and embankments, which were targeted as the sites for strip plantations. Participants did not want to risk their patronage relationship with the local elites and thus were unable to guard the plantations from grazing (based on ADB internal documents). Woodlot participants, in some cases, opted to abandon the participatory scheme due to the failure to realize immediate benefits. Research and understanding of the socio-economic issues were clearly inadequate. The main burden of tree protection for strip plantations fell on the poorer participants, although they simply did not have the resources to protect plantations. The production of biomass fuels increased and some (certainly not all) participants benefitted from the collection of pruned staff, leaves and twigs.

Land tenurial insecurity negatively impacted on the morale of participants. Government's commitment of reviewing and reconsidering the one-year land use permit was not translated into action. The attempts at organizing the participants into community organizations, coined as the 'forestry associations', were only partially successful.

As the executing agency, FD showed some promise in working with the community. However, there was a serious concern regarding the failure in effectively institutionalizing the capacity built up through the project by not incorporating a high proportion of project staff, who were in effect on temporary employment arrangements, into permanent work force (ADB internal document).

Forestry Master Plan (ADB TA No. 1355–BAN; EA: FD, Duration: 1991–1993)

The main goals of this Technical Assistance (TA) were to formulate a long-term strategic master plan for the protection and development of the country's forest resources, and thus, to provide a framework for maximizing the contribution of forest resources for environmental stability and socio-economic development. The 20-year (1993–2012) Forestry Sector Master Plan document was successfully drafted and it covered such thematic issues as forest sector status, environmental management, participatory forestry, wood based energy conservation, non-wood forest products, forest production and management, forest industries, forest policy and institutions, legal, forestry research and extension, human resource development, and investment scenarios. However, except for a number of (rather terse) occasional references, especially in the chapter titled 'Participatory Forestry', treatment of the social issues in general and poverty alleviation concerns in particular had been inadequately addressed in the main plan. In formulating the plan, stakeholder consultation, especially with forest-dependent communities, had been given scanty importance.

Forest Resources Management Project: Forest Directorate Component (IDA Grant and WFP Assistance; Duration: 1992–2001, EA: FD)

Among other activities, the project contained a component titled 'Participatory Forestry Development' (PFD) which represented the major SF activities within the project. The PFD component aimed at establishing 850 ha of plantation through participatory arrangement with the local people in Chittagong and Cox's Bazar Forest Divisions.

The physical target of establishing 850 ha of agro-forestry plantations in the Chittagong and Cox's Bazar was achieved reclaiming especially the encroached forestlands. Some 610 farmers were involved in the project, which extended over the districts of Chittagong and Cox's Bazar (under the administrative purview of Chittagong South, Chittagong North, Cox's Bazar South, and Cox's Bazar North Forest Divisions). Out of these 610 farmers, each 200 participants were allotted 2 ha of land and 410 participants have been allotted 1 ha of land, individually. Prior to the project, most of these lands, although designated as government forestlands, were encroached upon and denuded.

Although the participants were allotted plots, a good number of the participants did not receive formal documents stating benefit sharing agreement. The formation of 'participants' groups' seemed more of an attempt to fulfill a procedural requirement of the project, than an exercise towards developing genuine collective activities. Group activities were minimal and the concerned NGO involvement was ineffective in many cases. The protection of the plantation raised was a major problem. Some villagers, linked to local rural elites as clients, who were not included in the project, damaged plantations at a number of places. The FD staff faced serious pressure from local elites to employ participants of their choice, and as such a considerable number of well-off people were included as project participants. The relatively poorer participants were often engaged in off-farm activities, as they felt the income from the project activities was not enough. Because of this external involvement, they could not give adequate time to plantation protection and maintenance. After the initial work of selecting and training participants, the NGOs practically left the scene. The financial management at the grass-roots (participants') level was largely inefficient. In most places, even the bank accounts, as required by the project, were not opened. The participation of women was less or poor. There were some technical problems in relation to plantation development such as lack of provision of irrigation facilities and fertilizers after the thinning operation. The administrative problems included frequent and erratic change of the project leadership (the project saw 5 Project Directors during its nine years of operation).

Sundarbans Biodiversity Conservation Project (Currently suspended. Loan No.1643–BAN[SF]; EA: FD; Duration 1999–2006)

The development objectives of the project include development of a sustainable management and biodiversity conservation for the Sundarbans Reserve Forest (SRF) resources, and reduction of poverty of 3.5 m people living in the impact zone. The project is rated 'satisfactory'.

Activities towards achieving the physical targets are underway. The organizational and institutional structures, such as the Sundarbans Management Unit (SMU), Sundarbans Stewardship Commission and Stakeholder Advisory Council, have been in place, although the SMU remains understaffed. Plans for enrichment planting and sample plots have been prepared and reviewed.

The project aims at following a participatory and flexible approach for social progress in the impact zone, which should include assessment of baseline data on socio-economic condition, mobilization and organization of resource users, assessment of alternative sources of finance for micro-credit and mobilization of community-based micro-credit groups for employment and enterprise development, and development of social infrastructure.

The progress thus far achieved as regards the targeted 'socio-economic development of the impact zone' may be stated as follows: socio-economic baseline survey commenced with assistance from Khulna University; learning materials for school children are being developed, with assistance from a local NGO, with a view to raising environmental awareness, and local Government Engineering Department has initiated limited infrastructure building activities.

Since the late 2002, however, a number of ADB Review Missions have expressed concern over the project's 'lack of significant progress', especially in such areas as development of a participatory environment engaging the local people and other stakeholders, and effective financial management. Ultimately, in September 2003, the ADB suspended the loan for the project "on account of serious implementation delays and lack of proper financial management of the project" (ADB's letter to the Minister, Ministry of Environment and Forest, 4 September 2003). In order to consider lifting the suspension, the Bank has, however, advised the FD to proceed with such activities as the reformulation of the project plans through a participatory and consultative process, and to reconcile project accounts in compliance with ADB guidelines.

Coastal Greenbelt Project (ADB Loan No.1353–BAN[SF]; EA: FD; Duration 1995–2002)

The key development goals of the project were to protect and improve the coastal environment by increasing tree cover and alleviating poverty by creating supplementary income opportunities for the poor. The progress of implementation and of achieving the development objectives is rated 'satisfactory' and 'partially satisfactory' respectively.

The progress towards physical targets was generally satisfactory. Some 8,934 km of strip plantations and 665 ha of foreshore plantations were done, and about 143,936 participants and more than 100 NGOs were engaged. 12.56 m seedlings were distributed free of cost for planting in homesteads and institutions.

Participants received direct benefits from intercropping vegetables, and extracting fuelwood, fodder and fruits. Some 100,000 participants received payment for planting activities in the year

2000. The project helped in generating employment for more than 3.5 m man-days. Initially, less number of women were involved in the project activities; but female participation has gone up in the last two years. Lack of clarity in the land use agreement caused a low morale for participants in the initial months. This problem was subsequently responded to by incorporating the Participation and Benefit Sharing Agreements from the Forestry Sector Project. Activities towards building public awareness were limited. Some NGOs expressed dissatisfaction regarding the process and nature of NGO engagement in the project. Research support has been inadequate. Procedural delay in timely release of funds and frequent change of the Project Director have hampered smooth implementation of the plans. The project staff were recruited on a temporary basis, causing low staff morale and job insecurity. After completion of the project, some 400 'development budget' staff lost their jobs. Paradoxically, however, there is general shortage of staff in the local forest offices; 5 of the 9 Coastal Forest Divisions do not have adequate staff to continue even the basic plantation management activities. Some of the staff training programmes, notably study tours, were not undertaken at all.

NGOS' INVOLVEMENT AND PARTICIPATION

One major feature of the SF programmes is that they provide a platform and an avenue for forging a partnership between the FD (government) and the NGOs. Some 460 NGOs are currently engaged in the Forest Sector Project alone. A wide array of activities is prescribed for the participating NGOs in SF programmes such as the following: motivating and organizing SF 'farmer groups', facilitating the selection of community level 'SF plantation caretakers', arranging training for farmers on plantation techniques and management, and raising public awareness about 'homestead forestry'. In some cases, NGOs negotiate and make 'deed agreement' for benefit sharing among the landowning agencies, FD, and SF farmers. Some NGOs encourage members to set up nurseries not only to ensure supply of seedlings for SF plantations, but also to provide an additional source of income for SF farmers. Another notable area of intervention by NGOs is concerned with the promotion of public awareness on environmental degradation through continuous education and motivational campaigns.

Notwithstanding the above list of prescribed activities, however, recent evaluations (e.g., Davidson 2000; Khan et al. 2004;

ADB internal documents, Forest Department 2003) and the author's personal observations suggest that the level and extent of NGO participation in the major decisions and activities of the SF programmes have often been poor and restricted. A number of reasons and factors have been identified that can explain the predicament:

- NGO selection process in the SF programmes has often been faulty; most NGOs selected were very small and lacked necessary resources and skills to implement the programmes effectively. Furthermore, it has been observed in many instances that, the number of NGOs selected in each *thana/upazila* was more than the number of NGOs actually required to perform the task. Consequently, the work assigned to each NGO was very limited, and the meagre service charge paid to the NGOs was hardly enough to sustain their motivation and interest in the programmes.
- NGOs were not adequately involved in the selection of farmers/participants. Appropriate participants were not selected due to the interference of local political leaders and influential people. Similarly, NGOs had little voice in the technical operation of SF programmes such as the selection of species and plantation sites.
- In some cases, NGOs were not paid the required service charge as per the official agreement (between FD and NGOs). This created a feeling of distrust and lack of interest in SF programmes.
- There was a lack of necessary coordination between the FD and NGOs. Lack of provision for a regular monthly meeting between the FD staff and NGOs prevented development of a closer relationship and open flow of information.

Recent studies (e.g., Davidson 2000; Forest Department 2003, Khan et al. 2004; Khan 2002) suggest a number of measures towards strengthening the FD-NGO partnership and enhancing NGO participation in SF:

- NGOs should be given the total responsibility of selecting the farmers/participants in the SF programmes.
- There should be a system of holding regular meetings between local level FD and NGO staff for sharing ideas and evaluating project activities and visiting each other's offices to develop a better understanding and closer relationship.

- A limited number of NGOs should be involved in each *Thana* (maximum of two NGOs) so that the FD can monitor and supervise activities without much problem, and NGOs get enough work to justify cost effectiveness of their staff involvement for supervision work.
- NGOs having prior experience in SF (at least five years), having technical staff and local presence (office) should be selected as programme partners. NGO selection should be made through the involvement of senior level FD staff and donor representatives at the central level so as to prevent interference of local political leaders and other influential people.
- NGO involvement should be on a long-term basis. No service charge should be provided; instead payment should be made to each NGO towards employing a technical staff in each *thana* and grant a share (minimum 15 per cent) of the money obtained from the final harvest of SF plantations.
- NGOs should be made accountable for the money received from the FD in the form of effectively performing the tasks assigned to them. The FD should facilitate rather than implement the programme. The relationship between the FD and NGOs should be based on mutual respect, trust and transparency.

LESSONS LEARNT AND THE CURRENT TRENDS: IS GLOBALIZATION PLAYING A ROLE?

From the above review of selected SF activities, a number of observations and lessons may be highlighted. The implications and impact of the forces of globalization are discernable in at least three broad trends in the development of SF in the country:

- One may argue that the very growth of and enthusiasm for the concept of SF can, to a large extent, be traced back to international concern and propaganda (for details, see Khan 1998a, 1998d). Some analysts have gone as far as viewing the concepts of SF and 'participation' as 'western impositions' (e.g., Fox and Fisher 1990: 116–117). Along with the same vein, in Bangladesh, the externally assisted projects, especially those supported by the ADB, constitute the major and large-scale SF interventions in the country. Through just six major SF projects (namely, the CHT Development Project, Community Forestry Development Project,

Forestry Sector Project, Biodiversity Conservation in the Sundarbans Reserve Project, Coastal Greenbelt Project, and Upazila Afforestation and Nursery Development Project), e.g., the ADB has invested some Taka 5844.75 million or 47 per cent, out of the total costs of Taka 12472.25 m.

- The recent reforms and development efforts in forest policies and associated regulations are largely under the pressure of and prompted by the international agencies (e.g., ADB, World Bank) and relevant global events. A recent review of Bangladesh SF concluded that "many of the legal and institutional reforms have been done in response to the government's obligation to international aid agencies" (Khan et al. 2004: 123).
- The physical and quantifiable targets have often fared better than the social goals in the SF programmes. The emphasis on physical and quantifiable targets is also linked to exogenous factors, as Khan (1998a: 118) explains:

> ... in the field offices, donors' pressure channelled through the central line authorities contributes to the tendency of chasing physical and quantifiable targets of SF. Local foresters' concern for SF primarily centres around the achievement of physical targets which is the dominant criteria for evaluating SF's success.

Furthermore, the preoccupation with physical targets often led the central planners and field officers to neglect regional conditions and contextual realities (Singh and Khare 1993; Khan 1998a, 1998d).

Besides the above boarder implications, a number of other observations can be made at a more functional and (project) operational level:

- Considerable progress has so far been made in initiating reform of the institutions and policies, plantation establishments, creating opportunities of income generation and employment, and raising some degree of public awareness and interest about SF.
- Social and participatory goals are regulated and conditioned by the particular realities of the surrounding context and environment. These contextual regulators (e.g., patronage, social stratification, institutional biases) and their possible impact need to be carefully assessed and understood before launching any project.
- There is a need for more extensive stakeholder analysis and consultation in the formulation and (subsequent) management of development projects. The present level of consul-

tation and dialogue between project authorities and stakeholders is considered inadequate by many quarters.

- Land tenure status bears major implications for participants' morale and thus, the issue needs to be addressed. However, land management involves securing cooperation from an array of complex governmental regulations and institutions, which may pose a particularly difficult challenge for project authorities.
- In some cases, participants' preference and perception of project benefits and utilities are not in conformity with those of the project authorities. This may be responded to by a more rigorous process of interaction and field-level exploration.
- Research, especially on the dynamics of social regulators and implications of forestry projects, has been inadequate. Systematic and problem-solving research should continue to illuminate the process of project formulation and performance appraisal.
- The present and potential role of forestry in poverty alleviation has neither been made sufficiently clear, nor been explored in depth. Some of the recent projects (e.g., FSP) have started to recognize the significance of implications of poverty and other social issues for participatory forest management; however the focus has been on the impact of these issues on forest, rather than the reverse.

CONCLUSIONS

It is manifestly evident that Bangladesh has lately made considerable progress in consolidating forestry as a means of rural development and poverty alleviation. A comprehensive policy framework is now in place to support and nurture SF activities in the country, together with a growing interest in SF by the concerned quarters. The physical goals of, for example, plantation establishments, employment generation, seedlings and other input distribution, and infrastructure development, have mostly been achieved satisfactorily. SF programmes cover a large part of the country, and represent the most dominant intervention in the country's forestry sector. Despite these seemingly impressive results, however, achievements in terms of social goals of public participation, equity and farmers' empowerment have lagged far behind expectations, and are yet to produce any significant large scale change towards rural development. There has been little systematic effort in identifying and dealing with the social factors—for example patronage, status differentiation, distributive inequity – that have impact on and regulate the performance of SF in the programme implementation level. These unfavourable social realities also limit the farmers' ability to make use of and benefit from the otherwise conducive (central) policy environment relating to SF. Besides, our understanding of the impact of forces of globalization on SF currently is quite poor and far from conclusive. The situation calls for a great deal of further sociological research and exploration.

ACKNOWLEDGEMENTS

The article draws the observations and experiences of the author's involvements with the Government of Bangladesh (GoB)-commissioned *Review on Social Forestry in Bangladesh* (Forest Department, Ministry of Environment and Forest, Dhaka 2003) and Asian Development Bank's (ADB) *Regional Study on Forest Policy and Institutional Reform: Bangladesh County Case Study* (ADB, Manila 2001) in both of which he acted as the Team Leader. The cooperation of the fellow members of both the Study Teams and the respondent SF farmers is gratefully acknowledged. The views expressed here do not necessarily reflect those of ADB, GoB or any other organization; the usual disclaimer applies. This article comes as a sequel to a few earlier work examining the performance of social forestry as a means for poverty alleviation and rural development in Bangladesh (e.g., Khan 1998a, 1998b, 1998c, 2001, 2002).

REFERENCES

Ahmed, A.U. and Azad, A.K. (1987), *Social Forestry in Bangladesh: A Case Study of Betagi and Pomora Experiments,* University of Chittagong, Chittagong.

Alim, A. (1988), *Forestry with the People and for the People,* Institute of Forestry, Chittagong.

Arnold, J.E.M., Bergman, A. and Djurfeldt, G. (1988), Forestry for the Poor? An Evaluation of the SIDA Supported Social Forestry Project in Tamil Nadu, India, (SIDA Report 1987/8), Swedish International Development Authority, Stockholm.

——— (1990), Evaluation of The SIDA Supported Bihar Social Forestry Project for Chotanagpur and Santhal Parganas, India, Swedish International Development Authority, Stockholm.

Asian Development Bank (ADB) (2001), "The Draft Bangladesh Country Case Study Report", *RETA 5900: Regional Study on Forest Policy and Institutional Reform*, Asian Development Bank, Manila.

Chowdhury, J.A. (1993), Final Report of the Resource Survey Consultant, Thana Afforestation and Nursery Development Project, Forest Department, Dhaka.

Davidson, J. (2000), Social Forestry in Bangladesh and Social Forestry Research at the Bangladesh Forest Research Institute. Agricultural Resource Management Project, Bangladesh Forest Research Institute, Chittagong.

Forest Department (2003), Report on Review of Social Forestry with Special Reference to the Forestry Sector Project, Forest Department, Ministry of Environment and Forest, Dhaka.

Fox, J. and Fisher, R. (1990), "Community Organisations and Government Bureaucracies in Social Forestry", in Stevens, M.E., Bhumibhamon, S. and Wood, H. (eds.), Research Policy for Community Forestry in Asia Pacific Region, Proceedings of a Seminar, January 8–11, 1990, Report 5, Regional Community Forestry Training Centre, Bangkok.

Government of Bangladesh (GoB) (1995), *Development Perspective of the Forestry Sector Master Plan, Bangladesh*, Ministry of Environment and Forest, Dhaka.

Government of Bangladesh (GoB) (1997), *The Fifth Five Year Plan*, Ministry of Planning, Dhaka.

Khan, N.A. (1998a), *A Political Economy of Forest Resource Use: Case Studies of Social Forestry in Bangladesh*, Ashgate Publishing Company, Aldershot (England).

——— (1998b), "Land Tenurial Dynamics and Participatory Forest Management in Bangladesh", *Public Administration and Development*, Vol. 18, pp. 335–347.

——— (1998c), "Interview of the Sahibs: Bureaucratic Constraints on Community Forestry in Bangladesh", *Journal of World Forest Resource Management*, Vol. 9, pp. 73–93.

——— (1998d), "The International Aid Agencies and Social Forestry Management in Bangladesh: A Case Study", *Decision,* Vol. 25, Nos. 1–4.

——— (2001), *Social Forestry Versus Social Realities: Patronage and Community-based Forestry in Bangladesh* (Gatekeeper Series No.99), International Institute for Environment and Development, London.

——— (2002), "Current Trends in Social Forestry in Bangladesh", Discussion Paper Used for the ACF/DCF Training Course, Bangladesh Forest Academy, Chittagong.

Khan, N.A., Choudhury, J.K., Huda, K.S. and Mondal, M.I. (2004), *An Overview of Social Forestry in Bangladesh*, Forest Department, Government of Bangladesh, Dhaka and University of Chittagong, Chittagong.

Locke, C. (1995), Planning for the Participation of Vulnerable Groups in Communal Management of Forest Resources: The Case of Western Ghats Forestry Project (Ph. D Thesis), CDS, University of Wales, Swansea.

Oakley, P. (ed.) (1991), *Projects with People: The Practice of Participation in Rural Development*, International Labour Office, Geneva.

Poffenberger, M. (1990), *Forest Management Partnerships: Regenerating India's Forests*, Ford Foundation, New Delhi.

Roy, D. and Halim, S. (2000), "Forestry Rules of 2000", paper presented at the Workshop on the Forest Amendment Act 2000 and Social Forestry, organized by SEHD and associate organizations, held in Dhaka during 2–3 November, 2000.

Singh, S. and Khare, A. (1993), "People's Participation in Forest Management", *Commonwealth Forestry Review*, Vol. 72, No. 4.

Task Force. (1987), Participatory Forestry in Bangladesh: Concepts, Experiences and Recommendations, A Task Force Report to the Ministry of Agriculture, Government of Bangladesh, Dhaka.

Chapter 8

Globalization, Urban Environment and Role of Non-Governmental Organizations

Ravindra R. Patil

WE are in the era of globalization. Though millions of people are unaware about the global ization process, the term 'globalization' has already gained wider currency among the academic people and has become a 'catchword' of corporate world, professionals, media, social activists and the larger civil society organizations. Despite the fact that globalization has been the theme of many national and international seminars, and that various scholars have written extensively about the same issue, the impact of globalization on ecology, environment and human life and the role of NGOs in this context has not been explored enough.

The present paper is divided into four parts. While the first part illuminates the origin, nature and growth of globalization process in India, the second part opens a debate on globalization and urban environment with reference to growth of automobile industry and the effects of vehicular pollution on public health in Delhi. Part three brings out the fact of growth of environmental NGOs at national and international level in the context of globalization, and part four concludes the paper by providing suggestive measures for non-governmental organizations in reducing vehicular pollution.

GLOBALIZATION: HISTORICAL ORIGIN, NATURE AND GROWTH

The exact periodization of the origin of globalization is a matter of disputes. The wide literature on globalization provides various periods and dates of the origin of the globalization process. One opinion is that the concept of globalization dates back to the voyage of discovery in the 15th century (Valaskakis 1999: 153). However, many other sources trace the origin of globalization in the process of colonialism and industrial revolution of 17th–18th century. The early phase of globalization has brought a new economic system in the world in the form of capitalistic mode of production. Thus, the strong belief is that the emergence of globalization lies in the theory of 'capitalism'.

The theory of capitalism has a long history and stages, described particularly in the writings of Marx. Marx did not mention about the term 'globalization' per se but he did discuss the advanced form of capitalism, that would cross all the boundaries of nations and emerge as a new form of world capitalist development. As Marx held, the capitalist as one of the revolutionary class, which was more engaged with its own progress and development by inventing new technology and machines for the large-scale production and accumulation of profit. The increased productive capacity of capitalism and the capitalist further led to problems of market and consumers in the European and American society. The small population of western countries could not absorb the huge quantity of goods and finished products. Thus, market experienced the phenomenon of overstock of product. In order to avoid the recurring overstock of products, the developed capitalist countries captured overseas markets through colonial conquests of Asia and Africa. The overseas market served the capitalist countries in two important ways. First, it secured market for their manufactured goods, and secondly provided cheap source of raw materials. These two factors further greatly helped the expansion of international trade and commerce. With the emergence of a world-wide market, capitalism would rule over the world in terms of production, consumption and exchange. This new form of capitalism was foreseen by Marx prior to his death. In 1848, in the *Communist Manifesto*. Marx and Engles wrote: "The need of a constantly expanding market for its product chases the bourgeoisie over the whole surface of the globe. It must nest everywhere, settle everywhere, and establish connection everywhere" (Quoted in Hersh and Brun 2000: 106).

However, the advanced form of capitalism and capturing of world market for the clearance sale of overstock is not the sole reason behind the origin of globalization process. As per the Marxist view, 'imperialism' is another important factor which is instrumental to the present state of globalization. In this perspective, the current flow of capital from advanced capitalist countries to underdeveloped countries has more to do with political rather than economic and technological changes. The world was divided into two political and ideological blocks, one headed by the USA, and the other by the USSR. As a result, two parallel world markets came into existence, the so-called imperialist and socialist world market. The political victory of imperialism and demise of socialism gave a strong impetus to the unopposed growth of globalization process. The events such as the end of the cold war, dismantling of state socialism in the USSR, the collapse of the Berlin Wall, emergence of the USA as a super-power ruling the unified world market, advanced scientific and technological revolution were the important factors for the emergence of the process of globalization. Thus, the history of globalization though traced back to colonialism and industrial revolution yet the basic roots of globalization lie in the specific economic and political events of the world during period of 1980–90s.

The globalization process has created a new economic system (neo-liberal economy) in the world, transcending all boundaries of nation-states to establish trade, commerce, capital, commodity and communication in the world market. "The new markets were established in the form of service market, financial market and consumer market; new actors such as MNCs, WTOs, International NGOs, regional banks, policy coordination groups such as G-7, G-10, G-22, and OECD emerged to rule the world market; new rules and norms were governing the individualized liberalism, democracy, human rights movements, consensus on global environment and peace and multilateral agreements such as Intellectual Property Rights; and new faster and cheaper means of communication channel came into existence in the form of internet, cellular phones, fax, computer-aided design, etc." (Sengupta 2001: 3137).

The process of globalization has over shadowed the developing countries with the unique 'New Economic Policy'(NEP) framework. The NEP proposes lifting controls and restrictions on private enterprises; allowing free-trade and enterprise; privatization of countries' economies by disinvestments in public sector; selling state holding to private corporations of both national and foreign origin, removal of restriction on import and export and permitting free flow of foreign products and technical know how; removal of restriction on foreign capital investment and allowing multi-national companies (MNCs) to own share and invest in the national industries and service sector; reduction of subsidies on agricultural fertilizers, implements and essential consumer goods and services; closing down government enterprises and retrenchment in the existing government employees; etc. In a nutshell, the state minimizes its economic role and invites monopolistic capitalism to manage the economic affairs of country so that the national economy becomes more competitive in the international market. Thus, all these policy measures in the era of globalization have minimized the role of government and forced governments to withdraw from the economic and social sector, which gradually created an adverse impact on various aspects of human life and survival.

In pursuance of globalization and compulsion of international institutions and agreements such as World Trade Organization (WTO), World Bank (WB), Organization for Economic Cooperation and Development (OECD), General Agreement on Tariff and Trade (GATT), etc, the Indian government has introduced several economic measures for the growth of its economy in the form of liberalization of its trade with other countries and structural adjustment of its economy during 1980s–1990s. These economic measures of the Indian government are called 'Economic Reform' and came to be known as New Economic Policy (NEP) after 1991. The adoption of NEP by the Indian government has opened its doors for free-trade and commerce with foreign countries by providing market access to foreign goods and services (about 760 commodities), foreign direct investment, establishment of multinational companies, founding of foreign industry, etc. Further services like banking, insurance and education have been opened for national and international private sectors. Thus, the New Economic Policy of India has allowed free national and international trade, by drastically withdrawing government's role from the social and economic sectors.

GLOBALIZATION AND ENVIRONMENT: A DEBATE

As we have discussed in the section above the origin, growth and nature of the globalization process, the present section proposes to look into the contemporary debate raised by the environmentalists, social scientists, civil society organizations, UN agency, etc. on the relation between globalization and environment. The current debate on globalization and the environment has revolved around four major themes that explicitly highlight the complicity between globalization and environment in 21st century (Salih 2001). The first theme in the debate, a matter of common understanding, recognizes that the impact of any large scale development initiatives such as industrialization, raw material extraction, mega-irrigation projects, timber logging, mining, fossil energy exploration, mechanized fishing etc. will affect the quality of the environmental life support system (air, water and soil). Such large scale development initiative at the national and international levels will contribute to massive exploitation of natural resources, air pollution, climatic change, ozone layer depletion and greenhouse effect, etc.

The second theme in the debate is more concerned with the environmental consequences of the rapid trans-national industrialization and large scale manufacturing of technological and commercial goods, and services for the consumption of the growing world population. Certainly, if these current trends of industrialization, technological advancement and excessive use as well as misuse of non-renewable natural resources continue to go unchecked, the earth will soon be rendered empty of all its natural resources.

The third theme, especially propagated by the environmentalist, social scientists and civil society organizations of third world countries, expresses that the economically developed countries of North are the main agents of global pollution. Similarly, they strongly argue that the development of globalization and liberalization of trade and finance is not environmentally neutral, and largely 'hegemonized' by the developed countries of the North. They blame the developed countries of North for dumping hazardous wastes and locating polluting industries in the developing countries.

The fourth theme emphasizes that the global environmental protection could be realized by adopting the policy of sustainable development as a global idea. The main thrust of this theme is that the globalization and environmental protection should proceed simultaneously, and global environmental institutions and global governance should manage global environmental problems.

Thus, all these themes of debate on globalization and environment have different viewpoints to understand the growth of globalization and its negative impact on the global environment. However, the themes second and third would be more appropriate to understand the cyclical relation between globalization and growth of automobile industry, vehicular pollution and harmful effects on public health. The following section will highlight the growth of automobile industry and impact of increasing vehicular pollution on public health in Delhi city.

GLOBALIZATION, URBAN ENVIRONMENT AND HEALTH HAZARDS

The New Industrial Policy (NIP) announced on July 24, 1991 under the name of New Economic Policy (NEP) has abolished the pre-reform industrial licensing system and opened up various new sectors such as mining, banking, insurance, telecommunications, construction and management of ports, harbours, roads and highways, airlines, automotive, defence equipments, etc. to the national private sector and foreign companies.

The aim of the present paper is to highlight the globalization and vehicular pollution in Delhi. This section particularly deals with the post-reform growth of automobile industry and increasing vehicular pollution effects on public health.

It is now widely recognized that unplanned economic growth creates environmental problems. Going through scarce data available on the post-reform growth of automobile industry and vehicular pollution in urban India in general, and Delhi city in particular, it has been observed that the automobile industry is one of the major air polluters in urban India. The growth of vehicular population has reached its peak especially after the introduction of the NEP in 1991. The characteristics of automobile industry show that there has been a growth of all types of vehicles in the post-reform period. At present, there are 75 per cent two-wheelers (2-W), 11 per cent cars, 4 per cent medium utility vehicles (MUVs), 4 per cent carriage vehicles (CVs) and 6 per cent three-wheelers (3-W) in India. The Table on All India vehicle population gives details.

Table 8.1 reveals that the period between 1986–2000 has seen comparatively highest growth of all types of vehicles at all India level. The increase in the number of vehicles in India is due to proliferation of the automobile industry, after introduction of NEP measures in the form of liberalization of trade with other countries and structural adjustment of Indian economy partially in the mid-eighties, and more comprehensively, after the adoption of the NEP in 1991.

It is a fact that the post-reform period has witnessed the massive growth of vehicular population in all-India level. However, the

Table 8.1: All India Vehicle Population

	Pre-1986	*1991*	*2000*
2-W	6,133,771	14,046,764	38,770,000
3-W	389,542	763,573	2,510,000
Cars	1,278,654	2,281,569	4,715,809
MUVs	386,788	731,726	1,104,191
CVs	1,057,191	1,744,211	2,386,992
Total	9,245,946	19,567,783	49,486,992

Sources:

1. *Motor Transport Statistics of India*, Transport Research Wing, Ministry of Road Transport and Highways, 2001.
2. Sub-Group on Traffic Forecasts and Fleet Requirements in the Tenth Five-Year Plan, Planning Commission.
3. Society of Indian Automobile Manufactures, 2001.

urban India and especially the cities have seen a veritable explosion of vehicles due a to number of factors such as employment opportunities in the cities, rising income, pressure to travel, inadequate public transport system, etc. The statistics shows that 48.8 per cent of all vehicles in India are run in the three metropolitan cities, namely, Mumbai, Delhi and Kolkata. Hence, these cities are equally vulnerable to high level of air pollution.

Delhi has the largest number of vehicles in India, and vehicular population of Delhi has been growing in the wake of mushrooming automobile industries in the periphery of the city.

Table 8.2 shows that there has been very significant increase in vehicle population in Delhi. The increase in the number of two-wheelers and cars is comparatively higher than other vehicles. The increase of cars and two wheelers (personal vehicles) is due to inadequate public transport system in Delhi. However, this high growth of vehicle population is gradually contributing to higher level of air pollution in the city.

Table 8.2: Vehicle Population in Delhi

Vehicles	*1971*	*1985*	*1990*	*1995*	*1999*
Cars	0.56	1.58	3.45	5.76	8.37
2 Wheelers	0.93	5.79	11.13	16.18	21.31
3 Wheelers	0.01	0.03	0.59	0.75	0.75
Taxi	0.04	0.09	0.01	0.13	0.17
Buses	0.03	0.14	0.18	0.26	0.36
Goods Vehicles	0.14	0.52	0.93	1.25	1.52
Total	1.08	8.41	16.38	24.32	32.48

Source: Society of Indian Automobile Manufacturers, 2005.

Air Pollution in Delhi

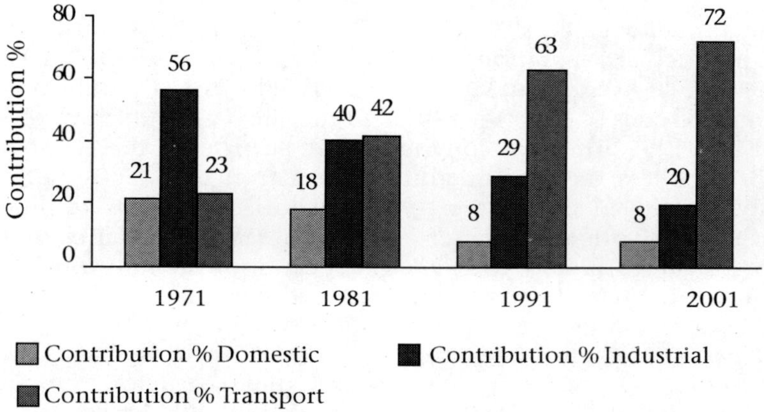

(**Source:** Society of Indian Automobile Manufacturers, 2005)

The above figure highlights that there are three major factors, namely, domestic, industrial and transport contributing to air pollution. However, two out of three factors of air pollution such as domestic and industrial have shown decreasing trends during the years 1971 to 2001. The transportation sector has emerged as comparatively one of the dominant factors contributing high level of air pollution in the city from the year 1981 to 2001, i.e., during the post-reform period.

VEHICULAR POLLUTION AND HEALTH HAZARD IN DELHI

For the most part of the primary pollutants are generated by motor vehicles and industries in cities and towns. The dramatic pollution of motor vehicles in Delhi is primarily caused by emission of various poisonous gases like Carbon Monoxide; Oxide of Nitrogen, i.e., Nitric Oxide; Oxides of Sulphur, i.e., Sulphur Dioxide; Lead; Polycyclic Aromatic Hydrocarbon (PAH); Suspended Particulate Matter (SPM); Benzene; Ozone; etc. All these poisonous gases are emitted by petrol and diesel vehicles.

Going through the limited data made available by the Centre for Science and Environment on three pollutants – SPM, NO_2 and Ozone and its effect on public health in Delhi for the years 1987 to 1996 show the following scenario:

Suspended Particulate Matter (SPM)

The annual average SPM level in Delhi's air remains consistently high, much above national standards almost everyday of the year. The annual average maximum level of SPM in Delhi's air ranged from 7.6 times to 16.7 times higher than the permissible limit from 1987 to 1995. The SPM consists of tiny particles in diesel exhaust PM-10 or less than 10 microns (one micron is one-millionth of a millimetre) in size on a regular basis in Delhi, called Respirable Suspended Particulate Matter (RSPM). These particulates cause the worst damage as they can penetrate deep into the lungs. In other words, the quantity of all particles in the air is called SPM, and on an average, nearly 40 per cent of total SPM in Delhi is PM 10. All particles are not dangerous. It is PM 10 or less that is more dangerous. On account of their size, these particles cannot be easily exhaled. They remain in the lungs for a longer period, corroding the cells, ultimately leading to the growth of tumour. The study conducted by the World Bank calculates that over 40,000 people are dying early because of air pollution in India. The annual deaths are 7,500 in Delhi, 5,700 in Kolkata and 4,500 in Mumbai. The study conducted by World Health Organization (WHO) revealed that air pollution was found to exceed in most of 23 Indian cities with a population of over one million. In Delhi, the annual level of SPM is at least five times higher than the WHO recommendation. The PM 10 is responsible for over 95 per cent of the health damages in Indian cities. The study conducted by the Scientific Review Panel of California Air Resources Board (CARB) has pointed out that chronic exposure to 1 micro-gram per cubic metre (mg/m^3) of diesel exhaust will lead to additional 300 cases of lung cancer per million people. Thus, for a population like Delhi, this means an additional 3,000 extra cases of lung cancer for a chronic exposure to $1mg/m^3$ of diesel exhaust.

Nitrogen Dioxide (NO_2)

The level of NO_2, a highly toxic gas, has been increasing rapidly in Delhi since 1987. The NO_2 level exceeded the permissible limits by more than 1.5 times in Delhi. Haemoglobin is known to absorb NO_2 more easily than Oxygen. About 80 to 90 per cent NO_2 inhaled are easily absorbed into the blood stream. This reduces the oxygen-carrying capacity of the blood. NO_2 causes lung tissues to become leathery and brittle and can cause lung cancer and emphysema (or severe breathing problems). Thus, NO_2 causes bronchitis and bronchopneumonia (*Down to Earth* 1999: 39).

Ozone

Ozone is considered a secondary pollutant because it is produced as a result of the interaction with other air pollutants, particularly Oxides of Nitrogen (Nox), which, in turn, are the result of diesel vehicle emission and hydrocarbons, emitted by both diesel and petrol cars. Because of a large number of two-stroke vehicles (two and three-wheelers), Delhi's air contains high levels of hydrocarbons. In the presence of sunlight, NO_2 reacts with hydrocarbons to produce ozone, a highly toxic gas, known to cause asthma. The studies conducted by Central Road Research Institute (CRRI) and the School of Environmental Sciences of Jawaharlal Nehru University have shown a very high level of ozone concentration in Delhi.

As per the World Health Organization (WHO), a safe limit for ground-level ozone is an average 50 to 60 parts per billion by volume (ppbv). Ozone in Delhi has often exceeded 120 ppbv. The CRRI study is based on tests conducted at seven locations in Delhi in the winter of 1993: Parliament Street, Daryaganj, Paharganj, Ashram Chowk, Karol Bagh, Maharani Bagh and Vasant Kunj. The average level of ozone at five sites out of seven over eight day time hours exceeded the WHO mean standard of 50–60 ppbv by 10 to 40 per cent. Even more alarming, the peak levels observed in areas with heavy traffic and congestion like Karol Bagh, Daryaganj and Parliament Street were as high as 119.0 ppbv, 125.8 ppbv and 123.9 ppbv respectively. In most cases, the maximum concentration of ozone exceeded the upper WHO limit by two times. The studies further reveal that the ozone is bound to rise in Delhi with increase in emission of oxides of nitrogen, carbon monoxide, methene and other hydrocarbons. The increasing number of vehicle population is the major reason for rise in such high ozone level in Delhi.

The studies conducted on the health hazards of ozone, which show that it causes inflammation of the air ventilators in the body (bronchus and bronchioles) and lead to typical respiratory problems, shortness of breath, wheezing and chest pain. Similarly, the ozone impairs the lung function and causes asthma. The children and young adults show greater risk to ozone exposure than older adults. One indicative study on the association of air pollution with asthma by S.K. Chabra of the Patel Chest Institute, Delhi shows that about 12 per cent of school children in the age group of 5–16 years suffer from asthma. Thus, the pollutants emitted by petrol and diesel vehicles are responsible for high levels of SPM, NO_2 and ozone in Delhi's air and higher health hazards in the city.

GLOBALIZATION AND ENVIRONMENTAL NGOs

We shall now present an overview of environmental NGOs at national and international levels. It is found, the acceleration of globalization process has also led the civil society organizations to show a positive concern for the environmental issues at various levels, national and international. By the beginning of the 1990s, some of the environmental organizations emerged as important actors at the global level. Apprehending the consequences of globalization on the global environment, non-governmental orginizations (NGOs), supported by the United Nations, have come in to existence, and they devote much of their time in international environmental negotiation, conference and lobbying activities. For instance, Green Peace and Friends of the Earth (FOE) have been deeply involved in the Antarctic minerals negotiations, a few NGOs seek to strengthen the Montreal Protocol on protecting the ozone layer, etc.(Basu 1997: 172). Later on, network and alliances of environmental organizations have been formed where NGOs have come across the national boundaries and a strong environmental movement of NGOs has emerged at the international level. This environmental movement on their part and initiative or the new social movement has broadened its agenda on international environment, from wildlife conservation and endangered species to rural development and community decision-making, free trade and patenting of biological materials, technology transformation and curbs on multi-national corporations, external debt and terms of trade, structural adjustment and 'conditionality', etc. (ibid.)

At the national level, the concern for environmental issues is quite recent. Moreover, the protests of small grassroots groups and *mandals*, against the deforestation and displacement of people led by governmental development project, are in the real sense NGO led environment movements in India. These NGO movements such as Narmada Bachao Andolan (NBA), Tehri Bandh Virodhi Samiti, Chilka Bachao Andolan have placed environmental issues on the national agenda. Similarly, in the urban areas, environmental NGOs have started addressing environmental issues related to air, water and noise pollution. The Centre for Science and Environment, a Delhi-based NGO, is actively involved in various environmental issues pertaining to air, water, soil, noise pollution, etc. and generating awareness among general public and pressurizing government, industry and corporate sectors for adopting environment-friendly policies, product and governance. Thus, the environmental movements led by national and international

NGOs have flourished during the globalization era in the form of protests against the ill effects of globalization on global environment.

CONCLUSION

The globalization process has been speeding high and is surpassing all the boundaries of regions and nations of the world. The basic tenets of globalization such as liberalization of trade and commerce, free flow of goods and commodities and capitalistic mode of production have started creating adverse impact on global environment and human survival. The discussion on the massive growth of automobile industry and health hazards caused by vehicular pollution in Delhi is one of the alarming realities posed by the effects of globalization process. There is the need to have some check on the harmful effects of globalization. The government should enforce and implement stringent measures and regulations to keep a check on automobile industry and prevent vehicular pollution in Delhi. Similarly, there is an urgent need that non-governmental organizations should take positive steps towards reducing vehicular pollution of the city. The prospective roles of NGOs in reducing vehicular pollution could be as follows:

1. Collection of scientific data related to vehicular pollution and it's effects on public health.
2. Conducting research studies and preparing reports on the state of vehicular pollution and its effects on public health.
3. Dissemination of scientific facts about vehicular pollution and related health hazards among the general public through media.
4. Working as pressure groups on the government to improve public transport system in Delhi and insisting on the public to commute by public transport system.
5. Inform the scientific facts about the vehicular pollution and related health hazards to the planners, decision makers and implementing bodies, and cooperate with them to evolve measures for reducing vehicular pollution.
6. Working as pressure groups on the government to improve the quality of fuel supplied by the state refineries.
7. Working as pressure group on automobile industries to invent and introduce improved and environment-friendly vehicular technology.

8. Working as pressure groups on the government to improve traffic planning and management.
9. Bring awareness among all personal vehicle owners about regular check up of pollution level and vehicle maintenance.

REFERENCES

Basu, R. (1997), "NGOs and Environmental Protection in India", in Noorjahan Bava (ed.), *Non-Governmental Organizations in Development: Theory and Practice*, Kanishka Publishers, New Delhi.

Centre for Science and Environment (1995), "Driven to Pollution", *Down to Earth*, Vol. 3, No. 22.

——— (1996), "SMOG INC", *Down to Earth*, Vol. 5, No. 12.

——— (1997), "Lurking Threat", *Down to Earth*, Vol. 6, No. 14.

——— (1999), "Fatal Attraction", *Down to Earth*, Vol. 8, No. 1.

——— (2002), "Limpfrog", *Down to Earth*, Vol. 10, No. 17.

Guha, R. (2002), "Environmentalist of the Poor", *Economic and Political Weekly*, Vol. XXXVII, No. 3.

Hersh, J. and Ellen, B. (2000), "Globalization and the Communist Manifesto", *Economic and Political Weekly*, Vol. X XXV, No. 3.

O'Neill, J. (2001), "Markets and the Environment: The Solution is the Problem", *Economic and Political Weekly*, Vol. XXXVI, No. 21.

Reddy, V.V. (2005), "Globalization: In Retrospect and Prospects", in Vinayak Reddy, A. & Bhaskar, G. (Eds.), *Rural Transformation in India: The Impact of Globalization*, New Century Publication, New Delhi.

Salih, M.A.M. (2001), "Globalization, Sustainable Development and Environment: A Balancing Act", in Frans J. Schuurman (ed.), *Globalization and Development Studies: Challenges for the 21st Century*, Vistaar Publication, New Delhi.

Sengupta, C. (2001), "Conceptualising Globalization: Issues and Implications", *Economic and Political Weekly*, Vol. XXXVI, No. 33.

Sheth, P. (1997), *Environmentalism: Politics, Ecology and Development*, Rawat Publications, Jaipur.

Society of Indian Automobile Manufacturers (2001), *Measures to Context Vehicular Pollution: The Delhi Experience*, Bangkok.

——— (2001), *Vehicle Emission Standards in India*, Chongging, PRC.

Valaskakis, K. (1999), "Globalization as Theatre", *International Social Science Journal*, June, No. 160.

Chapter 9

NGOs and the Disabled in the Era of Globalization

B.T. Lawani

THE taking care of the disabled is on the agenda of the social organizations since time immemorial. In the olden days, charity and philanthropy played a significant role in helping the hapless handicapped. Sympathy and encouragement remain the main source for such help. Today, the era of empowerment of the powerless and marginalized, there is a change in the approach, method and helping process. We have shifted from the welfare concept to rehabilitation model, and from rehabilitation to developmental model for helping the disabled. The handicapped no more remain as the helpless. They have been proved as capable people. In other words, it is said that they are differently abled. A new terminology has come up to refer to the handicapped, i.e., *challenged*. They are called physically challenged or mentally challenged and so on. The present paper makes an attempt to focus on the role of various partners engaged in the development and empowerment of the disabled community in the era of globalization.

DEFINITIONS AND CONCEPTUAL CLARIFICATIONS

The handicapped are "concerned with the disadvantages experienced by the individual as a result of impairments and disabilities; thus, handicapped reflect interaction with an adoption to the individuals' surroundings". The disabled people do not form a homogenous group. They include the mentally retarded, visually impaired, also hearing and speech impaired and those with restricted mobility or with so called "medical disabilities" and they all encounter different barriers, of different kinds, which have to be overcome in different ways.

The World Health Organization (WHO) makes a distinction between impairment, disability and handicap. Impairment is any loss or abnormality of psychological, physiological, or anatomical structure and function. Disability is a restriction or lack of ability resulting from impairment to perform an activity in the manner or within the range considered normal for a human being. A handicapped is a disadvantage for a given individual resulting from an impairment or disability that limits or prevents the fulfilment of a role that is normal for that individual.

TYPES OF DISABILITY

The disabled are broadly classified as physically and mentally disabled. Physical disabilities include spinal chord injury, amputated limbs, visual impairment, and hearing impairment. The mental disabilities incorporate learning disability, mental illness and mental retardation. A few researchers and practitioners classify disability into four sub-categories, viz. physical impairments affecting movement, such as post-polio syndrome, spina bifida and cerebral palsy; sensory impairments, such as visual or hearing impairments; cognitive impairments, such as autism or down syndrome; and psychiatric conditions, such as depression and schizophrenia.

THE EXTENT OF DISABILITY

India is a vast country with a population of more than one billion and nearly 70 million people with disabilities. Census 2001 says that persons with disability (PWD) constitute 2.13 per cent of the total population, but conservative estimates place Indians with disability between 5 to 6 per cent of the total population. This translates to approximately 6 crores of people. Almost 75 per cent of the people with disabilities live in rural areas, only 49 per cent of them are literate and 34 per cent are employed. The women constitute 42.46 per cent of the total population of persons with disabilities.

The U.N. officials claim that the percentage of the disability in India would be in double digits. Australia does admit officially that 18 per cent of its population is disabled. United Kingdom's disabled population is estimated at 14.12 per cent whereas, in the United States, it is 9 per cent only. In the neighbourhood countries, China has 5 per cent disabled population, Nepal has 5 per cent and Pakistan has 4.9 per cent disabled population (UN Manual: 1996).

Following figures state the extent and causes of disability in the developing world and are quite alarming. In fact, a considerable proportion of impairments in the developing world are a direct result of poverty, injustice and exploitation by the developed world:

- Over 100 million people have impairments as a result of malnutrition.
- 2,50,000 children go blind every year through lack of vitamin 'A'.
- 800 million people are at risk of preventable learning difficulties due to lack of iodine.
- Each year 1,00,000 women in Africa acquire impairments through childbirth complications.
- 40 per cent of hearing loss in children in the developing world would be preventable by early identification.
- There were 1,00,000 new cases of polio in 1994.
- Six million people worldwide are affected by leprosy each year.

NATIONAL POLICY FOR THE DISABLED

The National Policy for Persons with Disability, announced (February 2006) attempts to clarify the framework within which the state, civil society and private sector must operate in order to ensure a dignified life for persons with disability and support for their carers. The National Policy for Persons with Disability includes: extending rehabilitation services to rural areas; increasing trained personnel to meet needs; emphasizing education and training; increasing employment opportunities; Focusing on gender equality; improving access to public services; encouraging state governments to develop a comprehensive social security policy; ensuring equal opportunities in sports, recreation and cultural activities; and increasing the role of civil society organizations providing service to persons with disability and their families.

THE DISABILITY ACT 1995

The Persons with Disabilities (Equal Opportunities, Protection of Rights and Full Participation) Act, 1995 was passed by the Indian Parliament in December, 1995. It was notified on 7th February, 1996 and thus, it became the law of the land. Chapter VI of the Disability Act, 1995 is entitled for "employment". Clause 41 categorically mandates incentives to employers who ensure that at least 5 per cent of their workforce is composed of persons with disabilities.

GLOBALIZATION

Globalization has set in motion processes of far-reaching change that are affecting everyone. New technology supported by many open policies, has created a world more inter-connected than ever before. This spans in not only growing independence in economic relations, trade, investment, finance and the global organization of production, but also social and political interaction among organizations and individuals across the world. Globalization has led to increased material production, more open markets, employment and so on, all of which are very essential components in poverty alleviation. However, the current process of globalization is generating imbalance of outcomes, both between and within the countries. Wealth is being created, but too many countries and people are not sharing in its benefits. They have little or no voice in shaping the process.

These above mentioned effects of globalization turn out to be alarming for the disabled, since one of the important aspects of globalization is competitive market forces which entertain improved technology and skills, labour market that demands highly qualified personnel, etc. The disabled people, who have missed the opportunities of acquiring sustainable professional capacities and economical power, are definitely going to be the losers in this struggle.

GLOBALIZATION AND THE DISABLED

Given that 80 per cent of the disabled people live in the developing world (Charlton, 1998), it becomes crucial to examine how globalization impacts on the lives of the disabled people, and how new multi-scalar challenges are presented. In the global context, poor people are likely to be affected by impairment and disability, and disabled people are more likely to live in poverty (Stone 1999).

Disabled people tend to be the poorest among the poor, everywhere relegated to the status of surplus population. Poor countries include a disproportionate number of disabled people, because not only disability is a cause of poverty in the local context, but at every level from local to global, poverty operates as a cause of impairment. Diseases associated with malnutrition, illness, lack of health services and education often give rise to permanent disabilities (Harris-White 2002). The direct costs of impairment (what Amartya Sen calls "conversion costs") fall disproportionately on those with already scarce resources, and the socially imposed cost of disability further relegates them to the periphery. Though the Disability Rights Movement around the world has been influential in streamlining disability and development, its impact has been curtailed by the political economy of globalization marked by neo-liberal ideology and implemented through multilateral institutions like the World Bank, IMF, and so on (Holden and Beresford 2002).

Increasingly, international forces are shaping local and national responses to disability. Globalization, guided by neo-liberalism, has been reshaping the market and welfare systems around the world. Due to international monetary systems and global trading policies, states are becoming increasingly less autonomous or self-governing, and are undergoing major structural adjustments (Holden and Beresford 2002). In the process of structural readjustment, governments are downsizing, decentralizing and dealing with imposed debt restructuring and liberalization (Esping-Andersen 1985; Kaul et al. 1999). According to Holden and Beresford (2002), "International mobility of capital, people, governments leads into competition with each other for investment. They are thus constrained to follow policies of low inflation, low taxation, low public spending, flexible labor markets and privatization – that is, to minimize their economic and social involvement, except where it facilitates capital accumulation". Overemphasizing economic efficiency and downsizing social funding, globalization plays an important role in the social construction of disablement (Holden and Beresford 2002). Disabled people face disadvantages in the neo-liberal world order since it calls for excessive privatization of social problems and their solutions. Removal of disabling physical and social structures is unlikely to be prioritized within the imperatives of a globalized economy (Holden and Beresford 2002). Privatization tends to delink problems from their structural context, values, self-sufficiency over social justice and equity (Rioux 2002). This has had a far-reaching impact on those with disabilities as there is evidence that disability is being privatized (Rioux and Zubrow 2001). With significant reduction in social welfare, access is increasingly considered as an individual's problem and not a social concern, which in turn carries the risk of individualizing disability. Consequently, this shrinking public domain weakens the bonds of citizenship and the effective exercise of rights. Rioux argues that disabled people have never been included in the mainstream of social rights. Traditionally, their issues have been relegated to social development, to charity, to dispensation or to the determination of their best interests. But economic liberalization and globalization have highlighted the extent to which some people are excluded through the denial of their liberties and the restriction of participation in society. Those fundamental freedoms that governments promise to their citizens in democracies must also be protected for persons with disabilities.

The pressures of globalization and neo-liberalism are felt by all, but these forces hit the disabled people especially hard. Disabled people are directly affected when neo-liberal policies push states to cut social supports, and such cuts (for example, to public health programmes) also result in more impairment and more disability. As capital becomes more mobile across all boundaries, mobility becomes one of the few tactics available for labour. Since disabled labour is less mobile, less flexible than non-disabled labour, the demand for flexibility in labour and capital excludes those without flexibility from the market economy. This turns disabled people into unproductive subjects. In understanding the current dynamics of globalization, it is crucial to understand how traditional hierarchies of scale have been disrupted by what Neil Brenner (2004) calls "glocalization".

Bypassing the nation-state, global actors are becoming directly involved with local spaces, a change that creates new risks for the most powerless. The direct access of global powers to local contexts with less mediation of the nation-state creates a situation full of opportunity and peril for all actors. The state gains from this reconfiguration by shedding responsibility for the local in exchange for allowing global actors direct access to its citizens. The local space has the opportunity to be transformed by direct access to the vast resources of transnational actors, but find itself resultantly far removed from any access to power or opportunity to demand accountability. Global actors gain by creating an unmediated link to the objects of its projects, although perhaps at the cost of abandoning a vision of development on a grand scale.

SOCIAL EXCLUSION OF DISABLED

Unregulated globalization and liberalization have been seen to reinforce social marginalization and exclusion of the disabled people from development process and inaccessibility to services and resources. No doubt universal declaration of Human Rights adopted by UN General Assembly in December 1948, recognizing the freedom of individuals as well as their rights to equality was a matter of great importance but disabled people were not specifically covered by this important international declaration. This declaration did not include the prohibition of discrimination on the ground of disability specifically, even when disabled people constitute 10 per cent of the world's population. This reflects insensitivity and apathy of policy makers towards the disabled people. Disabled people are excluded from secured employment and access to property, housing, credit, good education, health services, enjoyment of their own culture, and a clean environment. Social exclusion has thus, in turn led to a disruption of social cohesion. These prevent full participation (economic, social, and political affairs) of disabled people in community and national development, thereby condemning them to abject poverty and to peripheral living in society.

POVERTY, INEQUALITY AND COMPETITIVENESS

Globalization has hit the disabled severely by cutting back welfare and unemployment programmes, privatizing state enterprises, reducing the regulatory role of the state, and promoting international investment and trade above other domestic interests. Against this scenario, the advocates of globalization keep arguing that conditions will improve overtime, and that expectations are still high with the conviction that prosperity is on the way, to be created by economic integration and more opening of economies. In fact, the income gap and poverty remains a reality despite the fact that the nations have dutifully followed the prescriptions of the IMF, the World Bank, NAFTA, and the World Trade Organization (WTO).

The neo-liberal form of globalization leads to more inequality, even if the economy is growing. The poor people and the environment are bound to suffer when economic systems emphasize cheap labour and exploitable natural resources as the key means of building competitiveness. This becomes worse for the disabled people as a marginalized and isolated group.

GLOBALIZATION AND EMPLOYMENT OF THE DISABLED

The proponents of free market argue that globalization creates jobs and prosperity by increasing business opportunities. On the contrary, internationally set employment rights, have had negative impact on the exercise of the right to association, collective bargaining, and the right to call a strike. In fact, the working people in many countries of the world have witnessed a tremendous loss of long-term, secured employment, which has been replaced by short-term, insecure jobs with fewer benefits and lower pay. The creation of an emphasis on the modern sector has resulted into there being fewer jobs, and promoted the expansion of informal sector employment, in which workers are excluded from benefits such as health plans, job protection, and social security, because their jobs are neither unionized nor registered with the government. This has disadvantaged the disabled people all the more. Even the very few who happen to get work are disproportionately represented in the lowest-paid jobs with the worst working conditions.

While contributing economically both to their economies and to their families, as well as enhancing the competitiveness of the firms for which they work, disabled workers and their families are nevertheless the victims of discrimination and mistreatment. They are caught between their desire of earning a living and the xenophobia of host firms to hire cheap labour services. In general, disabled people are the last to be hired and first to be fired. Governments are disengaging themselves from their obligation to guarantee full social rights to workers, in accordance with international conventions, and to promote balanced social and economic development, which would reduce the suffering of disabled people as a special category of workers. In fact, employment growth especially for disabled people in this era is no better than it was under the so-called "closed" economies of the past.

ROLE OF NGOs IN THE REHABILITATION AND DEVELOPMENT OF THE DISABLED

NGOs benefiting disabled people originated probably in the 1810s with public efforts to start a leprosy asylum at Kolkata. A long-lasting initiative was the opening of Raja Kali Shankar Ghosal's Blind Asylum at Benaras in 1826, involving the Raja as a concerned individual, his researchers who enumerated the local blind people, a group of British officials as trustees, with the help of the East India Company funds, some private and civic subscriptions. Many people subsequently started taking interest in the blind residents, and eventually some special educational provisions were made in the 1860s by European missionaries. In these activities at Varanasi no single modern-style constitutional NGO is clearly identifiable, yet a range of charitable and educational actions was initiated that were done neither by an individual nor by government, but by community action.

It is recognized that NGOs have played significant role in the development of rehabilitation services for persons with disabilities worldwide. This has been done regularly in the absence of government involvement and initially took an institutional, charitable approach. Present-day developments, however, favour a participatory, community based approach, complementing and liaisoning with government plans and services, and working with all the stakeholders' groups. Local NGOs are considered indigenous humanitarian organizations, and they work in coordination with the association of parents of children with disabilities and organizations of persons with disabilities. With timely assistance from local community members, local professionals or a combination of both categories, NGOs are able to extend rehabilitation services to the needy persons in a better way.

Nowadays, various international and national agencies are coming forward with financial assistance for extending services to the persons with disabilities. International agencies like the World Bank, WHO, UNICEF, UNESCAP, ILO, DFID, ACTION AID, etc. have established their country/regional offices in India and are extending financial support to the genuine organizations which are rendering valuable services to the community.

The Ministry of Social Justice and Empowerment is assisting the NGOs with grant-in-aid under the Deen Dayal Rehabilitation Scheme for persons with disabilities. The government is requesting NGOs to mobilize resources of their own for successfully implementing the existing schemes as well as their expansion.

The Disabled Welfare Department is promoting the performing NGOs in disability sector. Workshops/seminars are being conducted on 'capacity-building' of NGOs for improvement of skills in extending services to the disabled community as well as looking for sources for getting grants to run their organizations. With a view to improving the skills of officers of the Disabled Welfare Department to help the NGOs in this regard, orientation programmes are being conducted at State Level.

NGOs WORKING FOR THE RURAL DISABLED

Non-governmental organizations provide education, vocational training, and employment opportunities to rural disabled people. Goods and services like medical care and assistance devices are provided free to recipients. A sizeable number of NGOs, which serve disabled people, are charity organizations attached to religious faiths or institutions. They tend to operate on benevolent sentiments rather than socio-political objectives. These organizations are usually funded by foreign sources in order to address all varieties of disability, without a clear focus on region, type, gender or age, and with little or no administrative input by disabled villagers themselves (Erb and Harris-White 2002). Only a fraction of rural disabled Indians have access to governmental or non-governmental programmes. Moreover, participation and input of disabled people rate low on the agenda of the service providers. Generally, disability-related initiatives in rural India are based on the service delivery model, which holds that disabled people lack agency. This explains their marginal participation in the decision-making process. In brief, isolation, lack of opportunities, and the paternalistic nature of social services exacerbate the disempowerment of the disabled community.

NGOs AND EMPOWERMENT OF THE DISABLED THROUGH SHGs

In order to address the issues of empowerment and disempowerment of rural disabled people in India, and responding to a paradigm shift toward international participatory development, governmental and non-governmental organizations in India have been organizing disabled people into self-help groups (SHGs) since the mid-1990s. Several NGOs in southern India, and now the government of Andhra Pradesh, have adopted this SHG model as disability policy. A non-governmental organization called Action on Disability and Development (ADD) based in Karnataka has been at the forefront of organizing these groups for almost a decade (ADD 2001). Disabled people are organized into the self-help groups at the village level, and several groups are then federated at the district level to enhance the voice and visibility of disabled people. These groups seek to empower their members by providing micro-credit loans; facilitating access to health care, education, vocational training; and by advocating better services (ADD 2001).

NGOs IN ADVOCACY

There are more than 70 million disabled people in India who need special attention. Ninety-nine per cent of the organizations working with the disabled are welfare, rehabilitation and service-oriented. The National Centre for Promotion of Employment for Disabled People holds that it is time to get away from the welfare approach and focus on advocacy for the empowerment of the disabled. The National Centre for Promotion of Employment for Disabled People (NCPEDP) was registered as a trust in 1996, consisting of a board with representatives of industry, NGOs, disabled people and international agencies. NCPEDP stresses the need to move away from traditionally held views of charity and welfare to those of productivity and empowerment of disabled people.

QUOTA FOR THE DISABLED IN NGOs: NEED OF THE HOUR

The Chief Commissioner for Persons with Disabilities stated that the NGOs which avail assistance from the Union Government should accord 3 to 5 per cent reservation for physically challenged persons in jobs. "It is mandatory. Strict action can be taken against NGOs which fail to follow this direction", he said. Besides, the non-governmental and voluntary organizations that are supported by the Centre as well as the State governments should have a policy of reservation for persons with disabilities while making appointments. "We can recommend action against NGOs and also government agencies which fail to follow the direction," the Commissioner cautioned. Persons with 40 per cent disabilities are eligible to enjoy the privilege of reservation with NGOs. This reservation does not come under any provision. Though it came into force in 1996, it has not been properly implemented.

FUTURE ROLE OF NGOs

NGOs can take a very proactive role in ensuring implementation of laws, welfare programmes and working together to make their collective voices heard more powerfully. NGOs need to work through state-sponsored programmes in order to provide sustainable rehabilitation services. NGOs could play a bigger role in implementing community based rehabilitation programmes at village to district levels, and to organize disabled people and their families as pressure groups for ensuring that the state and all its administrative agencies such as the panchayats assist in seeing that persons with disabilities are supported and have access to services.

SUGGESTIONS

First, NGOs should be given an advisory role from the beginning of the planning process of urban and rural development. Local self-help organizations of people with disabilities should be represented on the committees empowered to finalize city master plans and rural development programmes like housing, road development, drinking water amenities, sanitation, etc. Secondly, NGOs and self-help organizations of people with disabilities should be closely associated with civic bodies and local community groups to assess in an ongoing fashion, the accessibility needs of persons with disabilities. Thirdly, a linkage should be established between self-help organizations of people with disabilities and professional associations and educational institutions, particularly those in charge of imparting education in the field of architecture, automobile engineering, etc. Fourthly, by NGOs working with disabilities should be represented on committees attached to state transport authorities responsible for surface transport, railway advisory committees and the committee for civil aviation. Last but not the least, in formulating legislations and policy provisions relating to the disabled, the NGOs should be involved, both in their implementation and enforcement.

REFERENCES

Action on Disability and Development [ADD] (2003), "Left of the Agenda?: Mainstreaming Disability in Development", A Conference Report, London.

Allen, T. and Thomas, A.(eds.) (2000), *Poverty and Development into the 21st Century,* Oxford University Press and the Open University Press, London.

http://www.helsinkprocess.fi "Democratising Globalisation Democracy".

http://www.oikoumene.org/en/activities/edan-home/resources/reports/06–11–04–disability – and – globalization - consultation/disability – and – economic - globalization.html.

http://www.infochangeindia.org/Disabilitieshistory.jsp?recordno+2639& section _ jdv+19.

http://www.deccanherald.com/deccanherald/jan132006/district172042006112.asp.

Nyanje, P. (2004), "Globalisation Report Proposes Parliamentary Group", *Guardian Newspaper*, 25th February 2004, Dar es Salaam, Tanzania.

Chapter 10

Child Health Care Services and NGOs in the Context of Globalization

Debotosh Sinha

THE United Nations Organization (UNO) declared 1979 as the International Year of the Child (IYC). Dr. Mahler, Director General of WHO in a special message on the World Health Day that year, drew attention to the fact that 12 million (mostly in developing countries) of the 125 million children born in 1978 would probably not live to see their first birthday. The majority of the 1,220 million children living in the developing countries suffer as a result of malnutrition, infections, poor housing, lack of safe drinking water and sanitation. Dr Mahler's message concluded with the hope that the activities generated by the IYC and World Health Day would create a socio-political climate of urgency in regard to the needs and problems of today's children and lay the groundwork for continuing and systematic action focusing on the health and well-being of the child.

Since then, all over the world, the perspective on health has undergone a revolutionary change contrary to the old paradigm of economic growth in which health was viewed as an item of consumption. Health is now recognized as a critical commodity of investment for development. In the development approach (Narayana 1998), improvement in health status is viewed primarily as a product of socio-economic development. By definition, development implies improved nutrition, hygienic living and working conditions, fall of high birth rate and infant mortality rate, conducive ante-natal and post-natal care, family care, family planning and reproductive health, greater awareness of health problems, and wider accessibility to health care services, which all have a favourable effect on the health status of the people. Improvement in health status as well as health care are treated as integrated components of the development process. Since health is a product of multivariable production process, impact of state intervention on health status depends on its overall socio-economic policies (Joshi 1999).

The UNICEF Health Strategy, revised in 1995, maintains the emphasis on reduction of child illness and death through such activities as immunization, breastfeeding, improved nutritional practices and sound management of illness. It also puts greater stress on the protection of children in the second decade of life and on reproductive health. A sharpened focus on the needs of adolescents aligns UNICEF health policy more closely with the Conventions on the Rights of the Child, and recognizes that the health, attitudes and behaviour of teenagers profoundly affect their capacities as adults.

The strategy was revised to respond better to economic, demographic and lifestyle changes affecting families throughout the developing world. The new strategy reflects the reality that, while the rate of infant and child mortality has fallen dramatically since the 1960s, communicable diseases such as malaria, diarrhoea, pneumonia and measles have become widespread. Further, health problems related to increase in poverty, environmental hazards and risky behaviour are growing at alarming rates.

Health indeed is a basic need and a fundamental ingredient of human rights. It is a positive right and it can acquire meaningful content only if the state is willing to ensure its implementation. The Constitution of India states in the Directive Principles of State Policy, "The State shall regard the raising of the level of nutrition and standard of living of its people and the improvement of public health as among its primary duties" (Article 47).

At this point, it is imperative to bring out the significance of the focus on child health. Child health is the greatest resource of our country. In a developing country like India, children form a wide base of the population pyramid. In India, 17 per cent of the population comprises of children under five years and another 35 per cent in the range of 5 to 16 years.

But it is not becouse of the number alone that the advocates of comprehensive health care for the child population stress their point. The most crucial period in a child's life is the first five years during which about 40 percent of physical and 80 per cent of mental growth and development occurs.

The foundation of healthy mind and body is laid in childhood. A healthy child, to state a truism, grows into a healthy adult. Only the physical, social and mental well-being can provide required energy to allow people to become productive and creative. Health of our children, therefore, is of fundamental value to the nation. However, the issue of child health cannot be understood without knowing the socio-political environment in which they are raised. The roots of ill-health of children lie in the social and economic structure of our society, and unless these are changed, children will continue to be in poor health.

Providing health care to ensure holistic development of 300 million children living in abject poverty and neglect, is an enormously challenging task. A child is exposed to many a type of deprivation right from conception stage. Disparity between the rich and poor, between rural and urban settings, gender discrimination, variations in geographical locations, illiteracy among parents are all contributing factors in the threat to the well-being of the child. Destitution and exploitation, children of AIDS affected families also pose additional threats to child survival, growth and development.

HEALTH SECTOR REFORMS

Many less developed countries are reforming their health systems in an effort to achieve public health goals more affordably and effectively. Many are also attempting to expand and improve reproductive and child health services, which include family planning, measures to ensure safe pregnancy and childbearing, preventing the spread of HIV and other sexually transmitted infections, and various measures to improve child health. The need to pursue child health objectives along with implementing health sector reforms poses a major challenge for health managers.

If health sector reforms work well, it would make basic preventive health care including child health services, widely available. Reforms should also make health providers more responsive to client needs. But some structural changes, such as decentralizing authority or integrating health services, can lead to a loss of focus and expertise to specific reproductive and child health issues. To avoid these and other pitfalls, child health specialists need to understand the reform process and engage actively in debates about financing, management, and structure of the health system.

Since the late 1980s, many developing countries have initiated efforts to improve their health systems. A number of factors have prompted these efforts: the movement from state-controlled economies to market-oriented economies; insufficient funding for health in times of financial crisis; the lack of basic health services for many citizens; and the poor quality, low accountability, and inefficiency of existing health services. To address these issues, many governments launched health sector reforms, which are intensive long-term efforts to strengthen and improve health systems, and ultimately, improve the nation's health.

Health sector reforms try to correct system-wide problems in health care that hinder the delivery of priority services. Five goals underline the reforms (*World Health Report* 2000):

Efficiency: health improvements should be achieved at the lowest possible cost.

Quality: appropriate and safe clinical services, adequate amenities, skilled staff, and essential drugs, supplies, and equipment should be available.

Equity: health should be distributed fairly so that nobody is denied access to essential care.

Client responsiveness: the system should meet people's expectations and protect their rights, including their rights to individual dignity, privacy, autonomy in decision-making, and choice of health provider.

Sustainability: the health system can continue to achieve its goals using available resources.

During the 1990s, especially after the International Conference on Population and Development (ICPD) in 1994, many countries have started to expand and improve reproductive and child health care. The ICPD agreement called for a wide range of social investments, and specifically, for primary health services that would provide a comprehensive package of reproductive and child health care. The agreement also called for services to be more "client-centred", that is, geared toward meeting individuals' needs so that women, men and children get the best possible health services.

Health sector reforms may involve a number of strategies, policies, and interventions designed to strengthen the health system so that it can better achieve public health goals. Country-wise approaches to health sector reform vary widely; some governments implement sweeping reforms, while others enact narrow changes. Most reform measures can be grouped into three broad categories, i.e., financing changes, organizational changes, and policy changes. A cross-cutting objective of these measures is to empower consumers by educating them and giving them more choices.

CHILD HEALTH SCENARIO AND SERVICES IN INDIA

The concern for health care and development of children in India dates back to ancient times. India had an inbuilt mechanism through the institution of joint family, kinship and other social institutions in providing child health care. In ancient and medieval periods, voluntary and community efforts provided the main platform for child health services. There were some enlightened rulers who also, in a limited way, promoted child welfare activities with special emphasis on health under their patronage. During the British rule, voluntary efforts rather than state endeavour was the main provider of child health services.

Prior to independence, the social, political and economic status of the people of India had degenerated to such an extent that hunger and malnutrition was widespread. Primary health care was non-existent and a majority of the population was illiterate. The number of health personnel was inadequate. There was only one doctor for 6,000 people, one nurse for 5,000 and one midwife for more than 10,000 population. Infant mortality was high; for every one thousand children born, 162 died before the age of one year, and 40 mothers lost their lives during child birth and post-partum period. Around half of the children died before the age of five years.

Again, the mortality rate of children under five, which is the best indicator of child health of any country, continues to be high. True, the rate has shown a consistent decline over the years 236 (1960), 177 (1980), 126 (2000), but this decline is still very slow. If we are determined to meet the target of Infant Mortality Rate (IMR) below 60 by 2010, we need to have 6.5 reduction in the 0–5 year mortality.

The mortality figures also reveal that the female child mortality rate is much higher than the male in all age groups. Out of over 15 million girls born in India every year, only 13 million live till their fifteenth birthday. The difference in 0–4 mortality between male and female is not so marked in urban areas but the variation is over 25 per cent in rural areas. A feature worth mentioning is the maldistribution of child health care system in India. The total expenditure in health care in cities works out to be Rs 160 per person, while in the villages the estimate is only Rs 16.

Post-independence years ushered a new era as regards the field of child welfare. Various provisions in our constitution regarding the need for emphasizing and improving child health inspired the efforts in this field. To reiterate, the Constitution of India provides a framework within which the constitutional vision of the rights of the Indian child can be given a concrete shape. The Constitution postulates the goal of a welfare state, and envisages child welfare activities as an organized part of national development. Article 39 (prohibition of employment of children); Article 45 (provision for free and compulsory education); and Article 38 (children should be given opportunities to develop in a healthy manner) have a bearing on the well-being of children.

India has the unfortunate distinction of having nearly 75 million malnourished children below the age of five years, the largest number of malnourished children in the world. Even at birth, one in every three children born in India is of low birth weight: the result of undernourishment in the womb. As the facts stand, children in Bangladesh and Nepal are more malnourished than Indian children.

It was also only after independence that the foundation for a comprehensive health care system was laid and the concept of universal outreach of primary health care was evolved. There has been a considerable expansion in the health system in the Five-Year Plans right from 1951 to 2002 (the ten Five-Year Plans). The maternal and child care too received considerable attention in planning and implementation of health services at the national level. The first three Five-Year Plans (1951–1966) focused on expansion of maternity and child health services, and during the Fourth Plan, an intensive family planning programme was integrated with health services. The current plan (Tenth Plan) has also given much emphasis on maternal and child health as well as family planning and reproductive health. The primary health care approach aims at integrating curative, preventive, and rehabilitative services to promote health status of children. The infrastructure facilities and the network of Primary Health Centres (PHCs) set up during different plan periods is available to a large number of families, both in the rural and urban areas of the country.

As on 31 March 2002, there were 1,852 community health centres, 20,531 PHCs and subsidiary health centres, and 1,30,390 sub-centres in the country. At the grassroots level, there were 5,98,793 trained birth attendants, 4,08,790 village health guides (VHGs),2,45,405 general housing midwives, 1,32,923 auxiliary nurse/midwives/health workers and 15,8817 health visitors. Currently the doctor population ratio varies from 1: 820 in the Union Territory of Chandigarh to 1:15,631 in Uttar Pradesh. Out of

141,99 million eligible couples, around 69.03 million are being covered by family planning measures.

The financial outlays under the health services have been increased over the successive Five-Year Plans. The total Tenth Plan investment outlay for all heads of development is Rs 100,000 crore out of which Rs 3,392.9 crore is allotted for health, Rs 3,256.3 crore for family welfare and Rs 6,522.5 crore for water supply and sanitation.

The Voluntary Health Association of India (VHAI) facilitated the Independent Commission on Health in India (ICHI) in 1995. The Commission with the help of policy makers and distinguished persons from the health and development sector, critically diagnosed the maladies affecting health services in the country and recommended remedial measures.

The Commission identified a few areas such as primary health care, medical education, Indian system of medicine, health sector reform, reproductive and child health, and private sector in health care and medical ethics for future attention in the present millennium. Among these areas, primary health care and reproductive and child health were emphasized much.

The ICHI report was very widely distributed and discussed at different forum. Active interaction between the Commission, the Planning Commission, the Prime Minister's office and the Health Ministry followed which culminated in the formation of the National Health Policy in 1999.

Keeping intact the very essence of National Health Policy, National Population Policy, 2002 has also made a number of commitments for the 21st century in the area of child health. These are:

- Addressing the unmet needs for basic reproductive and child health services, supplies and infrastructure.
- Reducing infant mortality rate to below 30 per cent per 1,000 live births.
- Reducing maternal mortality rate to below 100 per 1,00,000 live births.
- Full coverage of registration of birth.
- Convergence of service delivery at village levels.
- Empowering women to improve health and nutrition.
- Decentralized planning and programme implementation along with the emphasis on community participation.
- To integrate (Indian systems of medicine) in the provision of reproductive and child health services and in reaching out to households.

- Achieving universal immunization of children against all vaccine preventable diseases.
- Achieving 80 per cent institutional deliveries and 100 per cent deliveries by trained persons.

The latest child population in the age group of (0–6) years in India (Census 2001) is as follows:

	Persons	Males	Females
Total	150,421,175	77,322,151	73,099,024
Urban	116,828,332	59,963,100	56,865,232
Rural	33,592,843	17,359,051	16,233,792

For the benefit of such a vast child population, the National Policy for Children spells out that it shall be the policy of the state to provide adequate services to children both before and after their birth to ensure them full physical, mental and social development. All the children in the country should enjoy optimum condition for their balanced growth.

Universal Immunization Programme (UIP) was started in India in 1985 with the objective of achieving a coverage of at least 85 per cent in respect of infants and 100 in respect of pregnant women. The Government of India had taken up "Pulse Polio Immunization"(PPI) programme as a party to the WHO's resolution of eradication of Poliomyelitis (Polio), a major crippling childhood disease by the year 2000 AD. All new born babies are sought to be immunized before completion of the first year of their life with BCG (tuberculosis), DPT (Diphtheria, Pertusis, Tetanus) and polio vaccine. Recently, vaccine against measles, Hepatitis A, B and C, chicken pox and Manengitis for all children have been taken up as policy issues.

No one can claim that only immunization and Oral Rehydration Therapy (ORT) would improve health of the child. But it is fair to say that progress towards universalizing of these two particular techniques is both a measure and a means of progress towards health for all. ORT is a 100 per cent centrally sponsored scheme with the objective of reducing mortality amongst children below five years of age. Studies reveal, that 90 per cent of the children suffering from diarrhoea can be managed successfully at home by mothers by administering homemade fluids (combination of water, salt and sugar) at the onset of diarrhoea. Only 10 per cent of the cases need to be reported to the health facilities and only one per cent out of these require intravenous fluids. A little over a decade ago, ORT, the low-cost life saving method of preventing and treating dehydration caused by diarrhoeal diseases, was hardly known to the outside world. Today, it is being used by almost 40 per cent of all Indian families and saving about a million lives each year. Despite such phenomenal progress over the last two decades, 3 million succumb to diarrhoeal diseases.

Acute Respiratory Infections (ARIs) are among the most common childhood illnesses in India. They continue to be the major cause of death among children under five, where in 1995 more than 1 million children died of pneumonia and a further 1.1 million from ARI compounded by other ailments: ARI/measles, 6,40,000; ARI/pertussis (whooping cough) 2,60,000; ARI/malaria, 1,90,000; and ARI/HIV, 20,000. With as many as eight episodes per child annually, ARI is also a leading cause of sickness and serious disabilities such as deafness. India has taken up a training package to teach health care workers to look into these problems.UNICEF has supported ethnographic studies and found that peoples' own ideas about how to treat illnesses. An understanding of community perceptions is essential for the preparation of effective information and education strategies that can be adopted to a local context. Apart from many other countries, India has also started experimenting at a large scale.

GLOBALIZATION

The term 'globalization' has been on everyone's lips but very few people dare to define what exactly globalization means. We hear of 'neo-liberal globalization', 'capitalist globalization' and 'imperialist globalization'. When we ask people what they mean by globalization, they describe capitalism (a system based on the exploitation of workers and production for profit); imperialism (the political, economic and military domination over some states by others) and neo-liberalism (the policy of allowing the market to determine everything, including wage levels, health care, education, etc). But, if capitalism, imperialism and neo-liberalism can all be defined without reference to globalization, should it not be possible to define globalization without reference to them (Rohini 2004)? Surely it is. A reasonable definition would be the free movement of products, money, ideas and people around the globe. At present, the only major obstacles to such movements are national boundaries, so globalization would mean the weakening or eventual elimination of those boundaries.

To add to the above, let us use Kelly Lee's definition (2000) which describes globalization as the current reduction in barriers to time, space and ideas that used to separate people and nations in areas like health, the environment, the social and cultural environments, knowledge and technology creation and; political and institutional processes.The characteristics of globalization include: an increase in services at the expense of heavy industry and manufacturing; a move towards regional and global economies of scale; fewer national boundaries in the production of goods and services; the rise of the information economy (e.g., business being conducted via telecommunications); easier movement of money, ideas, goods and services and workers.

The benefits of globalization are hoped to include: economic growth and increased economic freedom; increased innovation and competition; improved information sharing, which has led to rapid advances in science and technology, improved democratic participation; rapid advances in farming technology, including the development of drought resistant and vitamin enhanced plants; and phenomenal development in medical science, and consequently, health sector development. Those who criticize globalization say that it may widen gaps in income, decrease democratic participation, limit cultural diversity, contribute to the degradation of the environment, result in less funding to the public sector (e.g., health and education programme), and promote nationalism and regionalism.

NGOs: A GLIMPSE

All NGOs are private organizations but they are different from the private sector on the following grounds: (a) Organizations operating as NGOs are registered either as 'trusts' or 'societies'. As a consequence, they are not supposed to make profit, unlike the private sector. (b) NGOs are fully dependent on external sources of financing for their activities. (c) NGOs are involved in the 'development sector'; that is, running programmes such as health, nutrition, family planning, education, water supply and sanitation, housing, research, training, documentation, etc. These constitute what one might call service NGOs. Another category of NGOs includes activist groups where members are involved in conscientious and struggle-oriented activities (Duggal 1988). (d) A large number of NGOs, especially in rural areas, run programmes of the government on a contractual basis because of their supposed dedication and flexibility. The government realizes that its own structure is insufficient, bureaucratic and incapable of reaching the beneficiaries.

The 1970s witnessed a mushrooming of NGOs for various reasons: (a) the government was encouraging NGOs by giving grants or permitting them to receive foreign funds directly; (b) the corporate sector in partnership with the government was encouraging and supporting NGOs, especially in the rural areas; (c) new tax reliefs encouraged donors by providing funds for rural development and social services to NGOs, therefore, there was greater willingness to donate funds to NGOs; and (d) the professionalization of the NGO sector offered opportunities to committed and motivated individuals to take up careers in 'development' (Duggal 1988).

Even the National Health Policy of 1983 recognized the need for relying, in a larger measure on the NGO sector for achieving the goals of 'Health for All by the Year 200 AD'. The policy envisaged a very constructive and supportive relationship between the public and NGO sectors in the area of health by providing a corrective to re-establish the position of the private health sector.

What appears from the above is that (a) the government has accepted its inability to provide adequate health care; (b) the active participation of NGOs is most necessary for achieving goals of the health sector; and (c) involvement of NGOs will result in better provision of health services.

There is a lot of variety amongst NGOs in India. They differ in terms of size, membership, structure, funding, relationship with the political parties and the State, philosophy, goals and programmes. NGOs are classified differently. For example, they can be grouped such as (i) techno-managerial, (ii) reformist, and (iii) radical. Likewise, it can also be clubbed as welfare-oriented, development organization and empowering NGOs. Another way of classification of NGOs is (i) relief and welfare organizations, and (ii) coalition building community organizations. Again there could be three types of NGOs: (i) charity, (ii) development, and (iii) empowerment NGOs. On the other hand, literature in the respective field also mentions about different stages of action groups, such as social welfarism, radical nationalism and socialist action groups.

NGOs have played a significant role in the development process (Alliband 1983; Cernea 1988; Mahtani 1992; Paul and Israel 1991). The potential strength of NGOs as development actors stems from their proximity to field realities, where people are in the central focus of their developmental efforts. NGOs have the latent ability to focus society's attention on existing inequalities both at local and national levels. They have been able to voice the concerns of a wide variety of disadvantaged and marginalized sections of society, such as tribals, dalits, the rural poor, children, women, and the urban poor. Many NGOs have demonstrated their ability to find innovative solutions to local problems, mobilize local resources, develop community based institutions, provide a platform to express social concerns, bring together diverse stakeholders in the problem solving process, and involve people in their own development.

While the several strengths of NGOs have been appreciated, it is also admitted that all NGOs do not have enough potentiality. The reasons for this are multiple, and include the following. NGOs have been constrained by inadequate planning, funds, and human resources. They tend to focus on local needs, without placing these in the macro context. They also tend to be reactive, rather than proactive, and their efforts appear to lack sustainability.

Despite these limitations, it is acknowledged that the work of most NGOs has been beneficial to the individuals, families, groups, and communities in whose interests they work. The NGO sector is the only one that has the potential to voice the concerns of those who are excluded from the mainstream of society and who do not have access to the benefits of development. It is because the NGO sector has the potential to counter the detrimental effects of the state and market forces, and strengthen democratic systems by promoting forces in favour of equity, and as development actors to fully achieve their potential. The impact of NGOs depends significantly on enhancing their internal abilities to effectively bring about the desired social change (Mahtani 1997).

In a democratic society like ours, the role of voluntary organizations becomes crucial for social development and it is also implied that each and every citizen has a responsibility towards social ends. Voluntary organizations have a proven record of sharing the developmental responsibility of the nation since independence, and even before. Since the government has realized its own limitations and scope in outreach and providing immediate relief to the needy, voluntary organizations have an extended responsibility towards community and child health. While big international organizations are collaborating with governments in providing international expertise in planning, management, infrastructure development, transfer of appropriate technology and technical expertise to other countries, training manpower and supply of sophisticated equipment, micro-level small voluntary organizations are doing the most needed task with the poverty-stricken, ignorant and illiterate, tradition-bound people at the grassroots level. Though the voluntary sector is miniscule in comparison with the country's population and economy, it nevertheless plays an important role as the conscience-keeper of our society.

The government shall of course endeavour in providing adequate resources for child welfare programmes, and see that appropriate schemes are undertaken. At the same time, voluntary organizations engaged in the field of child health will continue to have the opportunity to develop either on their own or with state assistance in the field of health and social welfare services. India, under the leadership of Nehru was influenced both by the British and Soviet systems of socio-economic development, and had chosen the socialistic pattern of society, and accordingly our voluntary organizations are working and should be working alongside the government to achieve this goal and make valuable contribution to the human well-being and also as delivery agents for providing child welfare services. It shall be the endeavour of the state to encourage and strengthen voluntary action, so that their efforts complement each other. The resources of voluntary organizations would have to be tapped to the extent possible for promoting and developing child health programmes.

NGOs AND GLOBALIZATION

At the beginning of the new millennium, NGOs, along with others, shared a sense of excitement about new possibilities, tempered by widespread anxiety about the future. The excitement stems from the quickly expanding opportunities for civic action that global trends are creating; the anxiety arises from the increasingly critical questions being asked about the role development NGOs will be playing in the future.

Confrontation with the globalization begins and ends at the grassroots level, where NGOs develop strategies to help disadvantaged people by way of addressing their position in global markets and help them play a creative role in reshaping economic forces. They are improving the endowments of the people, enabling them to compete more effectively and achieve a basic level of security, and voice, equality of rights. This continues to be the traditional the role of NGOs in developing skills, confidence, and forms of association and improving access to credit, services, and economic opportunities, but it also involves a systematic attempt to link different levels and socio-economic sectors (health in general, mother and child health, education etc). NGOs are attempting to turn market forces to the advantage of poorer groups by reclaiming benefits, normally siphoned off by intermediaries. Civic groups are exploring alternative modes of production, and exchange less costly ones in social and environmental terms, building more "social capital" (trust, cooperation, and honesty) for use in market settings, and supporting men and women to combine their market and non-market roles to distribute profits with a social purpose. These deeper changes are crucial in addressing "Achilles heel" of most empowerment strategies: a failure to think through what happens when people with less power obtain more of it. This challenge—the regulation of all exclusionary systems of power—is one that most NGOs have tended to ignore, but it is the key to an agenda for transforming capitalism rather than "humanizing" it. At the opposite extreme, NGOs continue their role as carers of last resort, operating safety nets and providing welfare to the casualties of globalization.

At the national level, grassroots innovations need support from pro-poor macro-economics and social policies. Although globalization does erode state authority, the redistributive and protective functions of the state remain paramount. There is a tendency among some NGOs to focus on global advocacy to the exclusion of the national level processes of state-society relations that are essential for any country in order to achieve progressive goals in an integrated economy. Few NGOs have given enough thought to their roles in the national arena.

At the global level, successful strategies must be connected to actions in other parts of the international system. Globalization means not only that NGOs must engage strategically with market forces on a bigger scale, but also they must do in so in ways that link micro to macro forces in a coherent way. With their international presence and connections, NGOs have a natural strength in this field, and in some areas this has begun, especially around ethical consumption, investment, and trading. NGOs have been key players in attempts to reform corporate accountability, verify multinational codes of conduct, reshape consumer demand, and alter patterns of global trade.

CONCLUSION

India being a vast country with different socio-cultural environments, no single strategy would be good enough to succeed in the field of child health. Specific strategies, therefore, will have to be evolved keeping in mind the socio-cultural settings. Interventions need to be introduced at an early age. Effective approaches like " child to child" education programme and other innovative ways need be experimented with. The special problems requiring focus are immunization and family planning, sexually transmitted diseases like AIDS are going to affect and cause a severe damage to society at large in the coming years and require immediate attention.

While government spending on health and family welfare has been steadily increasing, in absolute terms, the proportion of plan outlay spent on child health care has been declining from plan to plan. The pattern of health expenditure is yet to be geared fully to the concept of primary health care, which remains the main instrument for moving towards health for all. The holistic approach to child health requires integration of services like education, health, nutrition, mobilization of community support, etc. Two such programmes are already in existence, viz., Integrated Child Development Services Scheme (ICDS), and Urban Basic Services, have shown some positive outcome in improving the health situation of the children.

The health facilities and personnel can establish functional linkages with the expanding ICDS infrastructure, the school system, the water and sanitation programme, District Disability Rehabilitation Centre, nutrition support programmes and so on. This is the common aim of health education. The social demand for health care is linked not only to the ability in terms of time, energy and money to seek it but also to the perception of need through better awareness. Effective use of media for imparting messages can bring about the desired behavioural changes. Using folk media and traditional communication pattern such as puppets, street play etc are likely to be more effective techniques for imparting health and nutrition education, particularly in rural areas due to their familiarity and appeal. The 'health for all' goal presumes several changes, primarily a shift from an over-professionalized system to a redefined role for medical personnel, social workers, and common families. There is an unmet need to match skills and resources with requirement. It is clear that child health is more of a socio-political problem, and unless we integrate socio-political actions and work towards social justice much cannot be achieved. Appropriate strategies, giving recognition to the social workers, worked out to improve the status of women in the community, increased access to health care and health awareness, enhanced allocation of funds and rationalization of priorities, will result in better child health.

REFERENCES

Alliband, T. (1983), *Catalyst of Development: Voluntary Agencies in India*, Kumarian Press, New York.

Bajpai, P.K. (1999), *Social Work Perspective on Health,* Rawat Publication, Jaipur.

Brown, D., Pryzwansky, W.B. and Schultz, A.C. (1987), *Psychological Consultation: Introduction to Theory and Practice*, Allyn and Bacon, Needham Heights, MA.

Caroff, P. (1988), "Clinical Social Work: Present Role and Future Challenge", *Social Work in Health Care*, Vol. 13, No. 3.

Cernea, M. M. (1988), Nongovernmental Organizations and Local Development, *World Bank Discussion Paper (No. 40)*, The World Bank, Washington D.C.

Dhooper, S.S. (1999), *Social Work in Health Care in the 21st Century*, Sage Publication, London.

Duggal, R. (1998), "NGOs, Government and Private Sector in Health", *Economic and Political Weekly*, Vol. XXIII, No. 13.

Holosko, M. J. (1992), "Social Work Practice Roles in Health Care: Daring to be Different", in Holosko, M.J. and Taylor, P.A. (eds), *Social Work Practice in Health Care Settings*, Canadian Scholars' Press, Toronto.

Iles, P. and Auluck, R. (1990), "Team Building, Interagency Team Development, and Social Work Practice", *British Journal of Social Work*, Vol. 20, p. 151–164.

Joshi,S. (1999), *Child Survival, Health and Social Work Intervention*, Concept Publishing Company, New Delhi.

Kurpius, D. J. and Fuqua, D.R. (1993), "Fundamental Issues in Defining Consultation", *Journal of Counselling and Development,* Vol. 71, p. 601–606.

Lee, K. (2000), "Globalization and Cholera: Implications for Global Governance", *Global Governance*, Vol. 6, No. 2.

Maple, M.F. (1992), 'Teamwork: An Effective Approach to Team Building', *Journal of Specialists in Group Work,* Vol. 17, p. 144–150.

Mahtani, R.P.(1992), *The Strategies of Voluntary Organizations: A Study of the Content of Strategy and the Process of Strategy Formation* (Vols I and II), Indian Institute of Management, Ahmedabad (Unpublished Doctoral Dissertation).

Mahtani, P. (1998), "A Framework for Analysing NGOs: An Application of the Management Perspective", *Perspective in Social Work*, Vol. XIII, No. 1.

Narayana, K.V. (1998), *Health and Development*, Rawat Publications, New Delhi.

NIPCCD (2000), *Child in India: A Statistical Profile*, National Institute of Public Cooperation and Child Development (NIPCCD), New Delhi.

Pawar, S.N., Ambedkar, J.B. and Shrikant, D. (2004), *NGOs and Development: The Indian Scenario*, Rawat Publications, New Delhi.

Paul, S. and Israel, A. (1991), *Nongovernmental Organizations and the World Bank-Cooperation for Development*, The World Bank, Washington, D.C.

Rohini, H. (2004), "Globalization, Women and Work", *Economic and Political Weekly,* Vol. XXXIX, No. 3.

Saxena, D. (2000), "Trends and Determinants of Immunization Coverage in India", *Journal of the Indian Medical Association*, Vol. 90, No. 1.

UNICEF (1999), *Child Survival and Population Growth*, Oxford University Press, London.

WHO (2000), *World Health Report 2000*, WHO, Geneva.

Chapter 11

Non-Governmental Organizations and Income Generation: The Case of Meghalaya

A.K. Nongkynrih

MEGHALAYA was carved out in 1970, as an autonomous state with two hill districts of the United Khasi and Jaintia Hills and the Garo Hills of Assam and emerged as a full-fledged state in January 1972. It is one of the smallest states in India and is strategically located in the north-eastern region of India. This is mainly because it shares an international boundary of about 423 km with the northern part of Bangladesh. Meghalaya has an area approximately of 22,429 sq. km. The land surface of the state mostly comprises of steep hills and deep gorges, with valleys and plains being limited. The total population of the state as per the 2001 Census is 23,06,069 as against the 1991 census which was 17,74,778. The male-female density ratio per sq.km is 1000: 975. Nearly 81 per cent of the population of the state lives in the rural areas. As per the 1991 census, the state has a total of 5,492 villages indicating a rise of 12.04 per cent over the 1981 census. The ethnic composition of the state is 85 per cent tribal and 15 per cent others. The major tribes are the Khasi-Jaintia and the Garos. Smaller tribes are the Biate, Hajong, Lalung, Koch, etc. It is interesting to note that only the two major tribes named above practice matriliny, while the rest are patrilineal based ethnic groups. The others are the non-tribal groups like the Nepalese, Bengali, Assamese, Bihari, South

Indians, and North Indians. The religious persuasions of the state's population as per the 1991 census are: 64.58 per cent Christians (Presbyterian, Catholics, Baptist Mission, Church of God, Church of North India, etc); 14.67 per cent Hindus; 3.46 per cent Muslims; 0.15 per cent Sikhs; 0.16 per cent Buddhists; and the rest as others (Statistical Handbook 2000). If we take the population growth of the state of Meghalaya, we find that it is growing at the rate of 3 per cent per annum while its economy continues to stagnate. The poverty scenario of the state (1996–97) shows that 48.85 per cent out of the total population is below the poverty line, out of which 54.47 per cent is in the rural areas and 25 per cent is urban. The livelihood of the 75 per cent of the total population is primarily agricultural, and over the years there has been an increased incidence of landless labour and persistence of poverty (Government of Meghalaya, 2003–04).

BRIEF HISTORY OF NON-GOVERNMENTAL ORGANIZATIONS

Non-governmental organizations (NGOs) have been receiving enough attention from academics and social scientists in particular. Organizations belonging to this category are neither public nor private. We do not have sufficient information on NGOs in respect of the state of Meghalaya. The only substantial work that we find is in the form of a report of a study conducted recently in the state. One has to formulate and articulate in order to be able to provide some understanding on this subject of non-governmental organizations.

If we take the north-eastern states in general and Meghalaya in particular, we can safely argue that prior to 1829, that is the annexation by the British, there were no modern organizations or institutions in Meghalaya. Societies are politically administered by traditional institutions. It is only after 1829, when the British annexed the areas inhabited by these societies, and brought them under their modern system of political administration, that the colonial government invited and permitted the entry of religion-based organizations in this part of the Indian subcontinent, and the entry and establishment of non-governmental organizations in the hills. The religion-based organizations are the first organizations that have implanted the roots of non-governmental initiatives. After the formation of the Indian Union, we observed the gradual rise of all types of organizations like trusts, cooperative societies, associations, unions and clubs. In today's context, Meghalaya has two broad types of organizations. The registered organizations, and under this banner there are different types on the basis of registration, for instance, registered under the Meghalaya Societies Registration Act, 1976, the Central Cooperatives Societies Act, 1904, The Indian Trusts Act, 1982, the Trade Union Act, 1926, and the Section of the Indian Companies Act, 1956 (PRIA 2002: 9). The second category of organizations compries unregistered organizations. Under this category too, there are many like the students unions, the people's organizations and recently the Self-Help Groups.

THE CURRENT STATUS OF NON-GOVERNMENTAL ORGANIZATIONS

Before we describe the current status of non-governmental organizations in the state of Meghalaya, we would like to clarify that the report we are going to refer to later below uses the term non-profit organization (NPO) instead of non-governmental organization (NGO). We also observe that scholars or writers on the subject are using the term as 'Third Sector', voluntary organization, civil society organization, etc. We would like to make it clear from the beginning that we are not entering into this debate of plethora of definitions because that is not the purpose of this paper. The lesson we can draw from such confusion on the definition is that this particular area of study has been ignored for too long, and lack of comprehensive study and analysis has given rise to definitional impasse. We hope that this matter will be resolved and clarity will prevail. Coming back to our discussion and utilizing the findings of the report, *Exploring the Non-Profit Sector in India: Some Glimpses from Meghalaya*, prepared by the Society for Participatory Research in Asia (PRIA 2002), we understand that, the total number of non-profit organizations (NPOs) in Meghalaya is 8,757. Out of the total, 5,129 are registered and 3,628 are unregistered. The rural–urban divide is 8,407 rural as compared to 350 urban. The distribution patterns of NPOs in terms of primary areas of activity are: 4,133 NPOs are engaged in education, 8 in health, 3,204 in religions-based activities, 98 in social service, 1,331 in sports and culture, and 3 in others. The target groups of these NPOs are: children for 6,229, women for 2,394, youth for 2,945, senior citizens for 444, workers for 190, destitute for 873, slum dwellers for 648, the community in general for 4,983, and only others for 3. There are more than 20,000 paid employees and 1 lakh volunteers working in the state. The estimated distribution of paid employees is; 17,431 full-time paid employees and 3,376 part-time employees; and in the category of volunteers, 765 are full-time, and 1,01,538 are part-time volunteers. The significant observation we can draw from the report is that the NPO sector in Meghalaya is mainly centered on the religion-based organizations.

Religion-based organizations like the Christian denominations, the Ramakrishna Missions, the Waft Board, the Sikh and the Bhuddhist organizations are well established and engaged in various activities. Besides the religion-based organizations, we have other very active organizations in the state of Meghalaya. In the last decade, there has been a sudden spurt of activities initiated by organizations which are secular. The secular organizations are of two types: registered ones and unregistered ones. Their activities range from income generation, charity, culture and arts, sports and games, theatre, music, environmental protection, etc. It is not possible to examine all of them due to various limitations. In this paper we have selected only organizations registered under the Societies Registration Act, 1976 and Cooperative Societies Act, and the thrust is on those organizations engaged in income generating activities. Secondly, we have a large number in this category, and we are not in a position to discuss them severally. In order to be able to provide an in-depth picture of such organizations we have selected a few cases from the four districts of Khasi: Jaintia Hills, namely Jaintia Hills district, East Khasi Hills district, Ri Bhoi district, and West Khasi Hills district. The organizations we have selected in our study are partners of the Community Development Extension Programme (CDEP), an innovative project of the Department of Sociology at the North Eastern Hill University. The project is partially supported by the Department Research Scheme under the Special Assistance Programme of the University Grants Commission, New Delhi. The number of CDEP partners is more than 150 organizations and we have selected only twelve of them. The twelve organizations we have selected are the leading organizations in the area of income generating activities, and we shall focus only on the aspect of income generation.

The organizations that we have selected and will describe provide sufficient information and overall understanding of the role of NGOs and income generation for the people in particular and the state of Meghalaya in general.

NON-GOVERNMENTAL ORGANIZATIONS AND INCOME GENERATION

The NGOs we have chosen to describe are located in the rural areas. They are engaged in income generation activities and other types of programmes related with community development. The names of the NGOs are mentioned in Table 11.1.

There are twelve organizations, and out of the total of twelve organizations, the districtwise distribution is four from East Khasi Hills, three from West Khasi Hills, three from Jaintia Hills, and two from Ri Bhoi district. We can further divide the twelve organizations into two broad categories, i.e., three are registered as cooperative societies and nine are registered as association/ society.

All the organizations are located in their respective villages or townships but their area of operation differs from one to another. We find in Table 11.2 that only two organizations are covering the entire state of Meghalaya, six in their own districts, two in their community and rural development blocks, and two in their civil sub-divisions. The membership pattern in the organizations is as follows: six are youth-based organizations and out of six only one comprises male youth only while the rest have both female and male youth as members; five organizations have mixed members such as young, old, male, female, etc., and only one of the twelve organizations is a women-based organization. The members of the women organization are both adult and young females.

Table 11.1: Types of Organization

Name of Organization	*Type*
Iaitreilang Multi-Purpose Cooperative Society (ITMCS)	Cooperative
Khyrim Agro Multi-Purpose Cooperative Society (KAMCS)	Cooperative
Dalade Multi-Purpose Cooperative Society (DMCS)	Cooperative
Khatar Shnong Socio-Organization (KSO)	Association
Seng Samla Diskiangpungsior (SSD)	Association
Western Cultural Social Welfare Association (WCSWA)	Association
Mairang Farmer's Federation (MFF)	Association
Marchaphrang Development Society (MCDS)	Association
Sein Kyntu Lang Ki Kynthei Tuber (SKLKT)	Association
Nam Rhen	Association
Ri Bhoi Area Welfare Association (RAWA)	Association
Seng Samla Umbir (SSU)	Association

Table 11.2: Location and Type of Membership of Organization

Organizat-ions	*Location*	*Area of Operation*	*Member-ship*
ITMCS	Phlangwanbroi	East Khasi Hills	Youth
KAMCS	Mawryngkneng	East Khasi Hills	Mixed
DMCS	Sohra	Sub-Division	Youth
KSO	Khatar Shnong	Meghalaya	Mixed
SSD	Diskiangpungsior	West Khasi Hills	Youth
WCSWA	Nongstoin	Meghalaya	Mixed
MFF	Mairang	Sub-Division	Mixed
MCDS	Jowai	Jaintia Hills	Youth
SKLKT	Kyndong Tuber	CD Block	Women
NamRhen	Sohkha	Jaintia Hills	Youth
RAWA	Umsning	Ri Bhoi	Mixed
SSU	Umbir	CD Block	Youth

Earlier, we have observed that the area of operation of organizations is beyond their village. In the actual operational aspect, the organizations are yet to cover the total area, but are presently concentrating on some villages. The variation of coverage of villages till date ranges from 3 to 45 villages. It is found in Table 11.3, that four organizations cover between 0 to 10 villages, three organizations cover between 11 to 20 villages, four organizations cover between 21 to 30 villages and only one organization is covering 45 villages. The minimum number of villages covered so far is 3, and the maximum is 45. If we take the total number of villages covered by twelve organizations, it comes to a total of 227. The size of coverage is substantial, if not large comparing the fact that there are more than 5,000-plus villages in the state.

According to our findings, there are two categories of programmes and trainings which the organizations have undertaken. The first category consists of programmes related with leadership skills, political education, health camps and health awareness, environment awareness, low cost technology awareness, information on government schemes and guidelines on community development, youth and self-employment, youth and social problems like alcoholism, drug addiction, and drop-outs, basic entrepreneurship development, career choice for school children, village development, women and development, and the role of clubs/associations in community development. The second category undertakes programmes conducted by organizations for villages under their intervention are skills training for income

Table 11.3: Number of Villages Covered by Organizations

Organizations	*Number of Villages*
ITMCS	12
KAMCS	25
DMCS	5
KSO	45
SSD	15
WCSWA	30
MFF	25
MDCS	12
SKLKT	5
Nam Rhen	10
RAWA	30
SSU	3

Table 11.4: Types of Income-Generating Programmes and Sponsoring Agency

Organizations	*Programme and Training*	*Sponsoring Agency*
ITMCS	Livestock Management, Agriculture, Horticulture	Indo-German Social Service Society, GoM
KAMCS	Agriculture, Tea Plantation	Agriculture Department, Soil Conservation Dept, Government of Meghalaya (GoM)
DMCS	Fisheries, Piggery	Functional Vocational Training Forum, Bangalore
KSO	Bamboo Craft, Livestock, Petty Trade Agriculture	Action Aid India, Indo-German Social Service Society
SSD	Livestock, Vermiculture, Agriculture, Horticulture	Agriculture & Horticulture Dept, Bethany Society, NEDFI
WCSWA	Agriculture, Horticulture Livestock	GoM, NABARD
MFF	Agriculture, Livestock, Bamboo Craft	NEDFI, GoM
MCDS	Agriculture, Livestock, Micro-enterprise	GoM
SKLKT	Agriculture, Weaving, Tailoring &Knitting	GoM, North East Network
Nam Rhen	Agriculture, Horticulure Micro-enterprise	GoM
RAWA	Agriculture, Livestock, Micro-enterprise, Bamboo craft	GoM
SSU	Agriculture, Micro-enterprise	GoM

generating activities. Table 11.4 clearly shows that in most cases agriculture (cultivating turmeric, tea, vegetables, ginger) and livestock training (piggery) are most common, and other types of training are on horticulture, micro-enterprise, bamboo craft and fisheries.

It is also observed in Table 11.4 that the skill based programmes for income generation are being supported by different departments of the Government of Meghalaya; international donor organizations like the Action Aid India and Indo-German Social Service Society; and locally based organizations like the North East Network and Bethany Society. There are also two banks such as NABARD and NEDFI which are supporting the promotion of Self-Help Groups (SHGs) and micro-credit financing.

In the previous table, we have highlighted the types of income generating programmes and activities initiated by organizations. These programmes or activities are carried out and implemented in the villages by adopting new concepts. According to Table 11.5, we find that five organizations have adopted only the concept of SHGs as their tool of intervention, four organizations are adopting and applying both the concept of SHGs and micro-enterprise, one organization is adopting the concept of SHGs and village as a unit for intervention, and two organizations use both the concepts of SHGs and Village Development Committees (VDCs) in their programme intervention. If we take in general, the concept of SHGs is the most common procedure adopted and applied by the organizations. Regarding target groups of the

Table 11.5: The Concept Adopted and Applied in Initiating Income-Generating Activities by Organizations

Organizations	*Concept*	*Target Group*
ITMCS	VDCs & SHGs	Members & Villagers
KAMCS	SHGs & Village	Members & Villagers
DMCS	SHGs	Members & Villagers
KSO	VDCs & SHGs	Villagers
SSD	SHGs	Members & Villagers
WCSWA	SHGs	Villagers
MFF	SHGs & Micro-enterprise	Members & Villagers
MCDS	SHGs & Micro-enterprise	Members & Villagers
SKLKT	SHGs & Micro-enterprise	Members & Villagers
Nam Rhen	SHGs & Micro-enterprise	Villagers
RAWA	SHGs	Villagers
SSU	SHGs	Villagers

organizations, it is found that five organizations are for the village population and concentrated more on the poor households, and seven organizations provide opportunities to both the village population as well as their own members.

The approach the organizations have adopted and applied in the field is participatory development. It means that organizing of programmes or activities is done in consultation with the people or members. Take the example of training for the general population of the village. The process that is followed is that the organizations interact with the people and request them to identify the type of training they need. The organizations contact and request the concerned departments for support and collaboration. Such trainings are usually conducted in the village and in some cases lead farmers are taken elsewhere for training. The lead farmers are selected with the intention that they will be the village level trainers. The organizations themselves feel the importance of enhancing the skills of their manpower and solving the problem of technical knowledge dependency. Many of the organizations have been sending a few of their members for different types of skills training. As of now these organizations are capable not only in providing skill-based training for others but also utilizing it for their own income generation activities. Besides, they are also being called by government agencies as resource persons in various training programmes. The types of skill-based training provided by the organizations for the SHGs and the members of the village development committee are imparted by following the same process discussed above. The skill-based training for income generation process of SHGs is different. The formation of SHGs is the first part of the income generation programme. It is only when the group has reached a certain level and they would like to start income generating activity then only they are requested to identify training needs. The organizations only facilitate the process by providing avenues and opportunities for such training. Some of the specific skill based training provided so far are pig rearing and management, horticulture, pickle making, vermi-composting, knitting, sewing, flower making, bamboo handicraft, ginger plantation, paddy cultivation, community tea plantation, low-cost bakery unit, petty trade, managing co-operative stores and rural based entrepreneurship.

The most important initiatives of the organizations in income generating activities have been the promotion of SHGs and micro-credit. The organizations believe that the only way to transform and address the issue of economic backwardness of the poor villages and gradually replace that with sustainable income generation for livelihood is SHGs. All organizations are engaged in the promotion and forming of SHGs. In almost all their project villages there are SHGs. The process the organizations are adopting in the promotion of SHGs falls into two parts: one, SHGs, formed only by members belonging in the category of Below the Poverty Line (BPL) as per Government of India guidelines, are registered with the Community & Rural Development Block, and thereafter grading is done by the same block, Department of Rural Development Agency (DRDA) and the bank where SHGs are depositing their monthly savings under the Swarnjayanti Gram Swarozgar Yogna (SGSY), a programme of the Ninth Five-Year Plan of the Government of India. Such SHGs receive training support from DRDA and loan-cum-subsidy of Rs 25,000 from the bank. Once they repay the loan component, the group can prepare a proposal for accessing the second component of loan-cum-subsidy. This process goes on to the next stage till the group decides otherwise (Government of India, 1999).

There are SHGs with only BPL members or mixed members belonging to both categories of BPL and above poverty line (APL) or only APL members. The organizations have informed, that they did not register with the C&RD block. The reason is that APL members' SHGs and SHGs of mixed members (i.e., BPL and APL) cannot enjoy support under the SGSY scheme. It has come to the notice, in the earlier programme known as the Integrated Rural Development Programme (IRDP), many persons belonging in the category of BPL were given small loans and most of them had not been able to repay the same, and they had been classified as "defaulters" by the banks. The beneficiaries who have not repaid the loan under IRDP, they cannot have an access to the SGSY scheme. They can access the scheme only after repayment of the loan. For such type of SHGs or mixed SHGs or APL SHGs, the organizations under the study have sought solutions by adopting another new approach. There are three organizations who have evolved a new approach. These three organizations interacted with North-East Development Financial Corporation Limited (NEDFI) and requested to provide loan to them who in turn gave loan to the SHGs, and the SHGs gave loan to its members. It is a very interesting three-layer loaning system, that is, from the bank to the organization, from the organization to the SHGs and from the SHGs to individual members of the group. The SHGs from the village need not go anywhere, but can easily have access to the loan in their village and without too many complications. We shall share one example of this process and the transformation it has brought into the life of the poor and marginalized of a village in the interior of Rambrai area of West Khasi Hills district. The new approach which organizations have adopted to solve constraints in discussion with the banks for a direct partnership with SHGs and without any intermediaries in between. We give an example of the transformation that is taking place in a village after the formation of SHGs.

EXAMPLE 1: SENG SAMLA DISKIANGPUNGSIOR AND INCOME GENERATION FOR THE POOR

West Khasi Hills district of the state of Meghalaya is one of the districts that is known for its timber trade. With the entry of timber trade, majority of the working population from the villages shifted their occupation from subsistence agriculture to timber wage labourers. The change in occupation has taken place because of immediate benefits they received weekly in the form of hard cash. The same is not possible from agriculture being season-based production. On the 12 December of 1996, the Supreme Court of India passed the order of banning timber trade in the whole of India. The sudden halt in timber trade brought about one of the most shocking experiences for the daily wage labourers.

In Diskiangpungsior village, the effect of the above order was disastrous. The people did not know what they would have to do next. There was problem of food security since the villagers did not have money to buy their basic items and the land they owned did not grow anything since they left it fallow. It was the most vulnerable situation for the poor people and especially the children.

Under such circumstances, a village youth organization known as Seng Samla Diskaingpungsior emerged. In 1997, the organization was registered under the Societies Registration Act. From the same year, the organization organized the village by forming Self-Help Groups (SHGs). There are two SHGs in the village with membership of 15 and 10 each. With the formation of SHGs, the organization contacted various government departments and agencies for support. This process led to the gradual change in the life of the people because skill-based training was provided in the area in horticulture, agriculture and vermi-composting. Out of the three skills, the most beneficial of all was the vermi composting training since it was developed as a micro-enterprise.

The members of SHGs and the members of the organization are now generating income by selling the compost at the rate of Rs 8 per kilo, providing training to interested groups and individuals at the rate of Rs 50 per person per day and supplying of vermi-compost worms at the rate of 50 paise for one. Today, the organization and the village are known for vermi-composting. Besides the vermi-composting unit, the organization along with the people has introduced large-scale production of turmeric as part of their economic activity and sustaining their livelihood. Besides the activities mentioned above, the organization is also promoting plantation of fruit trees, medicinal plants, patchouli and vegetables. Other additional activities that have been taken up are education for the children, irrigation, and community water tank. These activities have contributed towards sustainable generation of income for the poor people.

In order to enhance the scope of village economic development and participation of women and youth, three organizations, besides promoting and forming SHGs, are also introducing another new concept that is known as Village Development Committee (VDC). The main reason of facilitating the process of formation of VDCs is that the concept of VDC is based on participatory principles. In the state of Meghalaya in general, and Khasi and Jaintia Hills in particular, village councils have been implementing various schemes and programmes of the government. Women and young people are not part of the decision-making process but only passive observers. The only way for the women and young people to be a part and be included as equal and active participants of the village development work is through the VDC. We cite below one example of VDC which is facilitated by Khatar Shnong Socio-Organisation (KSO). This is one of the leading organizations in East Khasi Hills district of Meghalaya. Its area of operation covers more than 40 villages with an approximate population of 6,000-plus. It has been in the forefront of development by applying participatory ideas and practices. It is the first to initiate and apply the concept of VDC in the villages of the East Khasi Hills district.

EXAMPLE 2: NONGTRAW VILLAGE DEVELOPMENT COMMITTEE: TRANSFORMING LIVES

The biggest constraint of development of this village is that the poor people do not own land. Out of total 30 groups, 80 per cent are without any land for agriculture or other economic activities. The landless have to lease the plot either on seasonal or annual basis. It is difficult for them to invest their small income to buy land or to invest into the land lease for long duration cash crop plantation. The village has never thought of collectively finding out a way in solving their problems. With the entry of KSO in the village and sustained dialogue with the village, the people have begun to think of the idea of VDC and gradually accepted and formed it.

The formation of VDC has contributed towards economic change and growth in the village. The key activities of the villagers are neither selected by themselves nor decided by KSO but they have evolved from VDC through the process of village level planning. There are few areas, in connection with income generation activities facilitated by KSO and the VDC, that need to be highlighted here:

- The VDC has a revolving fund and credit opportunity with no interest for the poor households. Every poor household from the village can avail this credit facility. They repay back only the principal amount according to the time fixed by the VDC. The credit is given for small economic investment with the intention that it will generate income. Many poor families are benefiting from this kind of credit opportunity.
- One of the stumbling blocks for economic development is landlessness. After sufficient thinking and several discussions, the VDC took another major decision to solve once and for all the problem of landlessness. Through the VDC, the members of the village came up with the idea of monthly contribution towards buying of land. This effort paid good dividend because they could generate Rs 25,000 from the village and KSO contributed Rs 20,000. With this amount the VDC bought a big hill. Having their own land has made the people to invest more on the land and generate more income. It does not stop here because people think of buying more lands in the future.
- It has been the objective of the VDC right from the beginning to promote the participation of women in the traditional village council which is male dominated. On the 28 of June, 2004, for the first time in the history of the village, women have been accepted in the village council as equal partners. This is one of the major achievements of the VDC in changing the attitude and behaviour of the villagers at Nongtraw.

CONCLUSION

One can definitely argue that the history of non-governmental organizations in the State of Meghalaya is the product of the process of colonization by the British from 1829 onwards. It was the British colonial government that permitted the entry of religion based organizations in the hills. These organizations were exogenous agents which have implanted the seed of voluntary initiatives. They set up educational institutions, health centres and organized other welfare activities for the people by using the charity-based approach. The second phase of the history of NGOs might have been evolved after the independence of the Union of India. The nation-state legitimized voluntary action by giving it a legal recognition. Out of such process, a number of NGOs were formed and registered under a particular act or law. Most of these NGOs are secular organizations and their activities include sports, culture, welfare programmes, etc.

The registered secular organizations can be broadly divided into different categories. They are youth clubs, youth association, women's association, general association/organization, and co-operative societies. The membership in such organizations varies. For instance, women's organizations are exclusive only to women, and the general type of organizations have mixed members, both young and adults as well as male and female. Majority of these organizations are rural and located in the villages.

The idea and entry of non-governmental organizations in income generation programmes started only in recent years. Much of their time and energy has been spent either on charity-based activities or welfare activities or sports and games. The 1990s can be said to be the beginning of the growth of the idea and involvement in income generating activities and the application of this idea is gradually taking roots in the programme framework of organizations, and the people too are requesting for such programmes. In the application of the idea of income generation, organizations have either employed the concept of SHGs or VDCs or sometimes both. It seems that these concepts are bearing fruits and gradually transforming the life of the people. By adopting and applying these concepts in the villages, organizations have also created a network between the people and the government departments, banks, like-minded agencies and other interested persons.

In one way, we can say that NGOs are playing an active role in addressing issues of livelihood of the people, and especially the poor. But they too encounter many constraints since they do not have enough professional skills and funds to develop their capacity, and also widen their engagement for generating more economic opportunities for the poor in the villages. The dimension which is beyond the control of these organizations is the market. Organizations, SHGs, VDCs and the general population are complaining about fluctuating market price of the local produce. They are not able to comprehend this aspect, and without any control on pricing many a time farmers are frustrated. This has been the most critical aspect of income generation activity of the poor farmers. With uncontrolled pricing of the produce, farmers are facing another brunt, and that is the fluctuating oil price. This directly affects them because the transportation cost of produce increases but the price of their produce does not in most cases. Last year, the price of ginger was 50 paise per kilogram; the farmers had to throw ginger away, and many lost their investments. This year the price is approximately Rs 1,200 per quintal. But this cannot compensate last year's loss.

It is a fact that NGOs are directly engaging in the promotion of income generating activities. In the case of Meghalaya, agriculture and horticulture are the major areas of income generation towards sustainable livelihood of the people. NGOs find it extremely difficult to handle and provide any assistance to the farmers and small growers in the pricing of produce. Organizations feel that their good intention, approach and process adopted in transforming the economic difficulties by providing various skill-based training and other linkages to the poor and those above poverty line are ultimately being determined by the global market forces. The power of the global market force is such that it can either increase economic opportunities of the poor or the poor become vulnerable by its power and decreases its poor people's chance of economic development.

ACKNOWLEDGEMENTS

I am very grateful to Prof. L.S. Gassah, Department of Political Science, NEHU, for reading, commenting and editing this paper. I also thank the various organizations mentioned in this paper for sharing valuable information. Without their support it would not have been possible for me to complete the paper.

REFERENCES

Government of Meghalaya (2002), *Statistical Handbook,* Directorate of Economics and Statistics, Shillong.

Government of Meghalaya (2003–2004), *Annual Plan-Draft Proposals,* Planning Department, Shillong.

Society for Participating Research in Asia (PRIA) (2000), *Exploring the Non-Profit Sector in India: Some Glimpses from Meghalaya*, PRIA, New Delhi.

PART II

ORGANIZATIONAL FACETS

Chapter 12

Funding Issues in NGO Sector in India

Swapan Garain

THE world in which we live is changing constantly. The rapidly changing socio-eco-political environment presents major challenges to NGOs in using its resources effectively and in keeping abreast of debates on development issues. Availability of financial resources from the state and the international institutional sources often mirror underlying priorities and values of the donor community and the country. For example, government funding allocation reflects the ongoing priorities of the government and also gives an insight into the significance of social development issues in the changing wider economic and political context. Similarly, trends in individual voluntary contributions throw light on the significance assigned to the role of NGOs by the general public. The fund-raising space for NGOs has changed in the last few decades with issues like foreign vs. indigenous funds, business funding vs. foundation/trust grant, institutional sources vs. individual contribution, and external vs. internal revenue generation. Issues concerning NGO funding are becoming more and more matters of debate.

NGOs in general depend on individual contributors, public charitable trusts, foundations, business houses and the government sources for procuring necessary financial and non-financial resources. Dominant funding sources can seriously influence the working of the recipient NGOs, forcing them to compromise on their independence in conceiving, planning and executing their activities (Biswas 2006). The legitimacy of an NGO is further challenged when the funds originate from foreign sources. As the sole monitoring of funding sources offers a limited perspective, funding trends need to be analyzed in the context of national and global policy debates.

Fund-raising is increasingly finding significance in the strategic planning and management of NGOs. As the institutional sources of funding, including foreign funding, become scarce over the coming years, NGOs with in-house competency of institutionalized fund-raising systems, including skilled fund-raising staff, will not only survive in the funding crisis, but emerge as strong organizations. Such organizations can continue to operate independently and remain credible to stay on their own with no fear of government reprisal (Biswas 2006). Fund-raising being a sensitive and at times an ethical issue, NGOs have to struggle to find, attract and retain suitably trained and motivated staff for the job.

In order to survive and prosper, an NGO must deal with current and future trends through a clear strategy. As a strategy, many NGOs in recent decades, attempted to move away from the charity approach and focused on need assessment, systems and procedures, sustainable programme design and implementation, and participatory processes. While strategy rarely aims at revolutionary changes, many NGOs often reacted to pressures to meet target group needs and the demand of funding agencies to be consistent, efficient and effective. The changing scenario contributed to NGOs building alliances/partnerships with other stakeholders for increasing scale and improving technical competence.

THE CONTEXT OF GLOBALIZATION

In the 1990s, the term 'globalization' was used to integrate Indian economy to the economies worldwide through economic reform that aimed at bringing prosperity to the country and its people. However, globalization has turned out to be the face of current onslaught by imperialism. In practice, gross distortion has often been reported. While labour (the real wealth of the poor countries like India) remains trapped within national boundaries, capital (largely centralized and concentrated in imperialist hands) armed with freedom of entry and exit worldwide maximizes the exploitation of labour worldwide. The working class in the imperialist countries that prospered from these processes did not benefit from globalization either (Rupe India 2003).

Globalization, along with liberalization and privatization, has left the world economically polarized between countries that enjoy unimaginable wealth and the countries that are crippled by poverty. As a tool of capitalism, globalization helps to perpetuate these inequalities. Globalisation not only created a massive gulf between the richest and the poorest nations on the planet, it also caused to limit the dominance of any single country.

While poor countries are exploited in the globalized society, though exploitative capacity is at times limited by certain factors over which the rich nations have limited control. The economic and political interdependence in a globalized world is one such set of forces that influence the policies and economic decisions made by other countries. However, the global economic institutions (e.g., World Bank, IMF, etc) and their policies are often in conformity with the policies and interests of the rich nations (like USA, UK and Japan), and loans are often linked to the poorer countries submitting to the neo-liberal capitalist policies. Such submissions often appear to be the only option, resulting in the poorer countries (like those in Latin America and Africa) liberalizing their underdeveloped markets prematurely (Stiglitz 2002; Vanita 1994).

The forces of globalization can be resisted, and even defeated, by collective efforts and struggles at various levels, in various countries, in various forms. Some opponents of globalization view World Social Forum as an appropriate platform. However, a careful analysis reveals WSF as a diversion from such struggle, far from being an instrument of it. WSF has tie with the existing system. Many political leaders of the imperialist countries have been attending WSF meet regularly. WSF as a body and the innumerable bodies participating in the WSF receive funds from sources that are tied to imperialist interests and operations. One such agency is Ford Foundation which is in close collaboration with the US Central Intelligence Agency internationally (WSF, 2004; Biswas 2006), and has helped to shape the Indian government's policies in favour of American interests. On the other hand, there are several political forces fighting for a change of the system that have been excluded from the WSF meets.

THE NGO SECTOR IN INDIA

India with more than one billion population is challenged by the problem of poverty, illiteracy and ill-health. Large-scale corruption in government, unequal distribution of wealth and lack of infrastructure, particularly in the rural areas to reach out to the poor, have aggravated the task of creating opportunities for the poor and thus alleviating poverty (Patnaik 2003; Robinson 1991).

About half of the population in India is reported to be living below the poverty line. The task of reducing poverty is enormous and the contribution of every concerned individual and organization will be critical in this mission. The role of non-governmental voluntary initiatives is significant due to their understanding of the issues and concern for the disadvantaged (Vohra 1990).

Two to four million non-government institutions (some of those will legally qualify to be called NGOs due to their incorporation under the relevant Acts) in India are engaged in various social sector activities helping the poor, deprived, disadvantaged and destitute (McGann and Johnstone 2006). Increasing fund flow to Indian NGO sector in recent years has led to a vast proliferation of NGOs (Biswas 2006). These NGOs are largely operating as service providers with concentration in the area of education, health, nutrition for mother and child, income generation, small loans for self-employment, and environment activities (Desai 1999).

Some NGOs focus on serving their members, and others on serving clients outside the organization. Some operate domestically, working on projects whose impacts may be felt from the village level to national policy to international arenas. At times, NGOs are set up to meet donor needs and programmes. For instance, due to the recent donor emphasis on HIV/AIDS programme, several NGOs have been registered to deal with HIV/AIDS issues. This has given rise to accusations that some NGOs are primarily concerned with making money and not eradicating poverty, and they appear and disappear depending on where the money is. Earlier, a similar trend had occurred with the mushrooming of NGOs dealing with women's issues.

NGO work in India has diverse ideological origins and underpinnings. Some have traditions that can be traced back to the ideologies of the Ramakrishna Mission, Mahatma Gandhi, Sarvodaya, Jesuit Missions and even Marxism. Many NGO establishments in modern India function as communes with community life for the staff and volunteers in isolated project campuses, and remain totally dedicated to the poor and deprived people in the area. There are a number of sincere individuals working in NGOs or associated with NGOs. Many such persons are moved by a desire to extend some immediate assistance to needy people. Seen in specific contexts, they do in fact reachout with some relief to sections of people. Without questioning the commitment and sincerity of such individuals, our concern here is to point to the broader political significance of NGOs' institutional performance (PRIA 1991; WSF 2004).

NGOs play an important role in linking communities and the government. NGOs, especially those working to provide various services—health, education, nutrition, rural development—act as a buffer between the state and people. NGOs ensure that the voice of impoverished people is heard (Desai 1999). As the government reduces budgetary allocation for various social sector spendings, NGOs come to the rescue of the needy to meet their most basic survival requirements. NGOs at times act as 'contractors' of the State for implementing government designed and sponsored schemes for the people. Such a scenario, absolves the state of its responsibilities and people cannot demand for such services.

The domain of traditional welfare oriented service providing NGOs' activities have been expanded to include activism, advocacy, support and intermediary services in the 1980s. This phenomenon served to further institutionalize people's movements and restrict the space of popular control. Nature of external funding sources contributed in determining the influence of institutionalized systems vis-à-vis popular control. Indeed, as NGOs proliferate and enlarge their domains, they set up organizations to protect and promote the cause of culture, human rights, environment, land rights of tribals, and consumer movement. In the process, NGOs bureaucratize people's movements. Traditionally, self-reliant people's movements become hybrid with professionalization and institutionalization. They are often launched at the instance of the parent NGO, external funding agency or an interested individual, instead of being popular home-made movement. They no longer raise their own resources. These new age movements are not led by their own representatives who have to be accountable to the people, its members. By contrast, NGO officials, while claiming to represent the people and paid by funding agencies, assume leadership of such NGO-led movements as a requirement of his or her job. They are usually career professionals with background in social work, rural management, law or business administration. Accordingly, they are neither accountable to the people, nor can they be removed by the people. Hence, these positional leaders of NGO-led people's movements are also free to decide and act on behalf of the people, without seeking mandate of the people. However, the parent NGOs running people's organization projects remain accountable to their funders (Agg 2006). Relevant examples could be found in the forums or campaigns for/against child labour, domestic helpers, project affected and so on. On the line of people's organizations, political life itself is increasingly getting NGOized, that is, bureaucratized and alienated from popular presence and representation.

NGO work is often referred to as "non-party political" work, as it involves mobilizing people around issues and demanding change. NGOs are emerging as a single non-party political formation in the country. They have unanimity on most issues. Their explicitly political activities span over a wide range of social segments. NGOs organize women, adivasis, dalits, fishermen, and slum dwellers around the issues that affect them. Invariably such deprivation is caused by the perpetuating or upcoming State policies at the interest or instance of the ruling political party or the coalition of political parties. For example, NGOs did admirable work on the issue of riot victims in Gujarat, in providing relief to the victims, and documenting the crimes against them. Some view this notion of "non-party political process" is the reason for the World Social Forum's (WSF) hypocritical bar on the involvement of political parties in WSF meet. However, leaders of political parties, appearing as 'individuals' do take part in the WSF, often pushing aside the people's organizations and grassroots movements from being heard or seen. Besides, the age old mass organizations (the trade unions, youth organizations, farmers associations, student unions, women's organizations) in most countries continue to be the primary platforms for mobilizing and meeting the masses of people. These mass organizations are traditionally affiliated with and often led by mainstream political parties. In the complex socio-political structure, WSF provides a platform and an opportunity to NGOs to legitimize themselves as a political force and expand their influence among sections to which they earlier had little access or command. Whenever the politicians find their omnipotence threatened, they view suspiciously the work of the NGOs that question the status quo. Accordingly, political parties find legitimate interest in penetrating the forums of non-party political formations in WSF and influencing its working through its leaders as individual members in the face of denial of organizational membership.

The NGO sector is facing many issues of concern today. There are many aspects of this sector that are raising numerous debates and discussions. These issues concern the NGOs, funding organizations and beneficiaries alike. While there is some focus, debate or discussion on the problems faced by NGOs and the target groups, it is sad that the problems faced by funding agencies are not given enough importance today. But it is to be remembered that their problems too are very crucial to the working of the sector, as it is they who bring the major resources onto the sector.

Another issue that dogs the NGO sector is about its image. The public never gets to know or see much tangible outcome of the work carried out by the NGOs. All they see or hear about are the NGO leaders (or owners) travelling in air-conditioned cars, occupying posh offices and undertaking foreign travels and using mobile phones. Such lifestyles are somehow incongruous with the image of sacrifice and penance adopted by the early leaders of the voluntary movements like Mahatma Gandhi or Vinoba Bhave. While working in NGOs is increasingly being considered as a good career option by the professionally trained, serious contradictions are emerging in the use of charity money for meeting personal needs for a reasonable livelihood, and the education and upbringing of children of the NGO leaders and other staff.

FUNDING SOURCES

The agencies and individuals who donate money to non-profit activities do so across varied causes. NGOs universally depend on funding from sources ranging from individual donors, foundations, corporations and governments. Funding sources can be broken down into three main components: the gift economy, the official aid and the market. The gift economy consists of voluntary income from the general public, for example donations given by individuals, groups and civil society organizations. Official aid (Farouk, 2002; Vanita, 1994), raised from the tax base, is channelled through bilateral (e.g., USAID, NORAD, etc.) and multilateral organizations (e.g., UNICEF, UNDP, World Bank, etc) and international aid agencies (e.g., Novib, Oxfam, etc). Besides matching grant from country's government, international funding agencies (from which smaller NGOs in various countries in the third world receive their funds) depend heavily on funds from corporate and institutional sources. International aid agencies are also seen as a separate segment of funding source as many of them maintain independence from their country's government by raising a large part of their funds from sources other than their government (Biswas 2006). In terms of the market, there are two main contributions to NGO financing: first, from the corporate sector, and secondly, from NGO enterprise and investment. The relative contribution of the three types of funding sources varies considerably from country to country and even between organizations. On an average, some two-third of northern NGO funding comes from voluntary income. However, the individual contribution in India is less than five per cent. A small percentage of NGO funding is derived from income-generation strategies.

The proportion of funds gained from various sources can be of particular importance to NGOs, as this can potentially influence their focus and autonomy. Critics charge that funding sources can seriously influence NGO policy, and thereby potentially transform these organizations into vehicles for promoting their interests and agenda. Either way, external funding entails the danger of compromising the credibility of the local NGO sector, as they are required to follow the agenda of the master donor (McGann and Johnstone 2006).

Charges of donor influence question the legitimacy of NGOs especially when funds originate from foreign sources, including foreign governments, corporations or aid agencies (Farouk, 2002). At the same time, NGOs around the world are raising the fundamental question of their own survival without international donor funding. In order to steer southern NGOs away from a detrimental dependence on international donors that are driven by northern agendas, some are promoting sustainable models of local resource mobilization in an effort to mainstream social causes by encouraging NGOs to innovatively garner support from local allies, such as the media, private companies, private individuals and the public in general (Farouk 2002). NGOs face a key challenge in building sustainable partnerships with the corporate sector as it is one of the few remaining sources of local funding (Farouk 2002).

As donor funding is withdrawn, many NGOs are closing, and those that survive will do so through taking a creative approach to raising funds, forging new partnerships, and finding a new direction for themselves. In this issue, NGOs, donors and government can share their experiences on the current problems that they are facing, and also present a vision of their future relationship, and the ways in which their goals can be realized. NGOs across the spectrum can be rated poorly at inventing creative resource solutions for their long term sustainability. Indian NGOs suffer from a lack of awareness with respect to local resource mobilization and there is a poor ethic of "voluntarism". The similar plane of ideas involves the lookout on the part of the funding agencies for organizations that have a right-based approach. This is to say, that the orientation is for and towards the idea of alliance building rather than service delivery alone. In this respect, the mission-led organizations are favourable to achieve more recognition than those based solely on ideology. There is a realization that alliances/partnerships are a very good way of increasing scale and improving technical competence through inter-organizational learning. In a shift from a traditional economy to a market economy riding on the back of an information explosion, it is these "successful" NGOs whose funding has become most dependent on their "Northern Partners". As a result, they have not developed the skills to talk to the public in India about their causes.

NGOs should not become hostage to the aspirations of those from whom they are receiving their money. Accordingly, an NGO must strive for diversity in his funding base, with substantial portion of its funds must be coming from governments, corporations, individual donors and foundations (BSDGlobal 2003).

NGO funding is mostly governed by the "whims and preferences" of donors. Personal relation reference or other consideration is often the key factor for an NGO in successfully procuring its funding from Indian sources, be it government, corporate or local funding agencies. Besides, donors prefer to steer clear of controversial issues, and hence avoid partnering and supporting rights-based and advocacy or networking NGOs (Farouk 2002).

THE STATE AND THE NGOs

A positive reallocation of state development expenditures towards more funding for the social sector, has increased the demand for external assistance, particularly for investment in social sector. The government reallocation policy must be seen in the context of the dictate by international development community to use its funding almost exclusively to the social sector portfolio. But emerging need for creating and supporting a responsive social sector delivery system is enormous. As the states are reaching out for international assistance for additional capacity building with a strong focus on social sector investment, the UN system faces a unique opportunity, having a long-standing experience and record in this area. On the other hand, partner organizations, such as the World Bank, are financing into areas that were traditionally supported by the UN system (Vanita 1994).

The state continues to be a major source of funding for the NGOs in India (Kudva 2005). The government has started playing a strong regulatory role in relation to fund allocation into particular streams like rural development, education or health, while NGOs that support state programmes are more likely to have access to bilateral or multilateral aid programmes. NGOs that receive international funding are unlikely to receive direct government funding. On the other hand, international funding NGOs prefer supporting NGOs that avoid state funding of their work.

The fund-raising space, particularly for large and urban NGOs, has thus been changed in the last few decades with issues like foreign vs. Indian funds, corporate funding, public contribution, etc. Also, NGOs have moved from one level to different level of organizational evolution, implying the need for organizational support beyond grants for service delivery (Desai, 1999). Besides, some NGOs find themselves out in the cold as foreign funders shift their aid in the direction of the government. Nonetheless, these NGOs have remained concerned about the involvement of the government in their work. While increasing funding potential from government sources (about 50 per cent of NGO funding comes from government) is an issue, why most NGOs like to maintain good relations (funding is one avenue) with the local level government bureaucracy to avoid any problems. At the same time, becoming an extension of the government will cause considerable dissonance for organizations that consider themselves "non-governmental" organizations.

Many of NGOs in the country's north-east with dubious origin served as a conduit for funding rebels both from foreign sources and international development aid. In 2003, Union Home Ministry blacklisted more than 800 NGOs for having alleged links with separatist groups (Bhaumik 2003). A large part of federal development funding for the region was reported to be finding its way to the rebel groups, because of corrupt politicians and bureaucrats who were helping them siphon it off. Incidentally, many of these NGOs belong to minority religious groups such as Muslims and Christians. In the face of such allegations, Leftist political parties are in favour of government abandoning its present posture of allowing free flow of foreign funds on the grounds that it contributes to the foreign exchange fund. The impact of foreign money flowing into India has been so great that the government had to enact a legislation called the Foreign Contribution Regulation Act (FCRA) in 1976 to control the foreign fund flow to Indian NGO sector (VANI 1994; Kudva 2005). The Act was welcomed since foreign founding was viewed a vehicle for massive penetration of imperialist funds to NGOs in order to influence the socio-political system of the country (Biswas 2006). Left political parties would like to see NGOs that claim to organize people for whatever form of non-party political process included in the list of prohibited organizations (just as political parties) for receiving foreign funds (Karat 1985, 1988). In view of the concern of the bureaucracy and of the political parties about the foreign sources of funding, NGOs are forced to opt safe and non-controversial issues, target groups and programmes to work on.

ROLE OF INTERNATIONAL AID

International non-governmental organizations (INGOs) or aid agencies are increasingly supporting programmes focusing on capacity building and sustainable development. Some of the specific areas that had been in focus in recent years include improving access and quality of education; poverty reduction and economic growth in an environmentally responsible way; sustainable use of natural resources through community based projects; capacity building of state and civil society functionaries for socio-economic development; good governance and so on. INGOs have had a substantial role in resource flows to developing countries like India (Kudva 2005). Their funding has largely come from private donations rather than from government grants. Most of the largest INGOs are of respectable age, and wisdom. They have changed and adapted to the times, but overall they have managed to keep their independence. This is a practice for CBOs (community based organizations) and national NGOs to follow. Co-operation between INGOs, national NGOs and CBOs is important to enhance the impact of development efforts. However, a healthy degree of competition is also needed for organizational development of the sector.

INGOs largely focus at the humanitarian level and their funding has limitations in engaging with issues of poverty and under-development at a fundamental level. Most of the large international NGOs started with relief work and still continue relief programmes as part of their mission. While they have started with a 'charity' approach, all of them support development work, raise funds over the internet and put their financial report out for all to see. All have a healthy amount of money coming from private donations so that they are quite independent from official donor agendas. Many are expanding their fund-raising efforts to the South. Some establish national offices or foundations and boards in developing countries. INGOs help the national NGOs and CBOs. They work to build their resource mobilization capacity. INGO-staff in developing countries are almost exclusively host country nationals or nationals of other developing countries. What large INGOs probably fear the most is the World Bank's Comprehensive Development Framework for donor co-ordination. This new organizational approach to development cooperation implies that donors give coordinated aid for a country's poverty reduction programme (Vanita 1994). The recipient country decides how the funds will be used for implementation and who will do the implementation – the private for-profit sector, CBOs, national

NGOs, international NGOs and government itself? INGOs fear that developing country governments may exclude them from the implementation scene.

The foreign-funded NGO sector has, with remarkable uniformity, propagated certain political concepts. For example, Ford Foundation's (FF) projects focused on 'identity', gender, ethnicity, caste, nationality, over class. Further, FF would specifically ensure that people's struggles against the government do not take the course of confrontation. The Foundation did not believe in conflict with government, as it operates at the invitation of the country's government. NGOs benefiting from the FF funding programme could be in confrontation with the government when they are working on issues such as welfare of dalits or adivasis. However, there is a conscious attempt to complement and cooperate with the efforts of the government. FF has chosen to focus on three particularly oppressed sections of the Indian society—adivasis, dalits, and women. All three are potentially important components of a movement for basic change in Indian society; indeed, some of the most militant struggles in recent years have been waged by these sections (WSF 2004). While acknowledging the concern about inequalities caused by the economic policies in tune with globalization and liberalization, FF views its projects to act as a corrective measure to off set the adverse impact of uncontrolled market forces, particularly among the oppressed people in India.

In 1983, the Development Grant Facility of the World Bank has set up Small Grants Programme to provide funding support to civil society organizations (CSOs) to promote information dissemination on development, and thereby aid partnerships among the key stakeholders in development. The specific purpose of this facility is to support activities related to civic engagement for the empowerment of vulnerable and marginalized groups. Besides, the projects approved by the World Bank mostly include the opportunity for NGOs and CSOs to participate in people related components of the project (WSF 2004; Vanita 1994). Critics view this as tiny well-publicized safety nets to catch a handful from among the masses of people thrown out by market forces, instead of attempting to control the uncontrolled market forces.

The 1980s and 1990s witnessed an extraordinary proliferation of foreign-funded NGOs in India (Biswas 2006). According to the Home Ministry, by 31st March 2005, 30,321 organizations were registered and 369 were granted prior permission during the year 2004–05 under the Foreign Contribution Regulation Act, though only 18,540 of them submitted their accounts to the government as required. Total foreign funds[1] received by these organizations rose from Rs 3,403 crore in 1998–99 to Rs 4,535 crore in 2000–01 to 6,256.68 crore in 2004–05 (MHA, 2005). In 2004–05, among the purposes, the highest amount was received for establishment expenses (Rs 948.20 crore or 15 per cent of total foreign fund flow of 6257 crore or 10 per cent) followed by relief/rehabilitation of victims of natural calamities (Rs 655.65 crore or 10 per cent or 9 per cent) and rural development (Rs 582.48 crore or 9 per cent). Despite the NGOs looking inwards for funds, there has been no let up for foreign support either. However, many foreign donors had stayed away from NGOs in the aftermath of the communal riots, not wanting to make a political statement by supporting them (David 2002).

The Communists in India and the Leftists have spent the last two decades in ideological struggle against foreign funds, against NGOization of political life and particularly against the way international donors set the agenda and create groups that are accountable to them and not to the people (Prashad 2004). Prakash Karat (Karat 1985, 1988) an important CPI(M) activist, now a politburo member, referred to sophisticated and comprehensive strategy, of foreign funding agencies to harness the forces of NGOs to their strategic design to penetrate Indian society and influence its course of development. He had cited instances of liberal fund availability to these groups, organizing the rural and urban poor to fight for their rights and against exploitation, and of activism by NGOs. He was critical of the role of ICCO-Netherlands, Friedrich Ebert Foundation; NOVIB, Ford Foundation, Canadian International Development Agency and Oxfam in promoting imperialist agenda in India. Karat was of the opinion that this open access to foreign funds allowed by the Government of India became one of the major avenues of imperialist penetration financially in the country (Biswas 2006).

Some NGOs have begun to be concerned about how foreign funding can be gradually replaced with Indian money. Since fairly substantial sums of foreign money are still available for NGO work, local fund-raising has not yet become a strategic objective for most organizations. If it was possible for Indian NGOs to raise their funds from within the country, at one stroke, it would release them from the government surveillance associated with the FCRA, and provide them with legitimacy and credibility to operate.

NGOs AND THE CORPORATE SECTOR

Increasingly, most NGOs have been unable to raise the sum of money they need from government, foreign or individual sources.

With limited donations from individuals on one hand and general suspicion on foreign funding on the other, NGOs are now facing constraints in maintaining and expanding their work. In such a tight funding climate, some of the visible and large NGOs have realized that the real money lies in the private sector and are increasingly looking up to the corporate sector funding. Corporate social investment is increasingly becoming a reliable source of income for large and well known NGOs. It is believed that private sector funding can play an important role in building the capacity of NGOs (BSDGlobal, 2003). Funding problem in the NGO sector is one of the factors which are bringing the two sectors closer.

While some NGOs may be skeptical of corporate funding vis-à-vis its independence, others may be 'too closely aligned' with industry. Some NGOs traditionally enjoyed good relations with the corporate sector and even introduced the practice of appointing business people to its board so as to build stronger relationships with industry. These include marketing relationships with media and other sponsors, sizable donations, brand affiliation, employee volunteering, etc. However, it may be difficult to single out a decision that has been improperly influenced by a relationship with a corporate donor. Even if corporate funding of NGOs cannot be shown to have influenced NGO decision-making, occasionally NGOs may find themselves caught in the crossfire between corporate competitors. Such a scenario is not very common yet in India in view of lack of media savvy outward posture of NGOs. Besides, NGO work and corporate partnerships with NGOs are not very much visible in the public domain. However, Consumer NGOs globally are at times subject to criticism that their lobbying against one product or company could benefit one company or sector at the expense of another (BSDGlobal 2003).

Not all NGO and business house relationships are centred on monetary contribution. The enthusiastic NGO representatives, who are open to work in a more collaborative way with the industry, are typically wary about relationships predicated upon a financial arrangement. NGOs should not become hostage to the aspirations of those from whom they are receiving money. Some NGOs are sensitive about the proportion of corporate contributions in the funding pie (BSDGlobal 2003). Hence, striving for diversity in funding base, with 25 per cent of the money coming from each segment, i.e., governments, corporations, individual donors and foundations is a good proposition.

The corporate being primarily concerned with profit, is motivated by business sense, long or short term, while responding to appeal from NGOs for support. This corporate-NGO interface is often based on fundamentally contradictory statements from two opposite sectors. While the corporate demands NGOs to fit into the condition laid out by it in order to release funds, while NGOs search only for such corporate grant that provides space to preserve their credibility. Nonetheless, funding problems in the NGO sector have brought the capable NGOs closer to industry.

Most business houses develop their social responsibility programmes in line with State priorities. However, NGO-business partnering is often driven by philanthropic interest of corporate CEO, and not the new found interest of the industry in sustainable development.

Any corporate funding would raise questions on NGO's credibility and autonomy. Even if an NGO draws most of its funds from charitable sources, it often faces criticism for accepting money from "socially irresponsible" companies. Some NGO leaders dismiss such criticisms, justifying that one must be free to use all the help one can get while fighting bigger issues. A healthy debate must begin among NGOs on the type of corporate funding arrangements that can afford them the greatest degree of autonomy. The NGOs will of course continue their search for funding relationships that will preserve their credibility and independence (Biswas 2006).

PUBLIC CONTRIBUTIONS TO CHARITY

In India, public contribution to social causes is negligible and many believe it to be less than five per cent of the money raised by NGOs. They have been unable to raise money from the individuals inspite of the increasing middle class population with high disposable income. Number of high networth individuals (HNI) has also multiplied in the last few years. NGOs in general have remained publicity shy and have not taken into canvassing their activities targeting individuals for donations. Besides, whatever monies raised from door-to-door canvassing often went right back to pay for the campaign, logistics and the fund-raisers/volunteers. Several NGOs are scaling back or trimming back their individual fund-raising activities targeting small and individual donors (BSDGlobal 2003). This adversely affects in enhancing the share of public contribution in the total funds flow to NGO sector in India.

Many large and urban-based NGOs, after remaining largely dependent on foreign funding for many years, have of late started exploring for local funds. These NGOs had indigenous funds, small and scarce. A conscious attempt to collect funds locally in the recent past has raised the confidence among NGOs about the availability of money in India. While a few NGOs have stopped looking for foreign funds, but many are planning to tap the middle class's growing desire to help a cause. Fund-raisers have realized the enormous potential of the middle class people to support a cause of their choice. Action Aid and their Aman Samuday programme have reported to have received about Rs 30 lakh through its national appeal for the Gujarat riot victims. The NGO collective, Citizen's Initiative (CI) is said to have collected about Rs 4 lakh in individual contributions, some of them as high as Rs 50,000 (David 2002). There are many such examples in different parts of the country.

The notion of charity, globally, has its roots in religious beliefs, while the practice of charity has developed along different lines in the case of Indian, European or American charities. The Christian notion of charity is based on love of fellow men, and on moving from an undesirable state to a better state of being. The Hindu notion is viewed to be inward looking, as spiritual advancement is the goal of Indian giving. The three key words in Bhagavad-Gita are "Yajna" (Sacrifice), "Dana" (Giving) and "Tapah" (Penance), all of which are good for the purification of the individual's soul. While solving problems of poverty could be the USP (unique selling proposition) of Western fund-raisers, Indian fund-raisers seeking individual contribution may talk of worthiness of one's charitable actions for spiritual advancement.

Local funds, particularly public contributions have advantages for an NGO. It allows NGOs to deal with sensitive issues more confidently, as they would be less afraid of being accused of being foreign agents. Besides, public contributions bring in more transparency and accountability as so many people are involved in it (David 2002). This is likely to make the system more humane and receptive. Hence, an NGO makes a choice between large contributions from only a handful of people vs. large number of people making small contributions to it. Nonetheless, the credential of NGOs who approach the Indian charity market is a determining factor in successfully raising money from the public. Involving the public in the cause of NGOs could be an important priority for attaining credibility. Hence, fund-raising from public has both communication and financial objectives.

The overwhelming response of public contribution in times of disasters—man-made or natural – has not found its way for development-related causes. Philanthropy in India has largely remained crisis-based. A lot of money has been generated through public appeal in the name of earthquake, cyclone or tsunami. People are also interested in donating for charity or welfare projects for street children, orphan or the blind, the old and the disabled or issues like opposing cruelty to animals. Such issues evoke sympathy (David 2002). However, there is little awareness on the basic issues of development, such as, dealing with marginalized groups, environmental degradation, infrastructural project affected people and human rights. NGO fund-raisers would like to see the public contributing for development-related causes as well. Although it is easier to raise money for charity, NGOs are increasingly promoting philanthropy and volunteering in development work among the general public. While general public views development projects to be the responsibility of the state, they find it convenient to stay away from controversial projects concerned with commercial sexual workers, bonded labourers, child labourers and dalit and minority issues.

NGOs IN BUSINESS

In the last decade, a number of NGOs, small or large, urban or rural based, began venturing into business as another activity. The basic motive has been two fold: first, to create income earning opportunity for its target groups, and secondly, to generate revenue for the organization. Either way, the business has to be run with a motive for profit so as to be able to pay to the people engaged in it. Unfortunately, most NGO functionaries do not have business perspective and skills to set up and run a business. In the event of their business incompetence, they take shelter under not-for-profit charitable mission of their organization. We need to make a distinction between profiting and profit distributing, within the context of not-for-profit organization. Not-for-profit does not entail not profiting or having surplus over expenditure or input cost, by an NGO. NGOs being not-for-profit entities are not allowed to distribute profit among their promoters, directors, trustees or members. However, profiting or engaging into any business activity can be permitted only if there is a provision for it in the Memorandum of Association or Trust-Deed of an NGO. While the constitution of many NGOs may or may not forbid them from engaging in any commercial activity, the real issue is in the ability and orientation of an NGO to set up and run a profiting venture. NGOs are structured to do social/ community work, and the structure and the ethos within which

NGOs work will create tension between social and business goals. The very idea of business plan, revenue model, business strategy and risk-taking with an eye on profiting appears to be a misnomer to NGOs. Many NGO stakeholders simply do not have the vision and skills to do any kind of business and that's why they have chosen to be in the NGO sector. If pushed into, they would prefer beneficiary business activities like dairying, goat rearing and poultry keeping rather setting up a production unit. While some NGOs like CRY have created separate division with dedicated core staff for its business activities, others (e.g., Kerala Shastra Sahitya Parishad) have even set up separate organizational entity for its business venture and the profit is given to the NGO as its income. There are also NGOs like Paraplegic Foundation and Annapurna Mahila Mandal that have imbibed business with their social activities by involving their beneficiaries in the business process. The experience of varied experiments in structure, process and mission of business activities of NGOs open new areas of learning. In the absence of case writings and their systematic comparative analysis, it would not be appropriate to address the question, whether or not NGOs should be looking at alternate structures for doing business and fund-raising.

Recognizing the need for separating business from social work, business houses that wish to contribute to society, set up a foundation as a not-for-profit body under an appropriate Act for doing social work. While some companies initiate and run corporate social responsibility activities as another business expense/activity, they obtain a distinct approach or method that governs such work. Considering similar structural arrangements even in the case of NGOs engaged in business, as in case of companies running social activities, it appears to make sense to separate one from the other.

In order to earn revenue, some NGOs have also started to offer consultancy services in the core area of their expertise like training, project monitoring and evaluation, household survey and programme development against fees. There are NGOs that are renting out space, farm equipments, vehicles and other productive facilities and earning some income. For example, renting out marriage halls in metros is a major revenue source for many public trusts. In rural areas, some NGOs give on hire tractors, pesticide sprayers, water pumps, etc. NGOs also take ponds/dams and farm land on lease for pisciculture or farming respectively to generate revenue. We know of an NGO which runs a STD booth or a community information centre which earns a steady monthly income for the project.

To ensure internal sources for meeting their overhead or core expenses (like salaries of core staff, rents, etc), many Indian NGOs have set up "Corpus Fund", and are asking their donors to contribute to build up their portfolio. Some Indian donors like Tata Trusts contribute to corpus building of its partner NGOs.

NGOs entering into business for earning revenue has become a debated issue within the sector. Some view that the NGOs getting into business may result in such NGOs gradually abandoning social work altogether. Another view refers to lack of business competency of the NGO functionaries that has brought them to the Sector. Otherwise, they would have been busy earning money. Many do acknowledge that they do not know how to do business. Apathy to business orientation, has even affected NGOs positioning themselves through marketing and public relations. Even if an NGO is not engaged in business, brand building is critical for any NGO to raise funds from any and all sources.

PUBLIC PERCEPTION

The perception of the Indian public about NGOs in general appears to be that of being centres of fraud, self-aggrandizement and destabilization. Most of the funds they get never reach the poor (Prasannan 1996; Upadhyay 2003). Council for Advancement of People's Action and Rural Technology (CAPART), one of the largest sources of government funding for rural development NGOs, is viewed by NGO leaders to be corrupt and charging commissions ranging from 10–40 per cent in return for sanctioning projects. Hence, opportunistic NGOs existing on paper alone crop up with political and bureaucratic patronage to siphon off easy money in the name of rural development, after paying the due unofficial processing charges or commission. In the last nine years, CAPART alone is reported to have sanctioned about Rs 330 crores to about 7,500 NGOs, besides grants to NGOs from other central ministries. Given the budget norms for projects sanctioned by government as such being very tight with little flexibility, a genuine NGO will be incapable of executing a sanctioned project with funding reduced on accounts of reasons mentioned above. Hence, such NGOs collect government fund and do nothing. Only a small number of unlucky NGOs come under the radar to get blacklisted for receiving further money from the same source. CAPART, Central Social Welfare Board, Ministry of Social Justice and Empowerment, among others, have blacklisted a number of NGOs in the last few years (Bhaumik 2003). Such NGO leaders either approach another government source for funding or open a new NGO entity to start operating once again. Hence, public perception is not totally unfounded.

Foreign-funded NGOs are looked down upon with suspicion by different constituents of Indian society for many different reasons (McGann and Johnstone 2006). Home Ministry that monitors foreign-funded NGOs, views them as trouble makers in sensitive areas. Politicians grudge their resources and grassroots influence, as it undermines their hold over the electoral constituency. Media attack on such NGOs centre around some of them pushing their donors' agenda in India.

One point of view is that many of the incompetent or fraudulent NGOs will disappear in the market-led selection for funding. In the age of information revolution, wide access of Internet and public as well as media scrutiny, the donor community is asking for credibility of the NGOs and transparency in their operation. Awareness among the Indian public about issues championed by NGOs is increasingly becoming a determining factor in NGOs' ability to attract donations. General people are slowly getting transformed as informed donors. Hence, the NGO community needs to work hard to improve public perception about the NGO world for getting the necessary funding.

CONCLUSION

In the contemporary funding scenario in India, institutional non-government funding sources (e.g., foreign funding agencies, corporate and Indian funding NGOs) search for innovative projects that can make significant impact in addressing an issue, and for credible NGO partners that have the ability to scale through sustainable approach in the long run. In addition, foreign funding agencies look for prospective implementing NGOs that attempt to influence state policies, laws and programmes rather than being limited to service providing.

Funding trend in India has found another interesting dimension. Funding agencies are recognizing the significance of core strength of the implementing NGO to perform. Besides funding programmes, funds are also being made available to enhance technical competency and managerial ability to ensure better organizational capacity for efficiency in service delivery and long-term impact. Role of intermediary organizations that help in scouting suitable partner NGOs for channelling funds to realize donor's objectives is another dimension in funding trends. Such intermediary organizations may operate either at the instance of a funding agency scouting for an appropriate NGO partner or at the instance of an implementing NGO looking for funding partner or source. The former may be seen as extension of a funding agency, while the latter is more of a consulting firm. While progressive and entrepreneurial funding agencies are looking for new and young NGOs or capable promoters with a viable business plan, the large well established funding agencies prefer to support those that have already developed a strong base over the years.

Social venture capital funding sources, quite a few such agencies having made their presence felt in India in the recent years, fund NGO efforts to accelerate social entrepreneurship, so as to help disadvantaged individuals achieve their full potential. Their focus is largely on issues of skill upgradation, entrepreneurship development, livelihood generation and support development programmes.

Certain funding agencies also adopt new approaches to problem solving through granting initial fellowship to enlightened individuals, followed by grant to set up new organizational entities to carry out the work initiated during fellowship in a more sustained manner. There are also a few foreign funding agencies that do not follow the traditional route to attract proposals from interested organizations. They identify genuine development endeavours on their own and invite proposals from the selected NGOs. Unsolicited proposals are not encouraged.

While the thrust area, the process of funding and the preferred implementing NGO partner may vary across different segment of funding agencies, they all look out for those NGOs that have sustainable objectives, and are capable of creating more social values from limited resources. The area of funding is increasingly getting concentrated on projects that have a long-term vision.

NOTES

1. Rajesh Tandon estimated the financial outlay for the entire voluntary sector (NGOs are a subset) as being Rs 160 billion for the year 1999–2000, by using Ministry of Home Affairs FCRA reports (Rs 40 billion), PRIA surveys on philanthropic giving in India (Rs 80 billion) and other estimates on total government funding to NGOs (Rs 40 billion). Direct funding and support received through bilateral and multilateral donors is left out of this calculation (*Planning Commission, Proceedings*, 2004: 40–41) (seen in Kudva, 2005).

REFERENCES

Agg, C. (2006), "Trends in Government Support for Non-Governmental Organizations: Is the Golden Age of the NGO Behind Us?" *Civil Society and Social Movements Program Paper Number 23,* United Nations Research Institute for Social Development: Geneva.

Bhaumik, S. (2003), "India Blacklists 800 NGOs", *BBC,* June 18, www.globalpolicy.org/ngos/state/2003/0619india.htm.

Biswas, N. (2006), "On Funding and the NGO Sector", *Economic and Political Weekly,* October 21.

BSDGlobal (2003), *Working with NGOS: Funding Issues,* May 6, www.globalpolicy.org/ngos/fund/2003/0506issues.htm.

David, R. (2002), "NGOs Go Swadeshi With Fund-Raising", *Economic Times, India,* July 10, www.globalpolicy.org/ngos/role/globdem/funding/2002/0710india.htm.

Desai, V.(1999), "Anatomy of the Bombay NGO Sector", *Environment and Urbanization,* Vol. 11, No. 1, April, 247–266.

Farouk, F. (2002), "A Global Dilemma for NGOs", *Mail and Guardian,* May 3, www.globalpolicy.org/ngos/fund/2003/0502dilemma.htm.

Karat, P.(1985), "Action Groups/ Voluntary Organizations: A Factor in Imperialist Strategy", *The Marxist,* New Delhi.

Karat, P. (1988), "Foreign Funding and the Philosophy of Voluntary Organizations", *The Marxist,* New Delhi.

Kudva, N. (2005), "Uneasy Relations: NGOs and the State in Karnataka, India", Cornell University, Paper Presented at the Karnataka Conference, ISEC/Cornell University/The World Bank, Bangalore, June 10–12.

MHA (2005), *Receipt of Foreign Contribution By Voluntary Associations: FCRA Annual Report 2004–2005,* Ministry of Home Affairs, Foreigners' Division, FCRA Wing, New Delhi, http://mha.nic.in.

McGann, J. and Johnstone, M. (2006), "The Power Shift and the NGO Credibility Crisis", *The International Journal of Not-for-Profit Law,* Volume 8, Issue 2, January, http://www.icnl.org/knowledge/ijnl/vol8iss2/art_4.htm.

Patnaik, P. (2003), "Agrarian Crisis and Distress in Rural India", *People's Democracy,* May 12, www.rupe-india.org/35/wsfmumbail.html.

Prashad, V. (2004), *Politics at the Venue: The WSF in Mumbai,* ZNet, January 11, www.globalpolicy.org/ngos/advocacy/conf/2004/0111venue.htm.

Prasannan, R (1996), *The Week,* Sept. 15, page 31.

PRIA (1991), *Voluntary Development Organizations in India: A Study of History, Roles and Future Challenges,* Society for Participatory Research in Asia (PRIA): New Delhi.

Robinson, M. (1991), *Evaluating the Impact of NGOs in Rural Poverty Alleviation: India Country Study, Working Paper No. 49,* Overseas Development Institute, London (seen in Desai, 1999).

Stiglitz, J.E. (2002), *Globalization and its Discontents*, p. 99, www.rupe-india.org/35/globalisation.html.

Upadhyay, A. (2003), *NGOs: Do the Watchdogs Need Watching?* Inter Press Service, 13 June.

VANI (1994), *Report of the Task-Force to Review and Simplify Acts, Rules, Procedures Affecting Voluntary Organizations*, Voluntary Action Network India: New Delhi.

Vanita, V. (1994), *The Bank's Cooperation with NGOs: A Background Paper*, Asian Development Bank, December.

Vohra, G. (1990), *Altering Structures: Innovative Experiments at the Grassroots*, Tata Institute of Social Sciences: Bombay.

WSF (2004), "The World Social Forum and the Struggle against Globalization", *II WSF Mumbai 2004 and the NGO Phenomenon in India*, www.rupe-india.org/35/wsfmumbai.html

Chapter 13

Nature of Job Satisfaction in NGOs

Asok Kumar Sarkar

JOB satisfaction is the expression of an employee's evaluation of his or her work life. It is basically an attitude which results from a balancing and summation of many specific likes and dislikes experienced in connection with one's job. The debates and discussions pertaining to job satisfaction in NGOs are very sensitive issues today. Whether NGOs are located in urban or rural or tribal area, whether they remain operating on welfare models of service delivery or act as dynamic grassroots organizations with policy advocacy, staff members are unhappy due to either exploitative nature of the management or leaving very little scope for self-improvement. This is the underlying cause of high staff mobility in NGOs.

NGOs are preferred by the government or international funding agencies because of their special characteristics like small size, more participatory approach, less bureaucratic functioning, more flexibility, cost effectiveness, etc. On the other hand, they are criticized and termed as contractors in development business. NGOs are blamed for their unethical activities, i.e., they change priorities of work every year as per the availability of funds. It is also heard that staff members in NGOs are discontented because of inherent contradictions as well as conflicts; lack of health care benefits and provident fund; absence of job security and career advancement scheme; incidents of corruption, exploitation, and sexual harassment; poor salary and long working hours; etc. In fact, when and where staff members are satisfied, they can contribute positively by meticulous work and respond immediately to the people's needs. In such cases, staff mobility decreases and overall productivity of the organization is augmented.

REVIEW OF LITERATURE

The term 'job satisfaction' came into vogue in 1935 when Hoppock published his classic work, *Satisfaction at Work* (Ganguli 1993). In order to understand the process by which job satisfaction of an individual is determined, five distinguished theories have been developed. These are: comparison theory, instrumentality theory, social influence theory, equity theory and two-factor theory. All these theories are not exclusive of each other but overlapping. Operationally, their validity and applicability depend on the career options of the staff, and other internal as well external factors of the organizations. The present study has been carried out within the framework of instrumentality theory. Because, it directly highlights how much benefit staff members get from the job. The basic assumption of instrumentality theory is that individuals assess their satisfaction with jobs by considering the extent to which the jobs lead to valued outcomes (i.e., pay, promotion, good working conditions, etc.).

Over the years, several studies on job satisfaction have been conducted. Ganguli (1957) administered a multidimensional attitude questionnaire and employed the method of analysis to study the scores of a group of satisfied and dissatisfied workers. The results indicated the existence of three morale dimensions including workers' satisfaction with the total organization and the benefits derived from it and two morale dimensions, relating to satisfaction with supervision. Sinha (1958) took research initiative to explore job satisfaction among office staff and manual workers and analysed the causative impacts on satisfaction and dissatisfaction. 'Interesting work', 'social status' and 'boss' were found to be crucial factors contributing to satisfaction whereas, inadequate salary and lack of job security were regarded as important factors causing dissatisfaction. Clerical employees were found to be lower in the satisfaction. Veeraraghavan (1960) made a study to understand the satisfaction and discontent levels among workers in three units of the transport industry, belonging to both public and private sectors. In general, the private sector workers had greater satisfaction and favourably inclined towards the management. Closer personal contact and greater interest by the management were the major causes for this. Sinha and Singh (1961) and Sinha (1965) had shown in their work the significance of job satisfaction in determining absenteeism. They found, there was a significant tendency for low-absentee workers to be more satisfied. Ganguli (1964) completed another study to find out answer of the question "what percentage of Indian employees can be considered as satisfied with their jobs?" The analysis indicated that in engineering industries in India, nearly five per cent of employees were highly dissatisfied with their total job situation, twenty nine per cent dissatisfied, nineteen per cent satisfied, three per cent highly satisfied and the remaining forty four per cent of employees were neither satisfied nor dissatisfied. Sinha and Nair (1965) studied the relationship between job satisfaction as well as different personal background factors and attempted to examine its effect on worker behaviour vis-à-vis attendance, productivity and general adjustment. The study set out that the skilled workers were found to be significantly more satisfied. Workers who had joined the organization recently or had put in long years of service were more satisfied than those whose tenures were of medium duration. Although the result was not statistically significant, the middle income group appeared to be the least satisfied. Satisfaction was also closely related to higher productivity, punctuality in attendance and better adjustment of workers as visualized by their supervisors. Desai (2004) analysed in her paper that management had specific role to inculcate job satisfaction among NGO staff. Management needs to consider boarder recruiting criteria that include personal aspects in addition to conventional ones, e.g., sensitivity and understanding others from their perspective; ability to listen and learn, experience, trust, honesty, etc. which are very difficult to assess in an individual. When recruiting from outside, NGOs should not have high expectations, but should develop the person's effectiveness by letting the him have long term contracts, and employ staff in such a way that they do not suffer from problems that arise from the employment terms. Desai feels, if these aspects are taken care of, accountability, sustainable outlook and working satisfaction of NGO staff will occur automatically.

RATIONALE OF THE STUDY

Having reviewed the above studies, we draw a few inferences such as job satisfaction reduces absenteeism, working attitude is positively associated with efficiency, increase in satisfaction is related to increase in occupational level, management bears responsibility to inculcate job satisfaction, etc. It is found that so far no study has been initiated to develop the mechanism for measuring the level of job satisfaction of NGO staff or to understand upto what extent they are satisfied in the context when NGOs are considered as one of the important development agents. Hence, the present study would explore the process of measurement and nature of job satisfaction of NGO staff. The study will be useful in understanding the degree of satisfaction of staff, and can suggest the means to improve satisfaction for sustenance as well as high productivity of the organization.

OBJECTIVES

The specific objectives of the study are as follows:

1. To develop a standardized scale in order to measure job satisfaction of NGO staff;
2. To understand the nature of job satisfaction of different types of staff members of NGOs under the study;
3. To verify whether there is any association between nature of job satisfaction and nature of staff in NGOs under study.

METHODOLOGY

There is paucity of data in the research area. It was necessary to explore different aspects and establish facts related to job satisfaction. The present researcher had to do literature review and case studies of some NGOs. Thus, the present study used exploratory design.

In order to fulfill objectives of the study, data were collected namely from the primary sources, i.e., NGOs. In this regard, two separate tools such as Information Proforma for NGOs and Job Satisfaction Scale for full-time paid staff were constructed. Information Proforma was necessary to understand the background of the NGO (i.e., history, name, address, objectives, operational area, organizational structure, programmes, staffing pattern, financial aspect, etc.). Job satisfaction scale helped to find out the degree of satisfaction of the NGO staff. Details of the construction procedure of this scale is mentioned are the next part.

The present study was conducted to understand the job satisfaction of staff members of NGOs of West Bengal. The main reason for selecting West Bengal was its unique socio-political background, which was unlike other states. West Bengal had a history of series of movements, such as, freedom movement, movement against social evils, *tebhaga* movement, Naxalite movement, land reform of the Left Front Government, environmental movement, women's movement, etc. These movements led to from a large number of NGOs. At the time of study, there were over 100,000 registered NGOs in West Bengal (as per information of Society Registration Office, in the year 2000). Since, now-a-days NGOs work in the specialized area, i.e. education, health, income generation, environment, etc., the present study considered only health care NGOs. According to many experts, nearly seven per cent of the total NGOs (i.e., around 7,000 NGOs) carry out health care programmes in West Bengal. Thus, 7,000 NGOs were the universe of the present discourse.

The present work focused on case study. In this connection, six NGOs were chosen purposively (purposive sampling) based on the following criteria: (a) NGO may be in urban or semi-urban or rural area but should locate within the territory of West Bengal; (b) only two NGOs should be selected from one division (West Bengal is divided into three administrative divisions, i.e. Presidency division, Burdwan division & Jalpaiguri division); (c) NGO must be registered, non-profit and welfare organization; (d) NGO should have at least thirty full-time paid staff and with yearly turnover of Rs 5,000,000; and (e) NGO must be having at least one full-fledged health programme which has specific project proposal, budget allocation and full-time paid employees. For administering job satisfaction scale, thirty staff members were selected purposively (purposive sampling) from each NGO. Efforts were made to include all types of staff (lower level, middle level and higher level) as per their availability, age, sex, marital status, educational qualification, etc.

CONSTRUCTION OF JOB SATISFACTION SCALE

In order to develop a standardized scale, the researcher had to work very extensively. It was found that a few job satisfaction scales were available in literature for the employees of private industries, autonomous organizations, government agencies, etc., but there was no scale for the staff of NGOs. Hence, this scale was constructed. It followed Likert's method. At the very outset, five dimensions (from where satisfaction came) were identified. Those were: (a) facilities available at the job, (b) relationship with the boss, (c) physical condition of working place, (d) career and self-improvement scheme, and (e) job security. A hundred statements were framed and gathered with the help of experts and relevant readings giving emphasis to all the five dimensions mentioned above. The draft comprising of hundred statements was sent to a few experts for cross verification of the items. After verification, eighty statements were retained. The researcher revised the draft several times and at last the list contained seventy items, both favourable and unfavourable equal in number, under all the five dimensions. All the seventy statements were shuffled, systematically arranged and finally the draft scale was developed. The scores of the favourable items were decided as 5,4,3,2,1 for the responses Strongly Agree (SA), Agree (A), Undecided (U), Disagree (D), and Strongly Disagree (SD) respectively. The scores were reversed (i.e. 1,2,3,4,5) for the unfavourable items. Table 13.1 shows the scoring key at a glance:

Table 13.1: Scoring Key for Job Satisfaction Scale

Degree of choice	*Scores for items*	
	Favourable	*Unfavourable*
SA	5	1
A	4	2
U	3	3
D	2	4
SD	1	5

This five-point job satisfaction scale with seventy items was tried out on a group of 54 employees of Seva Sangha (located at South 24 Parganas district). Having collected 54 filled-in scales from the respondents, scoring was made. The filled-in scales were arranged in the ascending order on the basis of total scores obtained by the respondents. Then, one-third scales from the top as well as one-third scales from the bottom were taken, and middle one third were put aside. Thus, two scoring groups, i.e., higher and lower scoring groups were formed. Then each item was taken and calculated to find out discriminating value (D), using the percentages of correct and incorrect responses of both the groups, with the help of following formula:

$$D = \frac{P_1 - P_2}{\frac{P_1Q_1}{N_1} + \frac{P_2Q_2}{N_2}}$$

Where P_1 and P_2 were percentages of staff respectively in higher and lower scoring groups who solved the item correctly; and Q_1 and Q_2 were percentages of respondents who solved the item incorrectly. N_1 and N_2 were number of staff members in higher and lower scoring groups respectively. In this regard, the researcher made it clear that 'correct' answer meant reply to the positive or favourable item as 'Strongly Agree', and getting five marks against such response. Similarly, a reply to a negative, or unfavourable item as 'Strongly Disagree' was considered as 'correct' answer and five marks were awarded to such response. Thus, the researcher gave the award of five marks against each correct answer irrespective of upper and lower group.

It is known to us (Asthana and Agarwal 1995), if the value of D is 1.96 or more, then the item is discriminating. Having calculated D value of all the 70 items, through above formula, best 38 items were selected whose discriminating values were more than four. These 38 items were mixed up irrespective of their specific dimensions, arranged logically and given the shape of final job satisfaction scale. The dimension-wise distribution of the items in the final scale was (Table 13.2) as follows:

Table 13.2: Dimension-wise Distribution of the Items

Dimension	*Nature of statement*	*Serial number of the statement*
Facilities available at the job	Positive (+)	20,21,24,30,32,36,38
Relationship with the boss	Negative (–)	2,14,19,34
	Positive (+)	4,8,9,15
Physical condition of working place	Negative (–)	25,31
	Positive (+)	5,26,37
Career and self-improvement scheme	Negative (–)	11,12,16,27
	Positive (+)	1,6,10,17,22
Job security	Negative (–)	28,33,35
	Negative (–)	3,7,13,18,23,29

In order to determine the reliability co-efficient of this tool, split half method (Rulon) was used. The final job satisfaction scale comprising of thirty-eight items was administered once again among the thirty staff members of Seva Sangha (located at South 24-Parganas). Researcher divided the scale into two equal halves by separating the odd and even items. Each haives contained nineteen items. The scores for both the halves were given separately. Each respondent had a score on first half and a score on second half. Having used these scores, reliability co-efficient was calculated by applying Rulon's formula. The process of calculation was (Table 13.3) as follows:

r_{tt} =Reliability coefficient of the whole test
$\sigma^2 d$=Variance of D= 45.0298
$\sigma^2 t$=Variance of total score =235.0989

$$r_{tt} = 1 - \frac{\sigma^2 d}{\sigma^2 t}$$

$$= 1 - \frac{45.0298}{235.0989}$$

$$= 1- 0.1915 = 0.8085 = 0.81$$

Thus, it was proved that the job satisfaction scale was reliable.

With regard to validity of this scale, content validity as well as face validity was ensured. The researcher took care of it while he selected the statements by undergoing statistical technique and experts's opinion. A copy of the standardized job satisfaction scale has been enclosed in Annexure I.

Table 13.3: Score Distribution of the Two Halves

Sl no. of the respondent	*Score of first half* (A)	*Score of second half* (B)	*Difference [D=A-B]* (D)	*Total Score*
1	70	70	0	140
2	70	64	6	134
3	59	53	6	112
4	66	75	-9	141
5	66	62	4	128
6	83	75	8	158
7	59	57	2	116
8	69	71	-2	140
9	68	72	-4	140
10	59	59	0	118
11	50	62	-12	112
12	65	70	-5	135
13	78	81	-3	159
14	78	80	-2	158
15	76	83	-7	159
16	63	67	-4	130
17	46	55	-9	101
18	53	66	-13	119
19	67	69	-2	136
20	51	66	-15	117
21	51	64	-13	115

Cont'd

Cont'd

22	57	68	-11	125
23	70	72	-2	142
24	74	66	8	140
25	74	66	8	140
26	58	58	0	116
27	60	59	1	119
28	63	69	-6	132
29	65	76	-11	141
30	64	65	-1	129

At last, it is necessary to mention that, in order to understand satisfaction of a staff, score was obtained through standardized scale and the following rules (Table 13.4) were applied to find out the level of satisfaction.

Table 13.4: Rules to Identify Levels of Satisfaction

Level of Satisfaction Dimensions	*Very low satisfaction (score)*	*Low satisfaction (score)*	*Moderate satisfaction (score)*	*High satisfaction (score)*
Dimension- 1	11–21	22–32	33–43	44 and above
Dimension- 2	6–11	12–17	18–23	24 and above
Dimension- 3	7–13	14–20	21–27	28 and above
Dimension- 4	8–15	16–23	24–31	32 and above
Dimension- 5	6–11	12–17	18–23	24 and above
Total Score	38–75	76–113	114–151	152 and above

JOB SATISFACTION OF THE WORKING STAFF

Profile of Staff Members

Table 13.5 illuminates the profile of 180 staff members who work in six NGOs (under the study) of West Bengal. The profile includes various characteristics such as sex, age, marital status, levels of staff, qualification and salary.

With regard to sex, it is found that numbers of males are more as compared to females respectively in the NGOs of Jalpaiguri division (53.4 per cent) and Presidency division (80 per cent). In the NGOs of Burdwan division, more than half of the workers (53.4 per cent) are female. Including all the NGOs, there are total 60 per cent male and forty per cent female. Table 13.5 also gives an account of age of the staff members. None of the NGOs is

Table 13.5: Profile of NGO's Staff

Organization / *Profile of staff*	*Two NGOs of Jalpaiguri Division*	*Two NGOs of Burdwan Division*	*Two NGOs of Presidency Division*	*Total*
Sex				
Male	32 (53.4)	28 (46.6)	48 (80)	108 (60)
Female	28 (46.6)	32 (53.4)	12 (20)	72 (40)
Total	60 (100)	60 (100)	60 (100)	180 (100)
Age				
21 to 30 yrs	28 (46.7)	4 (6.7)	32 (53.4)	64 (35.6)
31 to 40 yrs	26 (43.3)	16 (26.7)	18 (30)	60 (33.3)
41 yrs & Above	6 (10)	40 (66.6)	10 (16.6)	56 (31.1)
Total	60 (100)	60 (100)	60 (100)	180 (100)
Marital status				
Unmarried	16 (26.7)	6 (10.0)	24 (40)	46 (25.6)
Married	44 (73.3)	52 (86.7)	36 (60)	132 (73.3)
Widow	0 (0.0)	2 (3.3)	0 (0.0)	2 (1.1)
Total	60 (100)	60 (100)	60 (100)	180 (100)
Levels of staff				
Lower level	26 (43.3)	24 (40)	30 (50)	80 (44.4)
Middle level	24 (40)	24 (40)	20 (33.3)	68 (37.8)
Higher Level	10 (16.7)	12 (20)	10 (16.7)	32 (17.8)
Total	60 (100)	60 (100)	60 (100)	180 (100)
Qualification				
V to VII	Nil	8 (13.3)	Nil	8(4.4)
VIII to X	34 (56.7)	24 (40)	12 (20)	70 (38.9)
XI to XII	6 (10.0)	10 (16.7)	10 (16.7)	26 (14.4)
Bachelor Degree	14 (23.3)	14 (23.3)	36 (60)	64 (35.6)

Cont'd

Cont'd

Master Degree	6 (10.0)	4 (6.7)	2 (3.3)	12 (6.7)
Total	60 (100)	60 (100)	60 (100)	180 (100)
Salary				
Upto Rs 1000	6 (10)	20 (33.3)	Nil	26 (14.4)
Rs 1001 to Rs 2500	40 (66.6)	10 (16.7)	34 (56.7)	84 (46.7)
Rs 2501 to Rs 4000	10 (16.7)	14 (23.3)	12 (20)	36 (20)
Above Rs 4000	Nil	16 (26.7)	8 (13.3)	24 (13.3)
Reluctant to Disclose	4 (6.7)	Nil	6 (10)	10 (5.6)
Total	60 (100)	60 (100)	60 (100)	180 (100)

Note: Figures in parentheses denote the percentages.

having staff who are below 21 years. In the NGOs of Jalpaiguri division and Presidency division respectively, 46.7 per cent and 53.4 per cent of the staff members (i.e., maximum in each division) have age between 21 to 30 years. In the NGOs of Burdwan division, most of the workers (66.6 per cent) are 41 years and above. On the whole, out of 180 staff members, maximum belong to '21-30' category. We come across from the same Table that in the NGOs of every division, most of the staff members are married. Percentage of unmarried workers is less and only two widows have been found in the entire study. As far as level of staff is concerned, members who were having capacity to take decision and control activities at the higher level were considered as higher level staff such as president, secretary, programme co-ordinator, project incharge, etc. Supervisory level staff, accountant, warden, teacher, case worker, etc. were treated as middle level staff and bottom level staff like LDC, peon, driver, field workers, security personnel, etc. were taken into consideration as lower level staff. In every division, between 40 to 50 per cent staff are lower level workers, between 33 to 40 per cent are middle level staff and 16 to 20 per cent are higher level staff. The profile also highlights the qualification of staff members. Out of 180 staff members, 57.7 per cent have less educational qualification, i.e., upto XII. Regarding salary, it is understood that in the NGOs of Jalpaiguri division and Presidency division respectively 76.6 per cent and 56.7 per cent staff members get salary upto Rs 2,500 per month. It is very less according to cost of living. Only in the NGOs of Burdwan division, 50 per cent of the workers get salary above Rs 2,500 per month. It has also been noticed that 6.7 per cent and 10 per cent workers respectively in the NGOs of Jalpaiguri division and Presidency division were reluctant to disclose their monthly remuneration.

Job Satisfaction of Staff Members

Table 13.6 points out 180 staff members' levels of job satisfaction in different dimensions such as facilities at the job, relationship with the boss, physical condition of working place, career and self-improvement scheme, and job security. It is observed from the same table, in case of every dimension, in the NGOs of every division, most of the staff are moderately satisfied, and only a few have low level satisfaction or high level satisfaction. At the end, Table 13.6 has also shown, how is the overall satisfaction (including all the five dimensions) of 180 staff members. It is

Table 13.6: Job Satisfaction

Organizations Satisfaction (As per the dimension)	*No. of staff of 2 NGOs of Jalpaiguri division*	*No. of staff of 2 NGOs of Burdwan division*	*No. of staff of 2 NGOs of Presidency division*	*Total no. of staff*
Dimension 1: Facilities at the job:				
Very low satisfaction	2 (3.3)	–	–	2 (1.11)
Low satisfaction	26 (43.3)	14 (23.3)	16 (26.7)	56 (31.12)
Moderate satisfaction	32 (53.3)	46 (76.7)	42 (70)	120 (66.66)
High satisfaction	–	–	2 (3.3)	2 (1.11)
Total	60 (100)	60 (100)	60 (100)	180 (100)
Dimension 2: Relationship with the boss:				
Very low satisfaction	–	–	–	–
Low satisfaction	2 (3.3)	2 (3.3)	4 (6.7)	8 (4.44)
Moderate satisfaction	44 (73.3)	42 (70)	30 (50)	116 (64.44)
High satisfaction	14 (23.3)	16 (26.7)	26 (43.3)	56 (31.12)
Total	60(100)	60 (100)	60 (100)	180 (100)
Dimension 3: Physical condition of working place:				
Very low satisfaction	–	–	2 (3.3)	2 (1.11)
Low satisfaction	6 (10)	6 (10)	4 (6.7)	16 (8.89)
Moderate satisfaction	32 (53.3)	30 (50)	28 (46.7)	90 (50)
High satisfaction	22 (36.7)	24 (40)	26 (43.3)	72 (40)
Total	60(100)	60 (100)	60 (100)	180 (100)
Dimension 4: Career and Self improvement scheme:				
Very low satisfaction	–	–	–	–
Low satisfaction	2 (3.3)	4 (6.7)	12 (20)	18 (10)
Moderate satisfaction	48 (80)	40 (66.7)	30 (50)	118 (65.6)

Cont'd

Cont'd

High satisfaction	10 (16.7)	16 (26.7)	18 (30)	44 (24.4)
Total	60 (100)	60 (100)	60 (100)	180 (100)
Dimension 5: Job security:				
Very low satisfaction	–	4 (6.7)	2 (3.3)	6 (3.33)
Low satisfaction	14 (23.3)	18 (30)	18 (30)	50 (27.78)
Moderate satisfaction	46 (76.7)	28 (46.7)	32 (53.3)	106 (58.89)
High satisfaction	–	10 (16.7)	8 (13.3)	18 (10)
Total	60 (100)	60 (100)	60 (100)	180 (100)
Overall satisfaction:				
Very low satisfaction	–	–	–	–
Low satisfaction	8 (13.3)	2 (3.3)	6 (10)	16 (8.89)
Moderate satisfaction	52 (86.7)	54 (90)	46 (76.7)	152 (84.44)
High satisfaction	–	4 (6.7)	8 (13.3)	12 (6.67)
Total	60 (100)	60 (100)	60 (100)	180 (100)

Note: Figures in parentheses denote the percentages.

Table 13.7: Association of Levels (Nature) of Satisfaction with Characteristics (Nature) of Staff

Sl. No.	*Characteristics of staff*	*Total sample (n)*	*Degree of freedom (df)*	*Chi-square (c^2) value calculated*	*Table value (at 0.05 level)*	*Significant linkage*
1	Sex	180	2	5.28	5.991	does not exist
2	Age	180	4	3.5	9.488	does not exist
3	Marital status	180	4	.97	9.488	does not exist
4	Levels of staff	180	4	7.64	9.488	does not exist
5	Qualification	180	8	8.54	15.507	does not exist
6	Salary	180	8	20.8	15.507 20.090*	does exist

* Significant at 0.01 level

evident that 13.3 per cent and 86.7 per cent staff members respectively have low as well as moderate satisfaction in the NGOs of Jalpaiguri division; 3.3 per cent, 90 per cent and 6.7 per cent staff members respectively have low, moderate and high satisfaction in the NGOs of Burdwan division; and 10 per cent, 76.7 per cent and 13.3 per cent of the staff are respectively lowly, moderately and highly satisfied. Including all the NGOs, it is generalized that majority of the staff (84.44 per cent) are moderately satisfied and a few are having low 8.89 per cent as well as high (6.67 per cent) satisfaction.

ASSOCIATION BETWEEN NATURE OF STAFF AND NATURE OF JOB SATISFACTION

'Nature' refers to essence, character, composition, sort, tendency, affections, etc. In the present context, 'nature of staff' indicates six characteristics of the working personnel such as sex (male and female), age (21 to 30 years, 31 to 40 years, 41 years and above), marital status (unmarried, married and widow), levels of staff (lower level, middle level and higher level), qualification (V to VII, VIII to X, XI to XII, Bachelor's degree, Master's degree) and salary (upto Rs 1,000, Rs 1,001 to Rs 2,500, Rs 2,501 to Rs 4,000, above Rs 4,000) to understand them well. 'Nature of job satisfaction' points out whether somebody has low or moderate or high level satisfaction. In the following discussion, efforts are made to know whether any significant association exists between characteristics of staff and levels of satisfaction.

It is understood from the Table 13.7 that, in the respective degree of freedom, the calculated value of chi-square for sex (5.28) or age (3.5) or marital status (0.97) or levels of staff (7.64) or qualification (8.54) is less than the tabulated value at 0.05 level of significance. Hence, there is no significant linkage between sex and job satisfaction or age and job satisfaction or levels of staff and job satisfaction or qualification and job satisfaction. Only the obtained chi-square value for salary (20.8) reveals that linkage exists between salary as well as job satisfaction and the same is significant at 0.01 level. It proves, if salary structure fluctuates, levels of satisfaction do so as well. In another way, we can say, level of satisfaction of staff in NGOs under study can be improved by enhancing salary scale.

CONCLUSION

The present study shows, most of the staff members (84.44 per cent) are moderately satisfied with their job. The main reason is that the terms and conditions of the job and salary structure of the staff of NGOs under study are almost same as in public sector. NGOs too provide many facilities as government institutions do to the staff members. It is also found that the linkage between salary and level of job satisfaction is statistically significant and salary is a vital part. Staff mobility mainly occurs in NGOs due to low remuneration. This kind of trend proves that staff disquiets or changeableness or staff related grievances would no longer be a problem with NGOs if salary structure is designed properly. NGOs can contribute well if they take care of their pay structure.

REFERENCES

Asthana, B. and Agarwal, R.N. (1995), *Measurement and Evaluation in Psychology and Education,* Vinod Pustak Mandir, Agra.

Desai, V. (2004), "Emerging Staffing Issues in Grassroots Urban NGOs: The Case of Mumbai", *GBER,* Vol. 3, No. 1, p. 26–36.

Ganguli, H.C. (1994), *Job Satisfaction Scales for Effective Management-Manual for Managers and Social Scientists,* Concept Publishing Company, New Delhi.

Ganguli, H.C. (1964), *Structure and Process of Organization,* Asia Publishing House, Mumbai.

Ganguli, H.C. (1957), "Isolation of Some Morale Dimensions by Factor Analysis", *Sankhya,* Vol. 17, No. 1, p. 393–400.

Sinha, D. (1965), "Absenteeism and Job Satisfaction", Report on Seminar on Industrial Relations in Developing Economy, Sri Ram Centre for Industrial Relations, New Delhi.

Sinha, D. and Nair, R.R. (1965), "A Study of Job Satisfaction in Factory Workers", *The Indian Journal of Social Work,* Vol. 26, No. 1, pp. 1–8.

Sinha, D. and Singh, P. (1961), "Job Satisfaction and Absenteeism", *The Indian Journal of Social Work,* Vol. 21, No. 3, p. 337–343.

Sinha, D. (1958), "Job Satisfaction in the Office and Manual Workers", *The Indian Journal of Social Work,* Vol. 19, No. 1, p. 39–46.

Veeraraghavan, P.V. (1960), "Employee Attitude", Proceedings of the Second Conference on Human Relations in Industry, SITRA, Coimbatore.

Annexure - I
JOB SATISFACTION SCALE

Staff Identity

Serial No: .... Name of the Organization: ....

Name of the Staff .... Age .... Sex ....

Marital Status .... Educational Qualification ....

Experience .... Designation .... Nature of Work ....

Sl. No	*Statements*	*Response Category*				
		Strongly Disagree	*Disagree*	*Undecided*	*Agree*	*Strongly Agree*
		(1)	*(2)*	*(3)*	*(4)*	*(5)*
1.	My present job is as per my ability/qualification and experience.					
2.	Comparing the salary for a similar job in other organizations (NGOs) I feel my pay is better.					
3.	Taking up this job does not involve risks as it guarantees fair amount of security.					
4.	My supervisor keeps me informed about all policies or happenings of the organization.					
5.	My colleagues like me and give due respect at the working place.					
6.	My job has helped me to learn some new skills.					
7.	I often feel that my employer will not terminate me if I commit a mistake.					
8.	My supervisor increases team spirit in the work group.					
9.	My supervisor behaves properly (have cordial relation) with me.					

10. This job (of NGOs) helps for my professional growth.
11. We often face problems because there is crowding in our room (we are too many people in our room).
12. Physical condition of my room (such as lack of furniture or fan or sufficient light, etc.) gives maximum trouble to work during summer season.
13. If for certain specific reason I do not reach at my working place on time, I do not get threat to leave this work.
14. I have often felt that at our organization we have inappropriate leave rules.
15. My supervisor takes into account my wishes as well as work done.
16. Physical condition of my room leads to health problems during monsoon as it becomes damp or moist.
17. This organization has career advancement scheme. Whenever there is possibility, it sends us for further education and training.
18. I am really not interested to this job but circumstances force me to continue with it.
19. There is no facility related to social security provision or provident fund or gratuity or pension etc. in my job.
20. My organization provides good housing facilities to its employees.
21. I am satisfied with the medical facilities (for staff) provided by the organization.
22. On the whole, I have good prospects for advancement in my job.
23. If I get similar job with good pay in any other organization, I would like to quit this job.
24. Hard work as well as better performance is appreciated in my organization, which I like most.
25. The activities of my supervisor are governed by self-interest.

26. My co-worker does not create any tension or conflict talking too much on working problems (of this organization). He helps me in my work to reduce tension or conflict.
27. I often find myself disadvantaged at my working place due tolack of technical information.
28. My job (of this NGO) does not help to increase prestige or social recognition.
29. I am not interested to continue this job, as I usually feel tired at the end of the day's work.
30. Promotions are made as per qualifications and experiences in this organization. I have been getting it.
31. When my 'Boss' throws his temper at me I feel like protesting it to set him right.
32. Drinking water facilities are satisfactory and usually provided at work place.
33. My job does not provide opportunity for independent thought and use of my talents.
34. Recreational facilities are negligible in my organization.
35. My all the abilities are not utilized fully in my present job.
36. Canteen or kitchen facilities are well at working hours in this organization.
37. I seldom watch the clock when I am at office as time passes smoothly.
38. Childcare facilities (like Day Care Centre or Crèche) are very good in our organization to provide support to the working mothers (employees of this organization).

Chapter 14

Appraising Employees in NGOs: A New Trend of Performance Management in Social Sector

P.K. Ghosh

PERFORMANCE appraisal method came into being as a 'formal appraisal of individual performance' in the Wei dynasty (A.D. 221–265) in China, where an Imperial Rater appraised the performance of members of the official family. In industrial setting, Robert Owen's use of character book and block in his New Lanark Cotton Mills in Scotland around 1800 was the first recorded appraisal system. The character book recorded each worker's daily reports. The character blocks were coloured differently on each side to represent an evaluation of workers ranging from bad to good and they were displayed at each employee's workplace. Owen was quite impressed by the way the blocks improved workers's behaviour. Shortly before the World War I, the New York City Civil Service in the USA introduced formal appraisal programme. This exercise on performance appraisal slowly got into the industrial practices in the USA, European and other countries of the world, as it helped the organizations to develop the human resources who were the key to successful business and service enterprises. The evaluations of the performance of the army were an essential practice in the United States and it yielded a good result for the army men too to find the inadequacies and meet them by training and retraining. Following industrial revolution the need for training of the workforce for keeping the industrial enterprises updated and maintaining link with the development of technology and the market was keenly felt. The employers felt the need to make an assessment of the human potentials among the most important resources, i.e., human resources.

A couple of decades ago, the performance appraisal system emphasized employees' traits, deficiencies, and abilities. Of late, the modern philosophy of performance appraisal stresses employee participation in mutually setting goals with respective supervisors and heads of the section. The intention behind mutual goal setting is that the employees will work hard as they have participated in setting the goal to achieve within the stipulated timeframe. The system calls for the employee orientation to performance appraisal both for the appraiser and the appraised.

The voluntary organizations did not feel the need to have such practices except a few national and international organizations working for social development in myriad ways and means to reduce the cause of human suffering by making both short term and long-term arrangements. Civil Society Organizations (CSOs) believe that motivation to work is an innate quality; hence a driving force to work is emerging from and within the individuals. Performance of such workers is always is very good, so need not be monitored or evaluated. The persons joining such organizations are motivated and committed to help and assist people wherever and whenever needed. On the contrary, in modern complex society when development is to be managed with limited resources on a professional basis, the need for training of personnel in human service profession is felt. The universities and institutes in training and developing manpower could not meet the requirements of full-fledged professionals and need nurturing and monitoring. The actual problem lies in lower values and attitudes of the people working in CSOs, VOs and NGOs today, which have their roots in the social environment.

Douglas McGregor's theory X that describes basic nature of human being is to avoid work, hence needs to be driven, monitored and evaluated, seems to match with the modern context, theory Y, which advocates that the natural motivation of work-loving people is to seek opportunity to perform and excel if opportunities are provided. The employers of organizations need to recruit professionals for managing the projects efficiently, reducing the cost, and seeking the return on investment in terms of tangible and intangible services rendered towards the achievement of the goal. The project will be audited to make justifications for the development that has taken place in relation to the cost involved in it. At the moment, all state and national level organizations have some form of performance appraisal practice as a policy, probably to make employees accountable to the people and the organizations. The scientific system of monitoring and evaluation of performance of employees or performance appraisal of its employees adds to the credibility to the organization too.

Informal performance appraisal can be adopted by the organization to keep the employers informed about their day-to-day performance. The controlling officer can communicate what is desirable or undesirable and keep the employees informed as the traditional performance appraisal system benefitted both the employers and employees.

DEFINITION OF PERFORMANCE APPRAISAL

In society, people are generally assessed and evaluated in terms of his/her behaviour/activity with reference to their need and goal. Appraisal of an individual refers to his/her personality traits, knowledge, attitude, behaviour, practice and individual's adherence to the value system of the society and culture in which he lives. Evaluating the performance of the employees of the organizations in a systematic and scientific manner rationalizes the base for needed improvement without bias. The worth and ability of a person can be established through a scientific means for measurement, i.e., performance appraisal.

In other words, performance appraisal is a method, which is applied to assess the expected role of an employee in relation to his/her actual performance for appreciable contributions made by an employee or finding the gaps for improvement in his/her performance at the workplace. It may invite reward or punishment in the form of promotion or warning respectively, or recommendations for improvement of one's performance in the interest of the people and the organization. Performance appraisal is a tool for evaluating the individual traits and capabilities with reference to activities carried on in an organization towards the achievement of its goal. The individual may not perform his/her assigned task if he/she is let without a target performance within a given time to establish his/her capabilities. It is therefore, essential for each organization to assess the performance of its employees over six months or a year as deemed necessary by the development organizations. It is recommended that getting a self-appraisal done every six months to give an opportunity to the person to get interim feedback by the mid-year to decide the pace of his work performance in the last two quarters of the year. To begin with the organization may carry out performance appraisal annualy one to begin with. It should be fair and free from bias on the part of the assessor.

THE CONTEXT

The war against poverty, disease and unemployment can also be compared to the war in socio-economic and socio-political arena. Rabindranath wrote in one of his poems that those who want to go ahead with development leaving behind others, would be pulled back by their followers resulting in no development in true sense. The development has to be holistic in nature and the fruits are to be enjoyed by all together at a time. CSOs, VOs and NGOs therefore, are looking for those conditions of development, but the functionaries/personnel of the organizations are lacking in understanding of their role to perform in situation where things are difficult to do so. It is high time for the development organizations to adopt a performance review to provide feedback to managers, coordinators and workers informally or formally by appreciating their performance for development programmes as well as identify the gaps for improvement of performance of employees. In case of repetition of failure to achieve, it may lead to warning or some other punishments as appropriate.

Motivation to work is an innate quality, but now-a-days it is no more a driving force emerging from and within the individuals, and hence they need to be supervized or monitored against task accomplishment. The cost of supervision is a cost to service the people and the organization. The organization therefore, has to rationalize its cost, and benefit extracted out of the investment in social sector, adopting assignment-accomplishment mode of management. Industrial organizations can rationalize their output with the methods of quantifications, but it remains a hard task to the managers of CSOs, NGOs, VOs today to quantify all their benefit. The social sector today is mostly dependent on the funding organizations for the projects. Therefore, the need to make a projected cost benefit analysis before going for any social development programme is essential.

NEED FOR PERFORMANCE APPRAISAL

The need for performance appraisal has emerged due to the changing pattern of service delivery system as well as professionalism in social sector. The countries like India, Bangladesh, Pakistan and other south Asian countries are lagging behind with regard to service delivery system and management of the projects owing to various reasons as follows: (a) The Asian countries are highly dependant on the social sector organizations for mobilization and all-round development of the people, hence the performance of employees and organizations are key to the success of project goal achievement. (b) The persons who may not have professional expertise but run the organizations in their own ways of doing things; hence they need to have capacity to assess the performance of a person. (c) There is need for standardization of performance to add to the speed and professionalism to the ongoing development programme of welfare organizations. (d) The best way to standardize the employees' performance in social sector is to follow certain principles as common and regular practice to improve the quality of human service professionals and bring in the accountability to the people and the state.

India, after liberalizing its economy has changed its focus to outsource the social sector services and make it self-sustainable. The needs for performance apparaisal in this context are: it is an organizational necessity for the development of employee and organization, it is based on well defined objective criteria suiting to work requirements, it needs careful job analysis of each category of employees, this has to be used for job related criteria vis-à-vis the personality traits, it should be non-discriminating and help to bring out actual situation and performance of the employees.

SOCIO-CULTURAL GAP DUE TO PHILANTHROPIC ORIENTATION IN CSO/VO/NGOs

There are a few socio-cultural gaps in CSOs/VOs/NGOs due to philanthropic orientation. These include: (a) lack of orientation of the officers, leaders (government and non-government officials) in improving the service by motivating and developing the employees to perform; (b) vested individual interests including political interest; (c) corruptions everywhere within and outside the organizations; (d) interest of the people working for the organizations vis-à-vis a compulsion to retain their jobs; and (*e*) apathy/mismanagement of the government and non-government officials and their control on the work of the employees.

PERFORMANCE APPRAISAL IN GOVERNMENT ORGANIZATIONS AND NGOs

The government organizations and the departments concerning social and economic development have been following the state and central rules relating to performance appraisal system. The system is called Career Confidential Report (CCR), Annual Confidential Report (ACR), etc. The sections and offices annually do this especially at the time of considering the promotion of employee in his/her career or in circumstances like specific allegation/complaint against an employee. The rule says that the person should be informed about the adverse comments made by the reviewer(s), and those who have done well be appreciated to keep them motivated to perform better in the years to come. Good performance may result in easy promotion of the employee later when there is a vacancy at higher position. Unfortunately, today's government employees do not face any challenges or implications to such rules, as promotion has become a matter of seniority right and not of merit in many cases. The employee may say "I am in a wrong job, no satisfaction but still I have the seniority". The controlling officers normally do not make any adverse comments to avoid conflict with the employees and the trade unions. But in many cases, promotions become difficult when there are more departmental candidates for a limited number of posts. The end result is failure of the state departments to deliver the services at the time when required, as good performance is not taken as an essential criterion for career advancement. The frustrated people may raise questions but the office and the department run as usual.

The present paper proposes to examine the possibility of using performance appraisal for the employees in CSOs, VOs, Trusts and NGOs to improve their quality of services. The reason for not evaluating the employees' performance in NGOs may be due to non-implementation of performance appraisal system of the government organizations.

The approach to performance appraisal was initially judgemental, i.e., the performance of an employee was being adjudged by his/her superior, but now the focus on performance appraisal has been developmental, i.e., the purpose of performance assessment is to develop the employees to perform better if even he/she falls below average. The employees now need to be motivated to perform the assigned tasks efficiently and effectively with necessary development of skills, capabilities and attitude to improve their day-to-day activities.

NGOs emerged from the civil society organization (CSO) or voluntary organizations (VO) of the past. The objectives of such organizations were invariably to carry out benevolent work for people on religious and philanthropic interests, and almost all the functionaries who joined such organizations were either religiously motivated or concerned to work for prevention or alleviation of the human sufferings. The motivation to work for such causes was rather spiritual and out of their socio-cultural obligation to human society. It was expected that such individuals possessed a high level of commitment towards the accomplishment of the self-assigned tasks to earn virtue, fame and self-satisfaction of service to the mankind. Many a person moved by the tradition of their predecessors to create a healthy society.

The people and the society have changed over the period according to the needs of the situations overpowering the values, ethics and the social laws that governed them. The orientation of the CSOs, VOs and NGOs was to provide services selflessly without any expectations in return. But the time has changed and the need for professional education and training for rendering services indiscriminately is felt as harmful to the people in need and making them dependent. The workers for such organizations have also found that the charitable and philanthropic services in many cases are wasteful and discouraging for potential growth and all-round development of the target group. The transformation of kingdoms to states has made the modern states liable to provide services to the needy, and adopt a holistic approach in human development issues like health, education and employment, i.e. sustainable livelihood system.

The people who form and run organizations, need a high level of motivation to achieve the goal set by any funding agency. The performance of task by the people of the organization, therefore, is the key to success of any development project. The industrial houses are effectively managing the performance of the employees with their resources, knowledge and expertise at work place, but it's a fact that only a few VOs, CSOs and NGOs are concerned about the performance management of their employees, who are called or designated as managers, coordinators, and workers of the organizations. An organization implementing the programme of development for the poorer sections of the society would like to hire a person with moderate qualification with a minimum pay and benefit. Appraising the performance of these employees/workers is, therefore, essential in the voluntary sector. This paper suggests a common method of performance evaluation of the workers in VOs, CSOs and the NGOs working with the masses for their socio-economic and cultural ameliorations.

There are different methods of performance evaluation in industrial organizations, but a few are available for the voluntary and non-government organizations to evaluate, review and manage workers with continuous performance development programmes in the interest of the individuals, organization and the society. The functionaries and the administrators of such organizations are, therefore, in a dilemma as to what should be the model of performance appraisal when the funding organizations are evaluating the Result On Investment (ROI), be it a health service, an educational programme or awareness generation of the masses in myriad fields of social development.

MODERN PERFORMANCE MANAGEMENT SYSTEM

Performance management till now has been one of the prime activities in industrial and non-industrial organizations of the private and public sectors. The objectives of performance management are to identify the area of weakness of the employees and plan for their improvement over a period of time.

Let us review a few methods of performance evaluation in government and other organizations to answer the relevant questions: Why and how performance appraisal? What are its uses and effects in voluntary and social sector, which is now dominated by the professionally trained workers?

(a) J.C. Flanagan, introduced the *Critical Incident Method* for appraisal of employee performance. This follows critical or important incidents both good and bad as observed by his/her supervisor on the subordinates' conduct at the workplace during the period under review. All positive and negative contributions are noted down and discussed with the employee being assessed. This is one of the transparent methods of employee performance appraisal and acceptable to both employers and employees.

(b) The *Technique of Multiple Judgment* can be adopted in order to avoid bias of a number of people, i.e. the immediate superior, the officers at the higher level in assessing the performance of an employee. Most of the government and public sector organizations have a practice of having performance appraisal done by multiple people for any single employee.

(c) One of the mostly used forms of performance management is *Behaviorally Anchored Rating Scale (BARS),* which primarily relates to personality traits and individual's behaviour at the work place to assess his/her performance on a regular scale of assessment. Here the immediate supervisor or the head of the department mostly assesses the employee's performance. The assessor and the assessed may or may not be sharing each other's views and experience. There may be bias on the part of the employers or the employees but some amount of transparency and fairness has to be maintained to keep the organization and its people moving ahead towards its mission and vision.

(d) According to Rajesh Satyal, the ABC for performance management stands for Activators, Behaviours and Consequences. The organizations today need to follow certain basic and minimum standard of employee's performance by activating and motivating the employees for the expected behaviour towards the achievement of the goal set. He further states that the core advantage of this model is to remain proactive and inform the defaulting managers/supervisors/workers to improve their performance. The proposed achieve model given below may be a better option for the non-government organizations.

ACHIEVE stands for;

Ability	Knowledge and Skills
Clarity	Understanding or role performance
Help	Organizational support
Inventive	Motivation
Evaluation	Performance feedback
Validity	Valid legal, personnel practice, government rules
Environment	External and internal factors, policies, market

These are the key variables with regard to performance appraisal of an employee in any organization. The social sector organization will find it more relevant to make use the above model for appraising the performances of employees in social development as they need to achieve results of developmental work.

(e) *The Work Standard Approach*: The management fixes the target and standard norms of work performance of an employee. The employee has no other option but to fulfil the target set, which can be measured daily. Here, the job responsibilities of the employee are clearly stated with objectivity. The assessment of one's performance is done in comparison to the standards set for the employee. It is difficult to compare one employee with another due to varied nature of work and performance, but still a sizeable number of organizations having wider network and establishments spread over can follow the practice.

(f) *Management by Objectives (MBO):* In the work standard approach, the management fixes up the target task of an employee, while in the MBO system, the targets are decided in a democratic method. The targets are set in consultation with the person who has to work for the same. The final target is then decided by consensus. The progress of the plan is evaluated after six months to see where the people and the organization stand on the day of appraising the performance of the employee. This is a very good practice and may be suitable for the coordinators, programme officers and supervisors of the non-government organizations. These key persons then will discuss among the staff involved in implementation of the project and set the achievable target within the stipulated timeframe. The rationale in favour of this method is that it is not imposed but decided unanimously through participative style of management, hence may suit many social development and welfare organizations.

APPRAISING EMPLOYEES' PERFORMANCES IN NGOs/VOs/CSOs

The employers recruiting the employees to perform tasks of the organization naturally would like to get the person who is competent in the matters of knowledge, skill and ability. Naturally, the employers will have to assess their performance in using their knowledge and expertise towards the achievement of the project and organizational goal. Normally, the leaders of the organization will expect the employee to be disciplined with regard to their punctuality, devotion to work and leadership; skilled in public relations to deal with the people and other officials; quick in deciding an issue considering the situation; capable of planning, monitoring, and evaluating a development project; communicating across the people and the organization; organizing programmes efficiently and effectively; loyal to the people and organization; morally and ethically sound to cope with difficult situations; capable to manage self and others; perseverance for project goal achievement.

Therefore, the organizations need to develop a system to appraise the performance of the employees involving the employees, employers, colleagues and the beneficiaries to make it a feedback system for performance improvement, and follow the reward and punishment method to keep them motivated or compelled to work as the case may be.

PERFORMANCE APPRAISAL: NEED OF THE HOUR FOR NGO PERSONNEL

Among the experts who have worked extensively on performance management, T.V. Rao is the one who has given a new direction to appraising the performance of the employees. According to him, the assessor may be self, immediate supervisor, the leader of the organization and the beneficiary. If each one assesses 90 degree of the employee then all the four parties stated above constitute 90 degree × 4, i.e., 360 degree appraisal of performance of an employee. However, where the project staff is not directly related to the beneficiary he/she may be assessed by an independent external evaluator specialized in the subject. Alternatively, in such cases, the performance appraisal may be considered as 270 degree method of performance assessment.

Nevertheless, a strong and direct communication is essential among all the government and NGO officials and leaders for the improvement of performance of the members of the staff at work. The proposed method of performance can also be termed as 'scientific communication-feedback system in the process of organization and employee development'. It is also proposed that there shall not be any form of performance management system but each organization shall develop its own performance appraisal system depending upon its need and context in which performance is to be assessed.

Performance of an employee is always linked to reward and punishment system of any organization, though initial punishments may be nominal, like warning for improvement of his/her performance within a given time, but it may be severe for those who do not improve upon in spite of repeated warnings. The initial warning may be termed 'compulsion' for the employees to improve their performance over a period of given time. To avoid any conflict of bias or victimization, the method should be transparent and open to all interested in knowing the facts and figures about his/her performance in relation to the assigned task.

The government is withdrawing its direct services to the citizens since 1990s as a follow up of the liberalization policy of the State. Secondly, the government services have been found to be futile in most of the social welfare programmes that were being conducted in India. Therefore, NGOs/VOs/CSOs are having a major involvement in social development programme. The government's policy to shift its liability to deliver the services through NGOs is due to reasons stated below: (a) The government departments

are slow in operation owing to rigid rules and bureaucracy, which do not yield benefits to the people. (b) These departments are more expensive with regard to their payment to staff with social security benefits and a major part of the allocation goes to staff payment and other establishment costs. (c) Accountability of the government employees is lower than the non-government organizations and voluntary organizations. (d) Contracting out the tasks to CSO, NGO, VO and trusts is cost effective. (e) The accountability of the people in NGOs is higher as the control of such employees rests with the President, and Secretary of the organizations. (f) The government exercises greater control on the non-government organizations and may terminate the contract if services are poor.

CONCLUSION

The Chief Executives/Organizers of the NGOs/VOs/CSOs are to decide the need for appraising the performance of the employees engaged for a specific project and the period for such appraisal. The project personnel can be informed at the time of selection interview about the need to remain highly motivated to perform and get assessed every six or twelve months with reference to assigned tasks. There is no loss of face if even one falls below average, but one has remain open to accept the communication feedback process with regard to employee performance management. A growing number of organizations are now offering capsule courses for employees of social development organizations. The Presidents/Secretaries should be prepared to send the staff for training from time to time as staff development programme to address the needs of such employees and develop them by identifying their needs through performance appraisal for best and significant performance.

Let us consider a model (Annexure-I) for assessing the performance of the employees in CSO, NGO, VO, and Trusts of the modern state and society. While discussing the BARS and 360 degree performance appraisal for the employees in an organization, the former being the traditional and the latter being the modern, we can think of a system where the objectives of organizations and individuals could be balanced rationally. The proposed performance appraisal form shall be illustrative and not exhaustive. The organizations are to make necessary changes and apply them according to their requirements and contexts. As discussed earlier, government departments having a scientific system of performance appraisal do not follow it systematically, and in consequence, the service delivery by government officials is being questioned. There are a few departments which do not call for any appraisal but tasks are completed within cost and time limit satisfying the people, organizations and the state. It is high time that all VOs/NGOs/CSOs consider the need for performance appraisal without blaming the persons and the institutes of higher education for meaningful task accomplishments—the very basic purpose for which the employee, people, organizations, state and society exist. We must keep in mind that a person learns more from family and environment than the educational institutes offers training with degree or diploma. The employing organizations can mould and reshape the traits of the personnel through performance feedback at the end of the year.

REFERENCES

Armstrong, M. (1994), *Performance Management*, Kogan Page, London.

Beavens, S and Thompson, M. (1991), "Performance Management at Crossroads", *Personal Management*, November.

Boyett, Joseph, H. and Conn, Henry P. (1997), *Maximum Performance Management*, Vanity Books, New Delhi.

Chatterjee, N.N. (1984), *Management of Personnel in Indian Enterprises*, Third Edition, Allied Publisher, New Delhi.

Douglas, McGregor (1960), *The Human Side of Enterprise*, McGraw-Hill, New York.

Flanagan, J.C. (1954), "The Critical Incident Technique", *Physiological Bulletin*, p. 325–356.

Flippo, E.B.(1984), *Personal Management*, Sixth Edition, Mcgraw Book Company, New York.

Harrington, H. James (1995), *Total Improvement Management: The Next Generation in Performance Improvement*, McGraw Hill, New York.

Institute of Management (1992), *Performance Management in the U.K: An Analysis of the Issues*, London.

Marger, Robert F. and Pipe Peter (1984), *Analyzing Performance Problems or You Really Wanna*, Pitman Learning, Belmont.

Middlebrook, John F. (1996), "How to Manage Individual Performance", *Training and Development*, Vol. 50, No. 9.

Oberg, W. (1972), "Make Performance Appraisal Relevant", *Harvard Business Review*, p. 61.

Rao, T.V. (1997), "Human Capital", *Performance Management*, Special Issue, Vol. I. No. 6.

Robert Owen (1920), *The Life of Robert Owen*, Alfred A. Knopf, Inc., New York.

Satyal, R. (1997), "Human Capital", *Performance Management*, Special Issue, Vol. I. No. 6.

Silberaman, Mel and Hank, Karp (1999), "What is Your Feedback Quotient", *The 1999 Training and Performance Source Book*, Mc Graw Hill, New York.

ANNEXURE-I

Proposed Performance Appraisal Form for Employees in NGO/VO/CSO

(Name of the organization and address)

1. Name of the employee:
2. Designation:
3. Date of birth and age:
4. Date of joining:
5. Period of service:
6. Scale of pay/salary:
7. Last increment/enhancement/promotion:
8. Educational qualifications: Degree/Diploma/Others, if any:
9. Professional qualification:
10. Post held in the same organization:
11. Previous experience with post held:
12. Attachment to organization's other work/project:
13. Tasks assigned:
14. Time for completion of tasks:
15. Attachment to colleagues at the workplace:
16. Potentialities of the incumbent/core skills:
17. Ability to relate to the people:
18. Ability to take decision:
19. Advocacy skills:
20. Skills in human relations:
21. Employability in any other project:
22. Ability to drive vehicles:
23. Field work:
24. Reporting:
25. Perseverance:
26. Qualitative assessment of performance during the year under review

Area	*Excellent* 5	*Very good* 4	*Good* 3	*Poor* 2	*Very poor* 1
Punctuality					
Commitment to work					
Knowledge					
Skills					
Communication					
Work performance					
Ability to use knowledge/expertise					
Coordination with co-workers/supervisor					
Knowledge of budgetary control					
Quality of work					
Compliance with the project aim/goal					
Planning of work					
Execution of work plan					
Maintenance of records Inherent potentialities					
Ability to give leadership					
Integrity					
Honesty					

27. Overall strength of the candidate:
28. Overall weaknesses if any:
29. Suggestions for reward:
30. Suggestions for improvement including training need of the candidate:
31. Summary of discussion held between the supervisor and the employee

Signature of the officer assessing

Signature of the reviewing officer/Secretary with comments of agreement and disagreement on the review done:

Notes on Contributors

Rama V. Baru is at the Centre of Social Medicine and Community Health, JNU, New Delhi. She is the author of *Privatization of Health Care* and the Regional Editor (South Asia) for the International Journal *Global Social Policy*. Trained as a Medical Social Worker, Dr Baru has also worked with the Voluntary Health Association of India and the Andhra Pradesh Handicapped Persons Welfare Corporation, besides having been a Lecturer at the College of Social Work, Hyderabad.

Swapan Garain is at the Tata Institute of Social Sciences, Mumbai. He is a Senior Fellow of Johns Hopkins University, USA, and former Professor as well as Chairperson of the Centre for Corporate Citizenship, Jamnalal Bajaj Institute of Management Studies, Mumbai. He is also associated with several committees such as Government of India's Planning Commission Steering Committee on Voluntary Sector for the 10th and 11th (2007–2012) Five-Year Plans; Programme Advisory Committee of the Department of Science and Technology, Government of India; etc.

P.K. Ghosh is teaching at the Department of Social Work, Sriniketan, Visva-Bharati. Beginning his career in private sector industries as management trainee, he worked for three years before shifting to the Durgapur Projects Ltd, Government of West Bengal. He was with the Ministry of Labour, Government of India for a short period. He has also worked as Reader in the Department of PM & IR, Tata

Institute of Social Sciences, Mumbai. His current interest lies in management in social work, small enterprise development in rural and informal sector, rural development and human development thoughts of Tagore, etc. He is closely associated with intervention programmes on income generation as envisaged by Tagore in his rural reconstruction philosophy.

Sukla Deb Kanango is teaching in the Department of Social Work, Sriniketan, Visva-Bharati. She has been involved in working with people and organizations at the grass-roots level and developed action programmes in the field of non-formal education and disability. She was a member of the Social Work Education Panel of the University Grants Commission and also of the Executive Committee of the Association of Schools of Social Work in India.

Niaz Ahmed Khan is Professor of Public Administration at the University of Chittagong, Bangladesh and Institution Capacity and Development Specialist-CHTDF for United Nations Development Programme (UNDP) at Bangladesh Country Office, Dhaka.

B.T. Lawani is Director of Social Sciences Centre, Bharati Vidyapeeth University, Pune. He has been in teaching for the last 20 years. He has authored a couple of books of which *NGOs in Development* and *Social Work Perspectives* are of great importance. He is the Chief Editor of the journal, *Participative Development*. He has presented around 35 papers at the national and international conferences. His fields of interest are social work research, fieldwork training and NGO sector.

K.K. Mukherjee is Professor at the Department of Social Work, University of Delhi, New Delhi.

Sutapa Mukherjee is with Gram Niyojan Kendra, Ghaziabad, U.P.

A.K. Nongkynrih is Reader at the Department of Sociology, North Eastern Hill University, Shillong. He is coordinating an innovative project 'Community Development Extension Programme (CDEP)'. His areas of interest are sociology of development, social change, sociology of entrepreneurship and management, sociology of voluntary organizations, and sociology of environment. He is also a facilitator of participatory learning and action, and sustainable livelihood approach. He is a consultant to national and international organizations in the areas of development.

Komal Parmar is presently working as a Senior Faculty in the Research Department of the Indian School of Microfinance for Women based at Ahmedabad. She has worked previously as Research Analyst at EDA Rural Systems Pvt. Ltd., Gurgaon; Senior Programme Officer (Research & Documentation) at Friends of Women's World Banking, Ahmedabad; Research Associate, TALEEM Research Foundation, Ahmedabad; Research Associate, PLACON Management Consultancy Services, Ahmedabad; Research Assistant, Foundation for Research in Health Systems (FRHS), Ahmedabad; and Programmer, Mudra Institute of Communication (MICA), Ahmedabad.

Ravindra R. Patil is an alumnus of Tata Institute of Social Sciences, Mumbai, and Jawaharlal Nehru University, New Delhi. He is presently Lecturer at the Department of Social Work, Jamia Millia Islamia, New Delhi. His areas of interest are sociology of development, civil society, social inclusion and exclusion and issues of Dalits.

D. Rajasekhar heads Decentralisation and Development Unit at the Institute for Social and Economic Change (Centre of Excellence), Bangalore. He is currently directing three large research projects on 'Fiscal Decentralisation in Karnataka', 'Growing Rural-Urban Disparity' and 'Design and Management of Social Security Benefits for Unorganized Sector in Karnataka'. His research interests include local organizations, microfinance and linkages among the development actors. His recent books are *Poverty Alleviation Strategies of NGOs*, *Reluctant Partners Coming Together? Interface between Government, People and NGOs* and *Micro Finance, Poverty Alleviation and Empowerment of Women: A Study of Two NGOs from Andhra Pradesh and Karnataka*.

Asok Kumar Sarkar is Reader in Social Work, Indira Gandhi National Open University, New Delhi. Prior to this, he taught at the Department of Social Work, Assam University, Silchar, Assam. He is the author of *NGOs: The New Lexicon of Health Care*. Having completed M.A. in Social Work with specialization in Medical and Psychiatric Social Work from TISS, he has also worked with the Institute of Health Management, Pachod, Maharashtra before joining the M.Phil/Ph.D programme under JNU.

Debotosh Sinha is a social work educator, researcher and practitioner for more than two decades. Presently, he is a Reader in the Department of Social Work, Sriniketan, Visva-Bharati. He has published a number of articles, research papers in various journals and books. He is a widely travelled person in India and across the globe. He has close association with a number of professional bodies as well as non-governmental organizations.

Index